Secrets Of Buying Art

Secrets of Buying Art

Original Prints and Reproductions

Mary Ann Wenniger & Mace Wenniger

BETTERWAY PUBLICATIONS, INC.
WHITE HALL, VIRGINIA

Published by Betterway Publications, Inc.
P.O. Box 219
Crozet, VA 22932
(804) 823-5661

Cover design by Susan Riley
Cover art by Takeshi Hara
Typography by Typecasting

The glossary of conservation terms that appears in
Chapter 10 is excerpted from "Special Conservation Problems for Collectors: Basic Conservation
Terminology," by Judith C. Walsh, originally published in the September–October 1983 issue of
Drawing (Volume V, number 3). Copyright © 1983,
The Drawing Society. All rights reserved. No part
of the contents of this glossary may be reprinted
without express written permission from the
publisher.

Library of Congress Cataloging-in-Publication Data

Wenniger, Mary Ann.
 The secrets of buying art: original prints and repro-
ductions / by Mary Ann Wenniger and Mace Wenniger.
  p. cm.
 Includes index.
 ISBN 1-55870-158-3: $22.95—
  ISBN 1-55870-157-5 (pbk.): $14.95
 1. Prints—Collectors and collecting. 2. Prints—Re-
production—Collectors and collecting. I. Wenniger,
Mace.
II. Title.
NE885.W47 1990
769′.1—dc20   90-39098
                                                CIP

Printed in the United States of America
0 9 8 7 6 5 4 3 2 1

This book and the others in this series are respectfully dedicated to the hard working, hidden heroes of the art world, gallery owners, who are responsible for bringing art to consumers as well as to the lookers and lovers of art.

These self-directed entrepreneurs work unceasingly because, of course, they want to make a buck, but really it is because they love art. In the case of owners of the print galleries discussed in this book, it is because they are smitten primarily with printmaking and its marriage of paper and technique, the endless variations of imagery it produces, and the moderate price range of the prints they offer. Print gallery owners are to be saluted because they are self-controlled and friendly though beset daily by questions, skepticism, negotiation, even derision and jealousy.

If they are short with words, forgive them; they are tired out from combining janitorial duties with ambassadorship. A word of praise will make them smile and might permit them to slow down long enough to realize the wonderfulness of their services to printmakers and other artists, to clients, to art consultants, facilities personnel, designers, administrators, and to all the other ordinary people who value beauty in their daily lives.

CONTENTS

INTRODUCTION

When I tell people I own an art gallery, they tend to nod politely and change the subject, or gush with exaggerated admiration. Just once I wish somebody would ask, "What does a gallery owner do, anyway?" because the truth is, hardly anybody besides artists and bona fide art collectors know; and more often than not gallery owners, even to artists, remain mysterious creatures. In fact, an established gallery owner does not know what a competitor is up to.

This book describes the role of the gallery person in relation to the artist, the work, and the potential buyer, because the gallery has become a key point in the dissemination and marketing of art. The book focuses on step-by-step guidelines for people who want to develop their own taste and learn to trust it, and to indulge it by buying art. It is for people who are just coming out of the closet as secret art lovers, for those who want to begin to buy art intelligently and sensibly, and for the sheer pleasure of it.

WHY SHOULD RECORD COLLECTORS HAVE ALL THE FUN?

As a gallery owner who is about to reveal her age, I have watched the art scene change in the past forty years. During the 1950s art as an investment first became a rich man's game in the United States. Influenced by the growing acquisitiveness of the museums, especially in their purchases of the French Impressionists, wealthy Americans began to collect art not for art's sake, but for its future market potential. Although these privileged few purchased art chiefly for reasons of status and financial gain, they also bought art that they liked —at least some of them did.

Then in the '60s and '70s, new art—graphics and paintings and brand new art forms—became as available as fine recordings. With the same confusing array of prices, art flooded the marketplace, but with a significant difference. Record (now compact disc) collecting rapidly became an acceptable middle-class enthusiasm. People began buying sophisticated, expensive stereo systems, and conversation about systems and recordings became de rigeur. The jargon entered our language. Everybody had a stereo, then a tape deck, and the technology has continued to advance ad infinitum.

But not so with art. Art collecting, perhaps because of its long-standing aristocratic associations, did not become an acceptable middle-class activity. (People who can talk knowledgeably about tweeters still do not know what an intaglio is.) The idea of collecting art for pleasure simply has not caught on. Record collectors are still having all the fun.

Now, in the '90s, art has become a commodity. Like fax machines and rental limousines, it has never been so readily available to so many people, all of the time. People are eating it up like Lean Cuisine dinners and romance novels. Investing in and owning art, but not enjoying it. In fact, most people seem to have succumbed to one of the following syndromes when buying art.

The House Beautiful Syndrome: People who redecorate on an annual basis and new condominium owners tend to succumb to this syndrome. The most obvious symptom is their entrance into a gallery with mauve colored swatches in hand. They are frantically searching for anything that matches and will "work" above a new teak table on a 6-foot wide wall; preferably a floral print, or something with "an Oriental feel." Another name for this syndrome is "The Matching Complex." People who succumb to it buy art the way they buy wallpaper—with little or no regard for the work itself.

The Great Gatsby Syndrome: This is usually manifested in the single male. This person must maintain his corporate success image at all costs. He has just made the leap into upper management, has money to invest, and wants to spend it on the "right" young artist his friends will recognize. He must have the best of everything—cars, clothing, women, paintings—they are all the same. This is a particularly virulent strain of treating art as a commodity.

Kenneth Tyler printing the David Hockney lithograph, Potted Daffodils. *Photo by Lindsay Green, courtesy of Tyler Graphics Ltd.*

The Fast Food Syndrome (One Billion Van Gogh Sunflowers Sold): Young singles and young couples who are educated enough to know better may fall victim to this malaise. Although they know perfectly well that fine art exists, they never transcend their college dorm life mentality of a 4 foot by 6 foot room with five posters on each wall. They continue to buy poster art all of their young lives, forgetting what they learned about fine art in an undergraduate art appreciation course.

The Nude in the Bathroom Syndrome: This disorder often strikes latterday hippie couples. The woman affects Mexican skirts and Navaho jewelry; the man's beard has become a permanent fixture in his self image. They are part of what used to be called "the arty set." Neither of them has quite gotten beyond their graduate student mentality. They bought a Picasso, Renoir, or Matisse nude poster on sale at the college bookstores, tacked it to the bathroom wall when they got together, and it has been there since, suffering extreme water damage.

The underlying problem with this couple is that they are essentially puritanical and middle class, although they have free spirit pretensions (i.e., nudes can only be displayed in bathrooms). This couple ought to know better. Like the couples who succumb to the Fast Food Syndrome, they have the potential and the income to enjoy fine art.

The Solution: There is no need to feel guilty if you have fallen prey to one of these syndromes. If you have, the only problem is that you are selling yourself short. In childhood, we all had an innate aesthetic sense and need to express ourselves through art. But these sensibilities are delicate; they must be cultivated and nurtured.

Yet everyone collects art—an enlarged photograph of a family gathering at Christmas dinner; a porcelain elephant brought back from a trip; a Buddha from an uncle; even a bundle of flowers carried home in the hands of a tired business person is unspoken witness to the uplift expected from nature's artistic creation.

My striped jogging shorts, a glowing vase, our cat sunning herself in the sun on the window sill amidst my plants; these please my human need for the aesthetic, the need to arrange and appreciate, to escape or transcend the ordinary, without regard for usefulness.

We all collect art casually, unselfconsciously, and for pleasure. Something goes somewhere because it looks good there, because it comforts the spirit as a good chair comforts the bottom.

THE PROBLEM WITH ART

The problem with art in general and prints in this context is that they have been considered a luxury by most of us. Art is not measurably useful; you cannot sit on it or use it in any practical way, except to cover walls. The reason art was made, from the time when men drew on cave walls, was to tell stories. Think of art and prints as adding a human dimension to your home or office. It can tell you a story and relax you. It says who you are and what your interests are. My sister Katy bought a simple silkscreen of a huge lake with a dark slice of land separating the water from a twilight sky. It is well designed, strong but simple, elegant like Katy's house and clothes. She bought it because it reminds her of a favorite place and opens up her room and her mind.

IS ART A PRIVILEGE?

Part of the problem is that, historically, art was made for the privileged few. It was created either for the hierarchy of the church to teach the mysteries of heaven, or for aristocratic homes to delineate ancestry or illustrate mythology.

Americans do not think that we deserve art. We justify purchases from a pragmatic approach, not for our own enjoyment. The bottom line is that delight and pleasure are ultimately useful. They oil the wheels of our lives. Part of the problem for would-be art buyers has been the feeling that art belongs only to the privileged elite with extensive financial resources. With that in mind, there is a certain amount of reluctance on the part of many to approach the art dealer or gallery owner to ask simply if they might pay slowly for a piece of artwork.

To confront and to surmount these problems is the thrust of this book. The first question I will address is: Why should you buy art at all?

Collagraph print by Grace Bentley–Scheck.

WHY BUY ART?

Our thesis is that the viewer buys art because this artist enlarges his vision; in a special way, the viewer shares in this vision and feels the artist expressed in the work. If the artist were not there, or did not do his work, I would suffer a real loss; my experience would in some way be diminished.

But it is never too late to stake out your right to have beauty in your life, even to become an art junkie. For many people, this happens after a crisis point or major change in their lives: the end of a first marriage; graduation from law school; the end of six years of therapy that finally worked; the move into top management after years of combat on the corporate ladder; a major career change; or even just getting a credit card after college.

For late bloomers, this discovery or rediscovery of art for the love of it can be deeply rewarding. Some people actually become amateur or professional artists; others find great pleasure in buying carefully selected individual works of art as a treat every so often. Others become collectors, specializing in one artist, period, or subject. You probably have an idea of what is right for you. If you feel it is about time you had a meaningful relationship with a work of art, then this book will help you make the most of it. Whether you are the type of person who falls in love with art at first sight, or if you prefer long step-by-step courtships, the steps in the art-buying process described in these chap-

Silkscreen by Joe Price.

ters are the prerequisite to a long-term romance with art.

In fact, there is much more than just the work of art and you. There is the intimate relation between the artist and the work, between the artist and the gallery owner, between the gallery owner and the work, and you, the potential buyer, in relation to each and all. This multi-faceted relationship is one of the richest and most satisfying elements of the art-buying experience—one that many art buyers miss completely. The relation-

ship between the buyer, the gallery owner, the artists, and the art is an integral part of buying art as an aesthetic experience. That is, part of the pleasure is the exchange among the principals involved, and the shared experience.

There is too little intimacy and individual expression in all of our lives. The process of finding, choosing, buying, and framing art can be an exercise in intense personal expression and self definition; a growth toward learning to trust your own feelings and taste; a way of shaping and clarifying your relationship to your own surroundings. Creative art buying is an art in and of itself—an experience that is available to everyone. You do not have to have big money to be an art buyer. All you need is the commitment to include art in your budget and in your life.

Becoming an art lover also involves sharing the art you have purchased; in other words, you will want to invite people over to see your nude out of the bathroom. Art selected with new knowledge, care, and enthusiasm is a sincere expression of the best that is in you. Your private aesthetic experience makes waves; it creates many possibilities, including the involvement of your friends. It is participation in an artist's vision and a gallery owner's dream. That dream is to make art a part of everyone's life; to make art a necessity—not a luxury—for us all.

BASICS
Types of Original Prints and Where to Find Them
1

Bonnie complained, "I can afford to buy the prints we want for our walls, but how do I know what is good and worth buying? I do not want a fraud, and I don't want to be pushed by a high pressure salesperson. And galleries scare me. I need a handy guide that I can take along to the galleries that shows me how to make wise decisions that I will enjoy."

> Secret: When considering buying art, start by shopping for prints.

PRINTS DEFINED

Original prints are two-dimensional works of art on paper which are created indirectly. First, the image is made on a sub-surface, a block or a plate or a stone. Then the image is transferred by inking the sub-surface and printing it on paper. Hence, prints are not direct creations on a canvas, board, or paper. Yet prints *are* originals, like paintings, because they are made by artists directly working on the sub-surfaces and then printing the images; but they are also part of a *process* from which more than one copy can be made.

Unlike posters, limited edition prints and reproductions, which are made photographically and discussed in Chapter 2, are often worth buying as well. Original prints are made by hand in an amazingly labor-intensive way, by an artist whose professional designation is that of "printmaker." He or she creates an original design directly onto the surface of wood, limestone, linoleum, screen, or metal; this surface is called a

base or *plate*. Today, printmakers also can draw detailed images on plastic and transfer them photographically onto any of those printmaking surfaces.

There are, therefore, many types of original prints to learn about: woodcuts, wood engravings, lithographs, etchings, aquatints, mezzotints, engravings, drypoints, serigraphs, collagraphs, and monotypes.

The following description of an original print is taken in part from the 1978 definition promulgated by the Print Council of America.

An original print is a work of art, the general requirements of which are:
1. The artist alone has made the image in or upon the plate, stone, wood block, or other material for the purpose of creating a work of graphic art.
2. The impression is made directly from that original material by the artist or pursuant to his directions.
3. The finished print is approved by the artist.
4. There are four methods for inking and transferring the image to the paper: relief, intaglio, planographic or surface printing, and stencil.

> Secret: It's easy to learn how prints are made.

With the rapid increase of interest in original prints there is a corresponding wish to know how prints are made, how to distinguish one variety from another, and to learn something of their history.

There are numerous excellent books that describe in detail the technical aspects of each medium, some of which are listed in the Suggested Reading list at the back of this book. In this chapter, we will give a short description of the four main types of original prints: relief, intaglio, planographic, and stencil, and then describe the various techniques used within each medium in greater detail.

PRINTING METHODS
Relief Printing

In relief printing, the artist carves away from a block or plate what is *not* to be printed. What *is* printed is in higher relief than other parts of the block. The raised wooden or linoleum surface is then inked with a brayer and printed onto paper by means of hand pressure, rubbing the paper with a spoon, or by using a letter press.

Woodcut: Parts of a wood plank or plywood block are cut away, leaving a design in relief, which is then printed. To do a woodcut, one cuts *with the wood grain.*

Wood Engraving: Similar to a woodcut but the end grain of the block is used, enabling the artist to get a much finer line.

Linocut: Linoleum is used instead of wood, giving a somewhat similar result, although fine detail is not achievable.

Relief Etching: A print is made from an acid-etched plate whose top surface has been rolled with ink and printed.

Intaglio Printing

Intaglio is the opposite of relief printing in that the incised lines or textured areas of the plate (*not* the raised surface) hold the ink. After the artist has incised the image into the copper or zinc plate, the surface is inked and wiped clean, leaving ink only in the incised lines. The print is made when dampened paper is pressed into the incised lines in order to pick up the ink when it goes through the press.

A Plexiglas sheet to be used as a plate for a monoprint.

Intaglio prints can be recognized by the richly inked, matte surface variations which produce the image on the paper. The inked image is raised slightly and therefore has a texture. The edge of the inked and printed image is slightly recessed and clearly depressed. This depressed edge is the significant element that tells you that you are looking at an intaglio print. It is made by the edge of the metal plate pressing into the paper under press pressure.

Etching: A metal plate is coated with an acid-resistant "ground." The artist removes or scratches away parts of this ground to create the image. The plate is then put into an acid bath and the unprotected lines of the design are eaten into the plate.

Aquatint: Large tonal areas of the plate are often done in this manner. The plate is covered with a dusting of rosin, or lightly sprayed with enamel. The amount deposited, along with the length of time the plate is etched, determines the final tone.

Engraving: No acid is used in an engraving. Instead, the line is cut into the plate with a tool called a *burin*.

Drypoint: Similar to engraving. However, a sharp needle is used, which creates a burr along the cut line. Ink caught in that burr leaves a characteristically soft, velvety effect.

Mezzotint: A rocking tool is used which raises a texture or burr over the entire plate. A print taken from this plate would be solid black. Lighter areas have to be scraped or burnished away.

Collagraph: The surface of a Masonite® plate is built up by permanently cementing various materials to the plate. Relief and/or intaglio inking may be used. When printed, the paper will generally be embossed as well as inked, due to the thickness of the materials on the plate.

Planographic Printing

Planographic printmaking results in an even surface. The artistic work—a monoprint, lithograph, or silkscreen—is executed and printed from a flat surface or plane (hence *planographic*), which is not eaten into by incising with tools or acid, as in relief and intaglio printing.

Lithography: The image is drawn or printed on a lithograph stone or treated metal plate with a greasy crayon or ink. The stone is then weakly etched to fix the design. During printing the stone is dampened to prevent the ink (which is rolled on) from adhering to the untreated areas. The greasy areas repel the water but accept the ink.

Serigraphy: The artist prepares a stretched screen (usually silk or rayon mesh) and blocks out the areas not to be printed with glue, cut film, paper, or a photostencil. Ink is then "squeegeed" over the screen, forcing it through the open areas onto the paper, which has been placed beneath the screen.

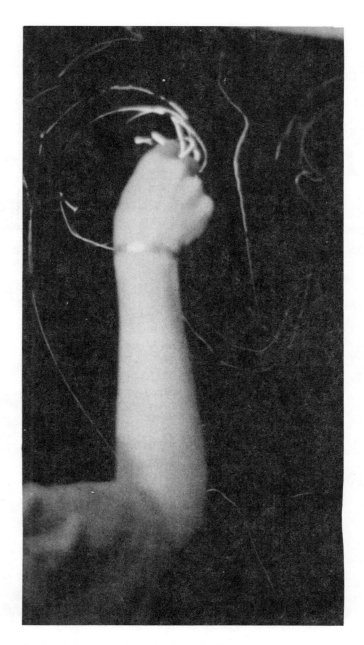

Sue Buck draws on the ink plate; the first step in creating the monoprint.

Monoprints: The image is drawn directly on a plate surface using etching inks, paints, or anything transferable. Paper is placed onto this drawn or painted surface and a single image is printed by means of a press. However, sometimes the "ghost" of an image remains on the plate, enabling the artist to create a second print.

Sue Buck rolling printing ink onto the plate.

Stencil Prints

Pochoir prints: This is a stenciling process in which each shape in an image is cut out of a thin wax paper or plastic sheet and then is recreated on paper by dabbing watercolor, gouache, or acrylic paints through the cutout.

RELIEF PRINTING
Woodcuts

Woodcuts are recognizable by noting the imprint of the grain of the wood. They are made by cutting areas out of wood blocks or large sheets of wood such as plywood, along the length of the grain. The distinct grain of the wood is usually visible in the print because the artist must cut *with* the grain, not across the wood grain because it would splinter. Sometimes variations, such as knots, are incorporated into the artist's design.

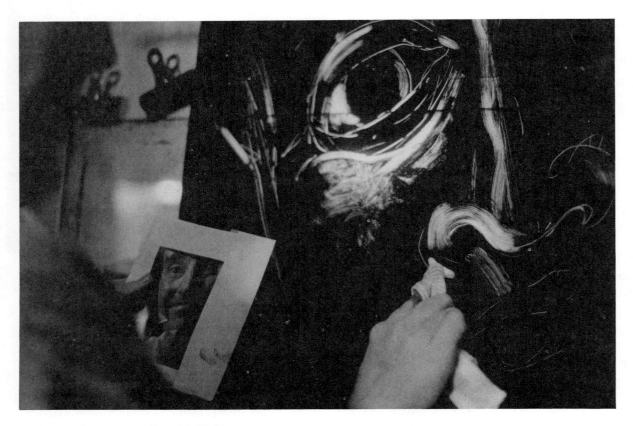

Working with a rag to pull out highlights.

Pulling the finished print from the plate.

The wood block is inked with a roller charged with a water-base or oil-base ink. The roller only covers with ink the raised portions of the wood. Special paper is used for woodcuts. This is often called *rice paper,* a misnomer since it is not made from rice, but is actually a fine absorbent Japanese paper made form the bark of kozo mulberry, gampi, or matsumata trees. It is thin but strong and since it is absorbent, it transfers the images easily. A press is not necessary when printing woodcuts, although some woodcut printmakers do use an etching press, made suitable by adding wood strips to each perimeter of the wood block so the etching roller doesn't bounce down to the press bed after the print is printed.

To print a woodcut, a sheet of absorbent paper is placed on top of the inked block and the back of the paper is rubbed vigorously with a spoon or a *barren,* which is a round firm pad of leather or palm leaf. The image is transferred onto the paper. Usually each color of the print requires its own wood block.

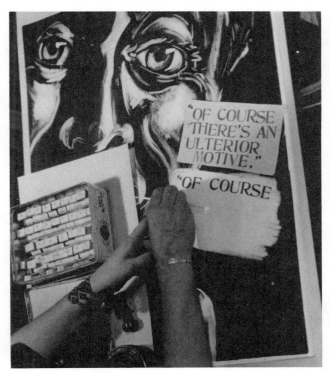

Sue Buck adds rubber-stamped words to the final print.

Artist Elizabeth Schippert working on a pochoir print. She sprays water-based paint through a cutout stencil using an airbrush.

The artist lifts the plastic stencil to expose her partially finished design before repeating the process.

Sabra Fields creating a woodcut. The drawing is transferred to the wood block, ready to be cut away. Photo by Molly Shallow.

Parts of the wood plank are cut away with the wood grain. Photo by Molly Shallow.

Parts of the image not to be printed are cut out of the wood block. Photo by Molly Shallow.

In Provincetown, Massachusetts during the early years of the 20th century, a unique form of woodcut printmaking was devised by a merry group of ladies who reportedly worked on their kitchen tables and produced genre scenes of American village life by means of a woodcut technique later known as *white line woodcuts.* These white line prints were invented by J. B. Nordfeldt in 1915. He had returned from Japan to Provincetown to teach his group of artist friends how to make Japanese Bohashi woodcuts using multiple blocks. With typical American ingenuity, he invented the more efficient white line wood block method, which calls for cutting and using only one block. The blocks had drawn areas which were isolated by a thin incised line. Each part of the image was painted with a color using watercolor paint and was printed separately by means of barren and hand pressure. These white line woodblock prints were printed one at a time, not in an edition. When one print sold, another print was made. The prints sang in full color of an earlier, innocent period in American life. Although white line woodcuts are made today, they do not have the

Printing ink is rolled out ready to be transferred to the wood block. Photo by Molly Shallow.

Another color about to be printed onto the print, which is held in register. Photo by Molly Shallow.

vivacity of the earlier prints, which are much sought after.

I was introduced to printmaking in Rockport, Massachusetts, by a small group of women calling themselves Folly Cove Designers who used woodcuts to imprint abstract motifs on paper and fabric. During the 1950s they formed an elite society by which a printmaker had to be accepted by their board members after offering her work for review. After the death of their leader, the group dissolved.

Wood Engraving

Wood engravings are recognized by the dense, intricate, and fine lines going in all directions, but not with the grain of the wood. Wood engravings are similar in technique to woodcuts in that un-

The print being pulled from the wood block after it has run through the press. Photo by Molly Shallow.

wanted areas are cut away leaving the raised surface to receive the ink. The major visible difference between wood engravings and woodcuts is that, in wood engravings, you see no grain since only the end grain of the wood block is used. The wood used usually has a very smooth, fine grain, such as fruit wood or holly. To make a wood engraving block, the wood is sliced across the grain of the tree and pieces of wood are glued together to form a large enough block.

Tools used to make the image are sharp pointed engraving tools, not the gouges used for woodcuts. Wood engraving cuts can be made across the grain in any direction, unlike woodcuts. Consequently wood engravings are characterized by intricately cut out areas and lines that define the inked image.

Wood engravings are usually small (since they are limited by the end grain blocks of wood); usually printed with black ink on smooth paper, often thin Japanese paper; and were originally used as book illustrations. Wood engravings are printed by using a screw-down type press similar to the ones used for letter press. Wood engraving is a very old art form developed in the 15th century to be compatible in depth with the wood letters often used in printing broadsides and later in 19th century advertisements. That is the reason the wood engraving block is traditionally "type high," thicker than other printing bases.

Linocuts

Linocuts are recognized by large, flat areas of ink, black or colorful, in bold styles. Because a linoleum plate cracks, this medium is not used for detailed work but only for gestural work and simple designs.

Linocuts or linoleum cuts are a more recent development of the woodcut process. Linoleum is easier to cut than wood. Besides being popular with grade school art classes, it is used by artists for special effects such as making large flat areas of black or color. Linocuts can be printed with the back of a spoon, a barren, or with a press on a smooth, thin paper.

Whitney Hansen cuts her final pearwood block.

Inking the final block, using a small brayer with the oil paint on it.

Preparing ink (in this case, oil paints) on the palette.

The Japanese paper is placed onto the inked wood block. The artist uses the back of a spoon to press the paper fibers onto the inked surface.

Pulling the multicolor woodcut.

Whitney Hansen exhibiting the final print. She comments on the texture of the handmade, unsized Japanese paper, which absorbs her inking and blends well with the textured print.

INTAGLIO PRINTING

Etchings

Etchings are made from a metal plate, either copper or zinc. The image is made by creating ink-holding gouges, crevices, holes, and lines in the metal surface. These incised markings hold ink in varying amounts.

How does this work? These inked marks get transferred through the pressure of a press onto a sheet of paper. This does not have to be a formal press. I have seen prints made by ink being transferred by the pressure of a car wheel or washing machine wringer.

Special viscous inks are required by the etching process so that the ink is sticky enough to stay in the plate gouges and crevices during the printing process. To explain further, first the etching plate is warmed and then covered with a greasy ink

which is then wiped off the surface using a smooth, semi-absorbent, hand-held mass of cheesecloth. What is left of the ink in the crevice is transferred in the following way: A printing "sandwich" is laid on the bed of the press. This consists of the plate, wet paper, a cover sheet, and soft blankets. This is run slowly through the press, which means the sandwich is squeezed through a pair of rollers.

Special paper is used for etchings. Generally it is 100% rag paper, created from cotton fibers. Hence, it has resilience, permanence, and strength. This paper is observably different from newsprint made from wood pulp, which is not acid free and will not last more than a few years. It is soft, warm in tone, and lends richness to the print.

The most exciting moment is when a print-maker "pulls" a print, i.e., when he or she pulls

Printmaker Siri Beckman cutting a wood engraving block. Photo courtesy of Siri Beckman.

The block being inked. Photo courtesy of Siri Beckman.

the paper up from the surface of the inked plate. Each etching in the edition requires re-inking the plate and going through the whole printing process.

Line etchings are made by first covering the plate with an acid-resistant coating. The artist scratches through this surface with a special tool, after which he immerses the plate in acid for varying periods of time, depending upon how deep he wants each mark.

Aquatints

An aquatint is a modification of an etching. It looks like a watercolor wash, but if you look at it closely you will see many fine dots created either by spraying a fine mist of spray paints or rosin dust melted onto the etching plate.

Soft Ground Etchings

Soft ground etchings are made by coating a plate with a very soft, waxy substance made of a combination of beeswax, lamb fat, and castor oil. The artist can draw into this by placing a sheet of paper on top of the ground and drawing into it. The ground lifts off into the sheet of paper or found objects, such as laces or flowers, may be pressed into the ground and then lifted off to create a ghost image which is then fixed by the acid bath.

Drypoints and Engravings

Drypoints are similar to etchings except the lines are made without the acid bite stage. Lines and textures are produced directly by scratching the metal surface. The burr created when an instrument drags through metal is like the furrow when a plow goes through earth. This burr holds the ink and gives a lovely soft, velvety quality to a drypoint line. The disadvantage of a drypoint is that only a tiny number of prints can be made from each plate because the pressure of the press and the motion of ink being wiped off eventually destroys the burr which is so coveted.

Engravings are variations of drypoints in that after the artist scratches into the metal surface with an engraving tool, the burr is polished away. Instead, light and dark tones are created by variations in the spacing and cross-hatching of the lines.

Mezzotints

This process was invented in Germany in the 17th century. A copper plate is first polished and then roughened with a rocker all over its surface. The rocker has minute sharp teeth which pluck the plate surface in several directions and leave crevices and burrs. These hold the ink in a particularly dense way when the plate is wiped and printed. The artist creates an image by scraping

Rolling the wood engraving block through the etching press using mat board as a "blanket" or felt. Photo courtesy of Siri Beckman.

off the roughness with a scraping tool, after the design is transferred onto the plate in reverse.

Mezzotint is a tonal process. The object is to reveal the image in light tone in contrast to the background's dark tones.

Collagraphs

Collagraphs are recognizable by surface textures, colors, and the indented images of the image area. Collagraphs are a form of printmaking which was begun about forty years ago when French printmakers made collages by attaching cut-up etching plates or glued found objects to their plates. Collagraphs are close to paintings in their immediacy.

Twenty years ago in America, a more permanent of the collagraph technique was made possible by the development of acrylic glues which permitted collages to be permanently attached to bases with attention to how the additive surfaces would hold ink. Artists inked their glued plates with colorful etching inks and oil paints instead of the traditional black or brown inks used in etchings.

Today collagraphs are made by using materials such as organza and other fabrics, tapes, papers, acrylic media, and other textures glued to a Ma-

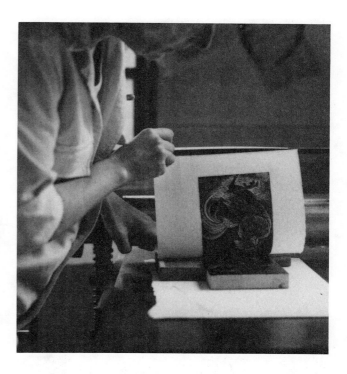

A proof being pulled off the block by the printmaker. Photo courtesy of Siri Beckman.

sonite® or cardboard base. Lines are incised into the base before inking. Collagraphs are also made by cutting cardboard into segments which are separately inked and then put through the press, together like a jigsaw puzzle or sequentially, in order to print them. In an intaglio print, such as a collagraph, the lines and textured areas print with a slight but palpable relief, above the paper's surface.

Collagraphs have the appearance of a manipulated print because the hand work of the artist is obvious. Since each collagraph inking is so carefully wiped before inking, editions tend to be small; hence, each collagraph print has value because more of the artist's attention goes into pulling each print than in any other print medium.

PLANOGRAPHIC PRINTING
Lithographs

Lithographs can be recognized by the dotted areas of crayon-like drawings or thin wash-like drawings printed on paper with no paper indenta-

Sticky printing ink is rubbed into the plate's gouges and lines. Photo by Randy W. Cole.

Grace Albee at work in 1982, cutting a wood engraving block. She was ninety-two years old when this was taken and, like many of her contemporary wood engravers, still working daily.

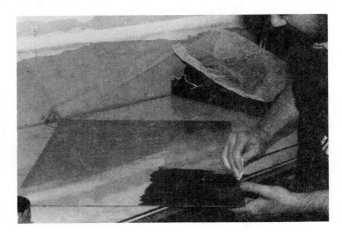

The greasy ink is wiped off the plate using a smooth semi-absorbent mass of cheesecloth. Photo by Randy W. Cole.

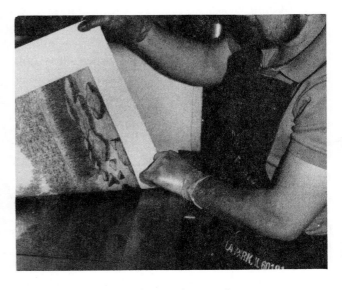

William Livesay scratches away the acid-resistant ground to create the image, which is then put into an acid bath. The acid eats away the exposed metal and makes crevices to hold the ink. Photo by Randy W. Cole.

Pulling the print. Photo by Randy W. Cole.

Mary Ann Wenniger inking a collagraph plate with a dabber.

Inking part of the surface of a plate with a roller so as to reach only the high points.

tion on the edge of the image. Lithographic printing ink lies thinly on the surface of the paper.

Lithographs are often similar in appearance to crayon drawings. A good impression reveals velvety blacks, soft grays, and rich, luminous colors. Many artists experiment and obtain fine wash effects with soft gradations of tone, which give their prints the appearance of watercolor paintings. Lithographs can be vivid or subtle in color; the creative possibilities for the lithographer are endless.

Lithographs are the most technically difficult prints to make. Therefore, not many lithographs are being printed today except by master printers, who print for artists, and by lithographers who still work on lithographic stones.

The artist draws with a greasy crayon or a greasy solution on the pebbled surface of a litho stone (a soft limestone from Bavaria) or on a metal offset plate that has a similar pebbled surface. The greasy drawing rests on the top of little hills that make up the lithographic surface. These marks are made permanent by means of chemical actions. First, they are dusted with talcum powder, then they are coated with a water soluble gum Arabic solution. Afterwards a dilute acid solution is applied. It indents the water soluble surface and gently eats around each greasy mark, making it stain the stone or plate.

Since the lithographic crayon which makes up the drawing is greasy and not water soluble, it resists water and remains to be printed by the lithographer, who works as follows. The stone or plate surface is sponged, isolating the greasy ink crayon image. Then a greasy ink-holding roller is passed over the whole surface, but the ink is repelled by the water in the dampened, non-image areas and attracted to the greasy areas.

To create an edition of prints, sheets of paper are laid on the inked stone one at a time, and the stone or plate and paper are then pulled through a hand-operated lithographic printing press under great pressure. The pressure of a scraper bar pulling across the litho stone or plate forces the transfer of ink from the stone to the paper. After each sheet of paper is printed, the stone or plate is dampened and inked again so that another print can be pulled.

Multicolored lithographs are made by drawing images on several plates, one for each color of ink. Each plate is placed in turn on the printing press and positioned so that, when printed, the color it holds will be perfectly lined up or *in register* with the colors already printed. If a color is *off register* (not properly aligned), it will overlap the outline and create an undesirable blurred effect. Colors are printed one at a time; the sheets of paper must

Wiping excess ink off a plate. Only a small amount left on the surface is sufficient when run through a press.

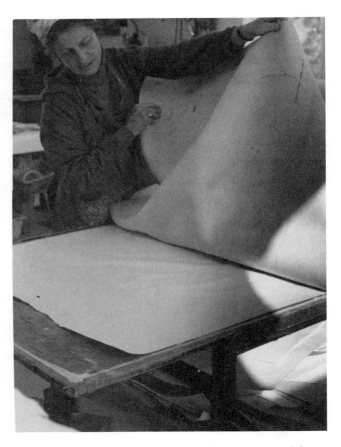

A sheet of protective paper has been placed on top of the etching paper to prevent staining the blanket, which is laid down next.

The artist lays a sheet of damp paper on top of the inked plate on the press bed.

be fed through the printing press one at a time for each color plate the artist prepares.

Because the crayons and inks the artist works with produce only black lines, the artist must imagine how each drawing will appear when printed in color. This is simple enough when only two or three areas of solid ink colors are added, but the process can become complicated if the artist decides to "mix" additional colors by printing them on top of one another. Each stone must be shaded with a different intensity to achieve a desired color, and the artist must position all the shaded areas on each of the stones in exact alignment.

When the artist and master printer print from the stones or plates, several proofs are pulled for the artist's inspection. When one finally meets with his approval as the finished image, he marks it *bon à tirer* which means "good to be pulled" or "good to be printed" and leaves it for a master printer to use as a guide when printing the edition.

Although the artist's drawings on the stones are capable of printing a thousand or more impressions, only a small number of original lithographs is normally produced, usually 200 or less. After an edition of prints has been pulled, the images on the surface of the stones are ground off in preparation for a new set of images to be drawn on them. If zinc or aluminum plates were used, they are usually destroyed or defaced to prevent unauthorized prints from being made.

Many contemporary artists such as James Rosenquist, Andy Warhol, Robert Rauschenberg, and Jasper Johns make use of the photo-offset

The finished print, Victorian Comfort. *Note the textures created by gluing an assemblage of doilies, tapes, and wallpaper to the particle board base (plate) prior to printing.*

method of printing, which until the 1960s was only used for inexpensive commercial printing. Since then, the use of the photo-offset process has become a highly controversial issue in the print world, because it employs the same printing methods used to make inexpensive art reproductions. This is explained in Chapter 2.

To make a photo-offset lithograph, an artist first creates a design or assembles the elements of his composition in the way he wants them photographed. The composition is then photographed through a special screen, which translates the tonal values into tiny dots. *Halftone dot patterns* are normally clearly visible on the finished prints. A negative image is then transferred onto a metal plate coated with a light-sensitive, water-soluble solution. This solution hardens when it is exposed to light. When the negative and plate are exposed to a special high-intensity lamp, the light penetrates the gray and light areas on the negative, causing the coating to harden on the plate where it becomes the image that will be inked and printed. The dark areas on the negative (the non-image areas) do not allow light to penetrate and harden the coating. Because the coating is water-soluble, these areas will be washed out later. The thin metal plate is then attached to a roller and placed on an offset printing press, which inks the image and transfers or "offsets" it onto a rubber roller. This roller rotates and prints the image onto sheets of paper.

Most prints made by the photo-offset process do not qualify as original prints, since the process is more often used to make exact copies of paintings and designs that were originally created in other art media. However, some artists have found photo-offset lithography well suited to creating certain visual effects, which they are unable to duplicate with other printmaking processes. If the

John Hutcheson sponging the stone with gum arabic and then drying during edition printing of Helen Frankenthaler's lithograph, Mirabelle. Photo by Marabeth Cohen, courtesy of Tyler Graphics, Ltd.

artist starts out with an idea he wants to express as a print, and if he decides photo-offset lithography is the best medium through which to translate his idea onto paper, then there is no reason buyers should not accept the resulting edition of prints as original. You must, however, be careful to distinguish between printmakers who employ photography creatively, and those who use it for purely reproductive purposes.

Buyers of lithographs should look especially for early lithographs, European and American.

Take care to ask for the *provenance* of an old print, i.e., documentation of where and how the gallery came to have the particular print.

Many lithographs made from 1920 to the 1960s were crayon drawn, in a narrative and figurative style that shows American rural and domestic scenes. These were often printed for the artist by lithographic printers such as Miller and Sons in New York. Always charming and unnumbered, they can be recognized by the rich variations of black and gray tones and rather lumpy, rounded figures.

Stowe Wengenroth spent his life drawing scenes near his homes in Maine, Connecticut,

Sponging the stone with water to clean it. Photo by Marabeth Cohen, courtesy of Tyler Graphics, Ltd.

Cleaning the stone with water. Photo by Marabeth Cohen, courtesy of Tyler Graphics, Ltd.

and Rockport, Massachusetts. He always sent his stones to Miller and Sons to be printed. Miller, meanwhile, would send him another prepared stone to work on. His images were gradually built up of successive layers of hard crayons covered with softer crayon until the blacks were dense but not smudged. This took weeks to accomplish to his satisfaction.

During the 1950s lithography was reintroduced as a popular medium by workshops in New York and New Mexico, where lithographic printmakers printed multiple images for American Expres-

sionist painters. Here the hired printers were as creative as their colleagues, the painters. Because this collaboration was an expensive process, the scenario was enlarged: a new commercial person was introduced—a publisher who paid for the printing and hence received most of the prints. At that time, the notion of strictly controlling the number of prints became commonplace in order to make this a profitable business, pivoting around the carefully created rarity of the prints. Print barons who waved banners announcing pre-publication prices and rarity came into the mar-

Preparing to place the paper on the inked lithographic stone. Photo by Marabeth Cohen, courtesy of Tyler Graphics, Ltd.

Placing the paper in registration on the stone. Photo by Marabeth Cohen, courtesy of Tyler Graphics, Ltd.

ketplace. Commercialism in the art industry was established with this renaissance of lithography.

Serigraphy

Serigraphy, or silkscreens, can be recognized by the flat areas of color making hard edged, crisp images on paper surfaces. Silkscreens do not have indented images or edges. They are now printed on 100% rag paper. They are pencil signed and numbered. The colored inks rest on the top surface of the printing paper. In a silkscreen, *skins* of color are laid flat onto the paper by a screening process to create the image.

To make a silkscreen a mesh fabric, not necessarily silk, is attached to a wooden frame. This screen is made into a stencil with closed areas which repel ink and open areas which allow ink to go through the fabric and onto the printing paper, which gradually adds layers or areas of ink and finally produces an image.

The inks used are oil-based or water-based emulsions. Be sure to ask your art dealer which type of ink your artist used because this affects the durability of the ink surfaces.

John Hutcheson pulling an impression from Helen
Frankenthaler's Mirabelle stone. Photo by Marabeth Cohen,
courtesy of Tyler Graphics, Ltd.

A silkscreen printmaker uses a separate screen for each color. An artist may use as many as a hundred screens in order to make a completed image.

The silkscreening process requires that each color be printed, one color at a time, for the entire number of prints in the edition. So, after making trial color prints (proofs) and deciding on what color will be used in each succeeding layer of ink, the artist determines the appropriate size of the edition according to his or her energy and hunch about the marketability and relative complexity or simplicity of making this particular picture.

For example, the artist must determine how many prints he wants to end up with—including the throwaway mistakes and trial colors. Since printing is fairly mechanical work after each color decision is made, professional silkscreen printmakers are often used to pull editions of 200 to 300 prints.

As part of his expertise, a professional silkscreen artist will conquer the problem of lining up the colors so that they go in the exact same place each time the ink is pulled through the screen onto another piece of paper. This action is called *registration*. It is crucial to successful silkscreen printmaking and is accomplished in various ways, more fully explained in books on how to do silkscreens.

Contemporary silkscreens are often printed by silkscreen machines or mechanical arms that pull the ink over the open areas of the screen.

Silkscreens with many layers of ink superimposed eventually get a cracked surface called *crackeux* by silkscreen artists, which the buyer has to accept as a normal condition.

> Secret: Making original prints is a labor-intensive process; therein lies their value.

ORIGINALS

Prints are originals because they are directly created by an artist known as a printmaker. They are signed in pencil, indicating that each print is an original work of art, in spite of the fact that printmaking artists, or print workshops working under

Pencil study of image for Joe Price's silkscreen print, Raincatcher.

their guidance, produce multiples in groups called *editions*. Every print in an edition is signed and numbered by the artist.

Making prints is a legitimate art form which allows an artist to create many originals of the same image, using labor-intensive methods. Prints are valued because they evidence in unique ways the handwork and decision-making power of the printmaker. In fact, there are as many different ways to make etchings, silkscreens, woodcuts, etc. as there are individual printmakers.

Limited in Number

Original prints are printed by the artist or in a printmaking studio by professional printmakers who are guided by the artist. There is a finite

Line drawing of the image—used beneath the screen to block out areas not receiving color.

number of copies made, usually no more than 200. Some editions are as small as two, or even one, in which case they are known as *monoprints*.

How can you tell the size of an edition? Look at the bottom margin of the print and in one corner you will note a fraction, such as 3/100, written in pencil. This means that the artist made this the third print out of the total edition of 100.

A low numbered print in the edition is not necessarily better than a high number with one exception: Prints created by the drypoint technique, which depends on the raised metal burr of the incised line to give the special quality to the inked print, rapidly lose that burr after repeated runs through the press.

When you see prints unnumbered or with edi-

tion sizes of 500 or more, they usually are no longer originals pulled by the artist, but mechanical reproductions made by an offset press. These can be high quality four-color reproductions, sometimes signed by the artist and commanding a high price, but they are not limited edition original prints.

Innovative

Each artist printmaker uses the media of his choice to achieve his or her aesthetic vision. Hence, printmaking results vary immensely and the more prints you see, the more varied the technique.

Affordable

Today, the price of many original prints is from $50 to $500, and therefore is considerably lower than that of paintings. The reason for this is the fact that the artist has made a number of prints instead of just one painting. During WPA (Works Progress Administration) days, original prints were printed to be sold for less than five dollars each...so artist printmakers could eat! Since then, even though printmaking is labor-intensive and time consuming, original prints are usually priced by the artist to meet the market and be saleable. Selling well builds an artist's reputation, as well as keeping the artist alive.

Prices of contemporary original prints can go as high as $2500 or more for work by name printmakers whose efforts may be paid for by backers (called "publishers") and promoted by expensive publications, brochures, advertisements, and other means of distribution.

Historical

In galleries, you will find both antique and modern prints to buy. *Master* prints are from 15th to 20th century Europe. *Vintage* prints date from the early days of printmaking in this century. *Contemporary* prints are made by artist printmakers today. Contemporary prints are made by the following artists:

1. Academics who teach printmaking in colleges and high schools and pursue one or several types of printmaking, may enter national competitions,

Tracing with pencil in order to block in the screen.

and are represented by galleries.

2. Professional printmakers who work for the sake of making original prints as their primary medium, and identify themselves as printmakers.

3. Painter printmakers who are artists in all sorts of media, who find that printmaking accomplishes their aesthetic goals. They often collaborate with master printers. Since they are successful as artists, they can hire master printers and often charge more money for their prints. There are also painters whose paintings are reproduced as limited reproductive editions, which are *color separated mechanically* and should not be confused with original prints. Your task is to ask the art dealer what was the level of the artist's involvement.

Large Selection

In the U.S. there are at least 200,000 printmakers producing an average of three new images per year, in editions of twenty to a hundred original prints. Subjects vary: landscapes, abstractions, humor, pathos, anger, street scenes, domestic scenes, portraits of people.

Decorative

Prints can be brought into a room, much as windows in a wall open up a blank wall, by introducing interesting subjects, colors, vistas, and dynamism. Print selection is large enough and inexpensive enough to justify matching fabrics, colors, and textures. Frames for prints are usually simple in design, modest in size, and not usually bulky. Thus, you can move framed prints easily to different walls in your home or to different houses or offices.

Transportable

Since original prints are works of art on paper, they are lightweight and easy to ship or take with you when purchased. The usual way to mail a print is in a tube. All galleries carrying prints have heavy-duty cardboard tubes in which they receive and ship prints. Ask for one when you buy a print. These tubes are also useful for storing artwork safely.

Tactile

The primary appeal of prints is their fresh appearance, provided by their paper-borne imagery. The combination of paper backgrounds and ink or paints transferred to the paper by means of a press or a hand's pressure, provides a crispness that is unique. James deWoody, pochoir printmaker,

The screen ready for printing.

wrote in an article in *American Artist* magazine, "I am in love with paper...the way paper takes paint is a delicious thing to see."

Technical Interest

The technical processes involved in printmaking are intriguing. Prints, unlike paintings, require a step-by-step procedural discipline in their execution by the artist which can be appreciated by the buying public.

For instance, a lithograph requires a series of intricate chemical steps which, if changed by a slight degree, can dramatically change the final result. A few drops of benzene added to the tusche background work creates beautiful textures in a technique known as *peau de crapeau* (frog's skin).

A complexity of technical procedures used in a range of combinations produces work immediately compelling to the viewer. Robert Rauschenberg's images incorporate photographs, washes, and transfers in striking lithographic statements.

Good printmakers often make use of technical "accidents," creating lovely effects which might not have been planned originally. Art buyers who have become more knowledgeable of printmaking techniques watch for these accidents.

PRINTMAKING MARKS AND SYMBOLS

Until about the 1920s, prints bore only the artist's signature. At first, the artist scribed his initials or name on the plate or wood block backwards so that it would read correctly when printed. Then it became more common for the printmaker to sign his name on the finished print in pencil on the bottom margin. Pencil, not ink, was used so that it would not bleed or fade.

As multiple prints became a popular and available art form, artists began to add the edition size to the bottom margin, such as "Ed. 50," so that the buying public would be made more aware of the limited availability of the print.

Finally, artists added the number of the print in a particular edition so that he or she could better record the location of a particular print as it was distributed to various galleries or dealers around the country. This was written in the form of a fraction, such as 3/100, three being the number of the print and 100 being the edition size.

Other symbols or information printmakers include on the bottom margin are:
• Trial Proof or T.P.—where the printmaker experiments or tries out different inking combinations.
• State Proof or S.P. I, II, etc.—when the original plate is significantly altered by adding to or sub-

Prints drying in the studio.

The final print.

tracting parts of the image and a new edition is printed.

• Artist Proof or A.P.—These are prints, usually no more than 10% of the edition, that the artist keeps for himself and for special exhibitions. These do not carry an edition number. These prints are selected and therefore considered by the artist and the public to be the best.

Other less common symbols that turn up on prints have to do with the printing of editions, such as Printer's Proof or P.P.—a print that the printer is authorized to keep as a thanks for his work; and B.A.T., which in French means *bon à tirer* or "good to print," signifying that this is the print that the master printer shows the artist and the artist okays, thus giving his approval on this inking for the edition.

Finally, no edition number or information on edition size, but just the artist's signature, means that the print is part of an "Open Edition." Either the artist expects an unlimited number to be printed and therefore more available, or he expects the print to be a best seller and wants to be free to print more as needed. The lack of rarity will have an effect on the price.

WHERE CAN I FIND ORIGINAL PRINTS?

Now that you know about the different types of original prints, where do you find them? You can look at and buy prints at the following places:

Artist's studios are fascinating places to discover. Do your research beforehand to find out if you like the artist's style of work and then make an appointment. Occasionally, larger urban areas may have Junior Leagues or other associations that organize "art tours," where local artists have open houses at set times.

Art associations have semi-permanent exhibits of the work of their members who have met certain qualifications to join the association. They are excellent sources of regional artists who might not be represented by the big-time galleries.

Artists' cooperatives have a relatively small, select group of artists who share in costs and administration.

Art galleries are a major source of quality work, both traditional and contemporary. They represent many artists whose work need not be as expensive as you think. Most galleries tend to specialize in certain artistic directions: Art Deco, 19th century, Impressionist, abstract, figurative, decorative, and so on. Art galleries are usually concentrated in certain city neighborhoods, so you can easily walk from one to another.

Resort galleries also show good work by a variety of artists, usually regional. They often are located in popular resort areas with reputations as summer art colonies. Big city artists spend the summer months there working, as well as selling their work. Prices are usually lower than art in city galleries, which have high rent and overhead costs.

Mall shops cater to impulse buyers and have volume sales at more modest price ranges. They concentrate more on inexpensive posters and ready-framed reproductions, but they also usually carry original prints at fair prices.

Frame shops carry prints of all types as an adjunct to their framing business. The work shown tends to be more commercial in nature and reflect the taste of the shop's owner.

Secret: Original prints are worth buying.

- They are original works of art.
- They are made in a limited number.
- They are innovative.
- They are multiples and therefore affordable.
- They are pencil signed, which signifies the artist's approval.
- They are often historical in background, part of a uniquely American print tradition.
- They are extremely tactile and can be explained in terms of a printmaking medium.
- They challenge you because of their technical interest.
- They offer a large selection from which to choose.
- They are decorative and frameable.
- They are transportable.
- They are a source of pleasure.

Secret: Learn the great names and great periods in American printmaking so you will be more informed when looking at original prints.

ETCHING IN AMERICA

Etching, with its likeness to writing and its spontaneity, was the favorite print medium in Europe during the 19th century. In America, the art of etching grew out of interest in the European tradition of the artist as printmaker—*peintre-graneur.* By the late 1870s the shared interests of many American etcher printmakers led them to organize etching clubs in the cities of Cincinnati, Philadelphia, Brooklyn, New York, and Boston. In 1887, the Boston Museum of Fine Arts organized an exhibition of the "Work of Women Etchers of America" which showed the work of Mary Cassatt.

By the late 19th century, galleries were actively selling etchings by James McNeill Whistler, William Stanley Hayter, Thomas Moran, and Joseph Pennel. These were mostly intimate landscapes of places familiar to the printmakers—Gloucester, Annesquam, Oyster Bay, Easthampton, Passaic, and other East Coast watering places.

Winslow Homer turned to etching in 1894, creating places and recording people at work and play. But Joseph Pennel was the great etcher recorder of the American and European cityscape, who influenced other artist etchers until the end of World War I. John Sloan memorialized people in their daily activities in New York. Edward Hopper and Martin Lewis continued exploring the city and urban figures during the 1920s, in dramatic black and white etchings. John Taylor Arms was another giant of this period. As the president of the National Society of American Etchers, he recorded etchings of all the cathedrals in Europe and preached about printmaking, as well as giving etching demonstrations to groups wherever he was invited. His grandson told me that he made a demonstration print at each talk, while he proselytized about the wonders of the etching medium. Then he gave a free print of the demonstration print to each person attending his lecture.

John Marin used the etching medium for abstracted images of boats and cities, expressively distorting and fracturing solids and spaces, foretelling the future abstract uses of etchings by artist printers in the mid-20th century.

WOODCUTS AND WOOD ENGRAVING IN AMERICA

Concurrently, during the late 19th and early 20th century, wood engraving emerged from an advertising craft into a highly original art form. Timothy Cole, William Baxter Closson, and Elbridge Kingsley formed a New School of American Wood Engraving, in order to make creative artists out of mechanical wood engravers.

Nineteenth century wood engraving workshops, which produced newspaper advertisements and magazine illustrations, were set up in a mode similar to chromolithography workshops of the same period. The wood engravers who cut portions of a block showing sky and foliage were called *printers;* those who showed draperies, *tailors;* those who drew people, *butchers;* and those who made machines, *mechanics.* Wood engraving blocks were cut apart, given to artisans to work on and then reassembled and touched up before printing.

Under the New School of American Wood Engraving, artists were encouraged to improvise new ways of cutting by cross-lining, stippling, and pricking the wood so that new effects in subtle tones and more intricate textures resulted.

Like the artist etchers in the late 19th century, wood engravers formed an organization, the Society of American Wood Engravers, which printed 100 copies of its members' works in an album, *Engravings on Wood.*

Originality in American wood engravings and woodcut prints was more pronounced than in etchings. In Provincetown, Massachusetts, unconnected with the turmoil in New York, a group of lady artists working at their kitchen tables evolved the technique of white line woodcuts, bought now as an indigenous American art form. Under the leadership of Blanche Lazell, they used their watercolors to print one color at a time on their simple one-block woodcuts of local province, street, town, and water scenes. They never numbered their productions but kept the wood blocks and printed them upon request and when needing money.

Ferol Sibley Warthen, who was in her nineties and still printing white line woodcuts when I met her, never caught up with her print orders because she printed each image color by color in a tedious production of a limitless edition, printed on demand. When she died, Warthen had no work left to show in our Provincetown gallery because she had sold everything she printed for $25 to $100, even in the 1980s.

After 1900, photo-mechanical processes were used in magazines and newspapers, so wood engraving was no longer associated with the printing trades but stood on its own. Wood engraving did not die, however, but flourished until the present, although it is far less spontaneous than etching, silkscreen, or lithography. If a wood engraver makes one slip on the block with his cutter, the block and months of work are ruined.

Among the famous American wood engravers who were supported by the WPA were Rockwell Kent and Fritz Eichenberg. Working independently of the WPA, Thomas Nason and Grace Albee cut intricate wood engravings of domestic and rural subjects, scenes close to home: outhouses and junkyards, stone fences and fields. Lynd Ward's wood engravings were made mostly during the 1930s. He illustrated his famous wordless books, allegories such as *Madman's Dream,* as well as his wife Mae Ward's children's books. A Socialist, Ward printed more images from blocks as his woodcuts sold for five dollars each. He was adamantly against numbering prints or making editions. Near the end of his life the day I visited him, his grandson was printing a block for him under his supervision. Ward's wood engravings have a peculiarly apocalyptic spirit similar to Grant Wood's lithographs.

LITHOGRAPHY IN AMERICA

Early in the 20th century, Joseph Pennel complained about the commercialism of the American lithographic industry, which focused on chromo-lithography and would have little to do with working with artist lithographers. He finally found a German lithographer working in Philadelphia to print his drawings on litho stones for his 1912 series on the Panama Canal.

Five years later, George C. Miller and Bolton Brown formed a company that still exists, George Miller and Sons, the nexus of great black and white lithographs in America. Among the famous lithographers printed by Miller and Sons were George Bellows, who memorialized scenes of America's past; and Grant Wood and Thomas Hart Benton, whose lyrical lithographs of rural America are unsurpassed and command high prices today.

Stowe Wengenroth created his first lithographs during this pre-Depression and Depression period. Always printed by Miller and Sons master printers, Wengenroth was popular from the start with his timeless fishing villages, lighthouses, and harbors. Living in Maine, Connecticut, and finally in Rockport, Massachusetts, where he died in 1976, he told me that he always had subjects enough without leaving his home. He spent at least a month drawing on one of Miller's stones, first using a light, hard crayon and gradually adding darker tones by successive layering of softer crayons, until one image fairly sung with rich tones. The stones were shipped to Miller in New York for proofing, whereupon Wengenroth was sent proofs to select a *bon à tirer* (okay to print proof), return it, and order an edition of twenty-five to 100 prints to be printed for him by George Miller and later by his sons.

The single most important event for printmaking in this country was the advent of the WPA workshops in the 1930s. With the several funded art projects of Franklin Delano Roosevelt's New Deal, lithography and wood engraving as art forms emerged and were taught to artists, so that they would have a way to readily make multiples which could be sold for one to five dollars, in order to attract buyers, not collectors.

Will Barnet, a famous painter, still prolific and making prints and paintings in 1990, tells of teaching lithographic printing at the Art Students League, under the WPA. Isaac Sanger told me about teaching wood engraving at the WPA printmaking workshop in Washington.

Herbert Waters, New Hampshire wood engraver, tells how this was the happiest period of his artistic life, when he turned in a finished wood engraving every two weeks, in return for his weekly stipend of $20.

Under the project, artists for the first time explored color printing and lithographs in four and five colors. Printing multicolor woodcuts was developed under the leadership of Louis Schanker. An exhibition of the new work, entitled "Printmaking, A New Tradition," was held at the project's Federal Art Gallery in New York. Jacob Kainen, WPA printmaker and later curator of prints and drawings at the National Collection of Fine Arts, wrote in 1972: "We should not overlook the importance of the WPA graphic arts division which bridged the gap between the old moribund etching societies and the flowering of the graphic arts, which would take place when William Stanley Hayter in 1940 opened his experimental etching studio Atelier 17M New York."

SILKSCREEN IN AMERICA

A silkscreen unit was launched within the Graphic Arts Division of the New York Federal Art Project, under the direction of Andrew Velonis, who had been trained in commercial screen printing and argued that silkscreen would be a facile and inexpensive medium for experimentation. Beatrice Olds, Adolph Gottlieb, Louis Lozowick, and Edward Landon worked for the unit initially. All of these artists' work can still be found in galleries and bought today.

In commercial shops during the 1920s, the silkscreen had been experimented with in various ways: with paper, shellac and lacquer stencils; tusche stencils used with glue that would be washed out to provide open areas to press ink through the silk mesh; and photo stencils.

These methods also were experimented with by a New England group: Adolph Gottlieb, George Shokler, Philip Hickens, and Edward Landon. In 1940, when they were planning an exhibit at the

Weye Gallery to sell their works at a dollar each, they wrote to Carl Zigrosser, Director of the Philadelphia Museum, asking him what to call their new art form in order to distinguish it from commercial screen printing. Zigrosser replied that the Greek root for silk was *ser*: "What do you think of the term *serigraphy*, silk drawing, by analogy to stone drawing, lithography." Thus came the confusion of the double name of serigraphs and silkscreens for the single process.

The Silkscreen Group, organized under the FAP, later became the National Serigraph Society, with Doris Meltzer as director; and exhibitions, classes, lectures, and a gallery for sales were established.

THE EXPANSION OF AMERICAN PRINTMAKING

Although most American printmakers, particularly etchers, clung to a black and white tradition, experiments in color printmaking led to the founding of the American Color Print Society in 1939. Stanley Hayter's Atelier taught the color-layering process of viscosity printmaking, where colors were kept clear and isolated when printing on a single plate, by means of using different amounts of oil in the rollers passed over the inked etching plate. The technique used was resist inking, which became a fad in printmaking, whereby one color which had little or no oil acted like peanut butter, as a tight layer resisting oil when rolled over a greasy layer of ink. I compare this technique to a mayonnaise layer being rolled over and repelling and being repelled by the peanut butter layer.

The next major event in the history of printmaking in the United States was the collaboration between lithographic printers, who became known as *master printers*, and the painter-artists, interested in using printmaking to further their growth by exploring the use of new media.

Tatanya Grossman in 1957 began Universal Limited Art Editions in her garage on Long Island; and June Wayne received a Ford grant of $135,000 in 1960 in order to found the Tamarind Lithographic Workshop in Los Angeles, whose goal it was to stimulate development of the lithograph

White line woodcut by Ferol Sibley Warthen, Violet. The white lines were created by gouged lines in the original wood block. Only the spaces between lines were painted with watercolors before printing.

and restore its popularity for American artists. Many workshops were formed in the 1960s, amidst the demands of a booming new print market, funded by a new species: Print publishers who added a new factor to printmaking. In order to stimulate sales, a new element of rarity was introduced by putting a strong emphasis on making a limited number of prints and cancelling or destroying the plate, stone, or screens after printing, thus facilitating competitiveness and higher prices in print sales.

Some of the artist printers in this new growth of master printing were Robert Motherwell, Willem de Kooning, Robert Rauschenberg, Helen

Frankenthaler, Jackson Pollack, and others whose prints are rare and expensive to buy now.

At the same time, workshops were opened for an independent new breed of printmakers, who cultivated printmaking as a medium in and of itself. Robert Blackburn, who worked as a master printer for Grosman, got federal grants to open the Blackburn workshop, which still flourishes under his guidance in New York. It is a warehouse housing several etching and lithographic spaces and offering memberships to interested artists.

Another segment of printmakers evolved, who might be called "academic printmakers." They teach printmaking and publish editions and sell their prints, usually at more modest prices than do the painter printmakers.

Academics such as Bruce McComb, teaching at Hope College; Arthur Werger, at Wesleyan in Ohio; Yuji Hiratsuka at Indiana University, to cite a few, use the facilities of their print rooms and often hire students to help edition their prints.

Will Barnet, who still teaches at the Philadelphia College of Art and the Art Institute, straddles both worlds because he paints and teaches while his prints are made as lithograph silkscreen combinations, not as copies of his paintings by master printers.

ONE PRINT BUYER'S STORY

Here is a story of a successful print buyer. Richard treasures his print purchases and shares his stories with me and many others. Over the years, he has given himself treats of art while raising a family on a journalist's salary. He had a drop-in friendship with an antique dealer who showed him vintage WPA prints and told him about the old-time printmakers he had known. As a result, most of his prints were bought for $10 to $30; they are now very valuable.

One day, he showed me his "Fondling Box." When he is a little down in spirits or lonely, he returns to visit the works of art on paper that he has bought over the years. He remembers the day and hour, how and from whom each piece was purchased. He has a story to tell about the acquisition of every one. He tells stories about the printmakers—who they were, why and how they worked.

This "Fondling Box," which is a specially built conservation storage box, has traveled with him on his writer's journey, and now sits under the spare room bed in his small retirement house.

REPRODUCTIONS
How to Recognize Limited Edition and Book Plate Prints
2

When Joe received, as a dividend from his book club, *Reproductions of Flowers by Redouté,* he was delighted because at last he was able to identify the old rose vine in his favorite aunt's garden. When he was Christmas shopping for her gift, he found an inexpensive reprint of Redouté roses that made a perfect gift. Though he usually bought original prints, this reproduction served his needs personally, aesthetically, and financially.

This flower book by Redouté was printed in the late 18th century. It has since been reprinted in many forms. This chapter will evaluate book plate prints and other reproductions available today.

Besides galleries, there are many public places where you can find prints displayed: outdoor fairs, art expos, craft shows, and art auctions are held each year all over the United States, and thousands of prints are shown. The print buyer may come away confused about what he has seen. As you wander down the aisles of art fairs, we want you to know why many prints look incredibly different from others. Some prints are textured, others are static. Why? We want you to know what you are looking at and what questions to ask to find out.

The subject of this chapter is the various types of reproductions, which are also called "prints" when you go to buy them. We want you to understand that these prints are completely different in quality than the prints described in Chapter 1. And we want to help you make an informed choice in considering them.

The confusion in the public's mind is that some of these reproductions are called limited edition prints because, although they are photographic copies of original paintings, they are pencil signed and numbered by the artist exactly as original prints are.

HOW DO YOU RECOGNIZE REPRODUCTIONS?

Secret: Look for the intentions of the artist when distinguishing between reproductions and original prints.

Original prints are those that draw the viewer into the process of making the prints. The artist's intention was to make an original print, not a copy of a painting or an illustration for a book, an advertisement, a guide, or a historical document. However, keep in mind that many contemporary wood engravings printed in limited numbers originate as book illustrations.

If you are considering buying reproductions you need to know what questions to ask before buying them and how to recognize the quality of what you are buying.

Reproductions can be any of the following: posters; offset-printed copies of paintings; Polaroids® and other facsimiles of paintings; the illustrations from old books known as bookplate prints.

You can recognize a poster because its surface is slick, the colors are flat looking, and the price is relatively inexpensive. However, in recent years, there has been a renaissance of art posters made by original print processes, in limited editions of less than 100, used to advertise causes. These often become collector's items.

Signature placement helps distinguish this as a reproduction. The signature is inside the image itself.

TYPES OF REPRODUCTIONS

Limited edition prints are contemporary paintings which are photo-mechanically reproduced in limited number (from 700 to 2500) on an offset press, often under careful supervision. These preserve a part of our artistic heritage and serve to distribute art at affordable prices to clientele an artist might not ordinarily reach. If you buy what you really like and buy from presses with reputations for integrity, there might be a secondary market for such prints in 100 years, just as there is today for the reproductions of paintings as printed in the 1860s.

Polaroid® copies of paintings are generically related to photography rather than prints, but are mentioned here because you should know that this method of reproduction is widely used, particularly for Impressionist paintings.

Thanks to a new Polaroid® process, your furniture store may carry these museum quality replicas of paintings, which are made by using a large format camera and digital image processing.

The film used is approximately the same size as the original paintings, and the camera makes its way in inchworm fashion across the screen, where each image is divided into millions of individual picture elements by a computer. The resulting image produces amazing verisimilitude. Works by Monet, Renoir, Chagall, Degas, Van Gogh, and others are available at prices under $100.

Book illustrations documenting natural history, botany, shellfish, and travel are called book plate prints. They command the most respected segment of the quality reproductions sold today and are discussed in detail later in this chapter.

Engraved, mezzotinted, and chromolithographically printed reproductions of 18th and 19th century paintings include the reproductions of American genre paintings sold today at high prices. The American Art Union, during the 1860s, printed engravings of George Caleb Brigham's paintings such as *The Jolly Flatboatman* and *The Country Election*. These reproductions of the most popular engravings were printed to popularize these paintings and distribute them.

> Secret: Limited edition prints are the most confusing of the reproductions available.

Limited edition prints can be recognized because their edition size is high, usually more than 300. A high number such as 956/2500 means that this print has been reproduced photomechanically and printed on an offset press.

Paintings are replicated by the artist through a company that arranges and pays for the painting and is called such and such press or publisher. Since this reference is the same as the name given

A reproduction print: Tobin's Barn. *Based on a painting by David Armstrong, a student of Eric Sloane, a realist whose style celebrates timeless Americana. Photo courtesy of Mill Pond Press, Inc.*

Reproductions of Paul Calle's oil paintings preserve and portray America's western heritage. Limited edition prints of his work are reminiscent of the now valuable chromolithographs made by Louis Prang of Thomas Moran's work in the late 19th century. Photo courtesy of Mill Pond Press, Inc.

to producers of books and original prints, the name of the company can be misleading. Some companies conveniently include the word "reproductions" and some do not, which might lead to the mistaken impression that the latter sells original prints.

However, many companies and artists are quite matter of fact about their processes. Popular artists like R.C. Gorman and presses like Mill Pond Press produce videos that tell the complete story of how they produce a reproduction.

HOW REPRODUCTIONS ARE MADE

Many publishers create extraordinary products in their reproductions, striving to be faithful to the original painting by consulting with the artist, and

This artist's painterly style distinguishes this reproduction. Summer Sketches by Robert Sarsony is a reproduction of an oil painting painted in a deliberately loose style. Mill Pond Press captures the work through fastidious attention to detail and many steps of printing.

making many careful corrections by adding plates to add depth and nuances. The following is a summary of how a limited edition print is made according to the Mill Pond Press.

A painting is selected and a contract is made with the artist. The painting is photographed onto four color continuous tone films. Then these are photographed separately with overlays of dot screens. They become "halftone film" with more dots for darker areas and fewer dots for lighter areas. Today, this translation can be computerized, hence truer to the original. Each halftone film is shot onto an aluminum offset plate with photo-sensitive emulsion on it. These four halftone plates are overprinted on a standard offset press in yellow, cyan (blue-green), magenta, and black inks.

Once the films are made and checked, they are exposed to a printing plate, with each color requiring a separate plate. The printing plate transfers the ink to a rubber blanket which then transfers, or "offsets," the ink to the paper. More plates may be added to strengthen details. The prints are inspected and curated for defects. The print papers are trimmed and stored or distributed by the publisher.

Although the original painting is clearly signed, which shows in the reproduction, many companies

Lincoln Graphics' electronic retouching department. Photo by Jack Slavin, courtesy of Lincoln Graphics, Inc.

An offset press. Photo by Jack Slavin, courtesy of Lincoln Graphics, Inc.

The laser scanner is used for state-of-the-art, top quality reproduction. Photo by Jack Slavin, courtesy of Lincoln Graphics, Inc.

The color manager marking corrections on the pre-proof after comparing to the original. Photo by Jack Slavin, courtesy of Lincoln Graphics, Inc.

The reproduction artist discussing corrections with the color manager. Photo by Jack Slavin, courtesy of Lincoln Graphics, Inc.

Final inspection before approval to run edition. Photo by Jack Slavin, courtesy of Lincoln Graphics, Inc.

ask the artist to pencil sign and number the finished prints. On the one hand, this could be considered reprehensible because it confuses them with original prints. On the other, if the print is valued and valuable a hundred years from now, the signature will make it more collectible.

> Secret: The price of limited edition prints reflects the technology and quality of the reproduction.

ASSESSING PRICE AND QUALITY

Print pricing corresponds to the time spent finding paintings to print and negotiating and promot-

ing the company's artists, as well as the advertising, marketing, and printing costs this type of speculative business requires.

Reproductions are part of the American culture. Commodities of the good life—pictures, flowers, music, and wine—are part of our tradition. Chromolithographs to cheer the hearth at less than five dollars were mass produced for the American home, along with the family broom, in the latter part of the 19th century. Some Currier and Ives prints are documented to have sold 200,000 copies.

The number of reproductions which can be made is unlimited, except by business prudence. A typical initial printing run will be 700 to 2500 prints. More reproductions can be printed as needed from the color transparency of the painting, which is made as step one in reproducing it and can be stored for later printings.

The difference between reproductive prints and original prints is that, although both are prints on paper, original prints are artworks on paper conceived by the artist to be printed as multiples, and not conceived to be paintings. Think of the artist's intention when you distinguish between an original print and a reproduction. The artist whose painting was intended to be an acrylic, oil, or a watercolor painting in and of itself can be copied by taking steps to reproduce it photographically and photo-mechanically on a printer's offset press.

Since reproductions are cost efficient to print and are mass produced, they are usually relatively inexpensive. But many publishers work extra hard to produce prints that look exactly like the original, by adding many more plates than strictly necessary in order to create colors with depth and strength. Hence, their print prices are high. These companies work speculatively, much like book publishers, bidding on an artist's work and hoping it will sell. And they cover their guesses by charging enough for the works that sell to cover the ones that do not.

Many reproductions are priced according to the fame of the artist. As long as you realize that you are paying for the artist's reputation, the quality of the reproduction, and the marketing that promotes him, and you have no misconceptions about buying a valuable print, then if you enjoy the print, buy it.

If you like the image and realize that it is a reproduction, make sure that it is printed on good paper, and make sure that you know how and where it was printed and by whom before buying it.

A contemporary poster that memorializes a much-loved subject, the Brooklyn Bridge. Although the quality of paper it was offset printed on is questionable, this poster might someday be a valuable vintage collectible.

REPRODUCTIONS ARE AN IMPORTANT PART OF THE ART INDUSTRY

Reproductions are works of art which are printed on paper. They make up a huge part of the art industry today. One company that houses nearly 3000 images, from reproductions of old masters to reproductions of Wyeth paintings, sells close to half a billion pieces of paper with pictures printed on them, each year.

Reproductions can be sold as copies of works of art. You can help yourself determine the quality of reproductions by developing a discerning eye and by asking for full disclosure about the artist, his medium, and the method used for printing the work under consideration.

Secret: Reproductions are decorative.

What makes reproductions worth buying? The thesis of this book is that buying art enriches all of us, so buying reproductions makes today's paintings available to all of us without much of a financial burden. Reproductions enable you to buy copies of loved famous paintings in order to decorate your home so you can enjoy copies of an artist's work daily.

Reproductions are a safe beginning for a lifelong addiction to buying art. Once you start hanging prints, your confidence in your taste will grow, your eye will become more educated, and you will buy other prints more easily.

The paintings selected for reproduction by publishers and reproduction companies such as the New York Graphic Society or Rockport Reproductions are chosen because they have a broad decorative appeal. It is hoped that they will be bought by customers overseas as well as those in the U.S. Therefore, the subjects of reproductions are evaluated and carefully selected to reach a large market. You will find little abstract work; the images are historical, landscape/beach, countryside, village and city scenes, people, boats, families, flowers, sports. They are generally upbeat, positive, and not depressing. They transcend localism and are intended to be universally popular. If they have any fault, it is that they are printed in trendy colors and follow fads in home decorating.

Secret: Reproductions are not investment art.

Reproductions are sold in art galleries, frame shops, and furniture stores. They are intended to be sold like a piece of furniture and to be enjoyed for a limited amount of time. Even if their paper is not 100% rag, if they are not hung in direct sunlight, they should last for many years. Most reproductions are not printed on 100% rag paper (although this is a question you can ask when considering your purchase).

On the other hand, limited edition prints printed on 100% rag paper of paintings of today, judiciously chosen, weighing the beauty of the reproduction and the fame of the artist, might be viewed as an investment someday. Most of these reproductions bought today will fall into disrepair or will be discarded just like the chromolithographs of the 1870s. Those left, cherished by families as favorites, could become treasures in a hundred years.

STEPS INVOLVED IN MAKING A REPRODUCTION

1. A painting with broad general appeal is selected from an artist's body of work or from a museum. If it is from a museum, it will be a popular image, such as a Monet garden or Renoir's dancers, not an exotic image by an unknown artist. The reproduction company obtains permission to reproduce the artwork. In return for this, the company pays the museum for reproduction rights and royalties, and gives living artists money and/or a certain number of reproductions and royalty for each reproduction sold.
2. A color transparency is made and taken to a printing company.
3. There the transparency is scanned by a laser beam, and information regarding its color values, densities, textures, and tones is recorded digitally onto a computer. There it is analyzed and a digitally encoded spectragraph of the image is recorded onto data tapes.
4. Tapes with data are loaded into a computer which generates high resolution television images, which can then be altered by a computer graphics expert until a color balance is reached. The machine can add and subtract, magnify and diminish parts of the image until it looks just great and the sought color balance is achieved.

What used to take eight to ten separations can now be divided onto four color separation films, which are sent to the plate maker.

5. The plate maker photographically and chemically transfers the image from the film to an aluminum offset plate.
6. The plate maker brings the plates and the original paintings to the pressman, who sets the painting up near his press and proceeds to print each plate successively, passing thin veils of colored ink onto the paper in a wet ink onto wet ink process. In this important step, he adjusts the color intensities as he visually checks his color proofs against the painting. He keeps trying to get the printed copies to look like a good facsimile of the original painting. I have watched pressmen make seemingly miraculous, minuscule adjustments in order to get the print to "read" like the original.
7. The copies are printed quickly once the color adjustments have been made. All four colors are printed at the same time, with no waiting for colors to dry between the laying on of colors. The printing is usually done on ordinary paper, usually on 80 or 100 pound cover stock, although sometimes 100% rag paper is used.

In reproductions, there is usually no great interest in the paper as a part of the artist's intent as there often is when a printmaker conceives and prints original prints. Printmakers often experiment with papering, using different European and Japanese papers, carefully chosen as a sub-surface for their print.

HOW TO RECOGNIZE REPRODUCTIONS AND QUESTIONS TO ASK

• Note the rich look of painting; the discernible brush marks.
• Note the quality of the image on the paper. If it is perfectly printed, it is probably a reproduction.
• Note the lack of richness. Each of the original print media creates special effects when the print in ink is transferred from the printmaking base to the paper. Silkscreens and lithographs deposit thick, even skins of ink on print paper; intaglio prints deposit textures and thick inks, which are absorbed into the paper.
• Note that a signature printed as part of the image

itself may indicate a reproduction, though early printers often included a signature on a lithographed or etched work. Any print that is not pencil signed by an artist is in the copy or poster category except vintage prints, which sometimes were sold or given away without a signature in the early 19th century.

• If the print is pencil-signed and you think it might be a reproduction, research the artist. Ask if the artist made an original painting first. Ask if the artist printed the edition and if so, where and how.

• Note edition numbers. If an edition is larger than 300 prints, it probably is a reproduction.

Original artists' paintings reproduced in four color process and printed on 100 lb. buffered, wood pulp-based, coated cover stock. Priced at $40, unframed. From Rockport Reproductions, Inc. Left: Early Sunday Morning, by George Shedd, from a 16″ × 24″ watercolor. Right: Charles Street, by Jean Cain, from a 18″ × 24″ oil painting.

• Pull out your magnifying glass. A dot pattern is obvious in reproductions. Photo-mechanical printers use a dot screen to transfer the image in halftones; a dot screen step is used between the color separation step and printing.

• Ask about the print paper on which the image is printed. Require full disclosure about the quality of the paper. Is it 100% rag? Is it American made or French, handmade, etc.?

BOOK PLATE PRINTS AND REPRODUCTIONS
Original Book Plate Prints

Book plate prints were originally taken from books. They were printed to decorate the books and inform the reader, as well as to classify nature and history. They include maps produced for atlases and to glorify travels and guide travelers.

Above: French Bouquet, *by Rigmor Washburn, from a 24″ × 30″ watercolor.* Below: Faded Red, *by Nathalie Nordstrand, from an 18″ × 24″ watercolor.*
All photos courtesy of Rockport Reproductions, Inc.

Other period reproductions include chromolithographs made to provide inexpensive decorations and glorify American history and institutions; reproductive copies of paintings, engravings, and mezzotint methods of printmaking made to be sold popularly; and posters made by printmaking methods or by photomechanical means of advertisement or decoration.

The story is told that an early printed book with thirty-four hand-colored pages, cited as most fascinating by decorators and collectors alike, is the 19th century publication by an English medical doctor named Thornton: *The Temple of Flora*. The pictures are unique in that the flowers are brilliantly painted against a romantic landscape background with churches and villas set in hills and valleys.

The Temple of Flora was listed in 1890 book catalogs at twenty British pounds. After the second World War, it was priced at 500 pounds. By 1965, according to its condition, it cost between 4000 and 5000 pounds. In 1979, it sold for 12,000 pounds, which was about $18,000.

Thus, reproductive prints from books do have investment value. People buy them because they are decorative; they have diverse subject matter, and contemporary reproductions of them are universally available. The challenge is to recognize them as being exactly what they are—copies, not original prints. However, as the story above suggests, many of the original book plate prints have become very rare and hence, very valuable.

Book plate prints are available in many qualities and price ranges from $40 on up. Color plate prints illustrate nature and history. They are usually the decorative botanicals, maps, animal and shell prints that people buy primarily for decorative reasons.

Original old book plate prints, which came from leather bound books of the years 1700–1860, are now rare. These page illustrations were printed on handmade paper and painted with brilliant watercolors and then hand sewn into the books. The old books were printed by many of the same printmaking processes found in original prints: engraving, mezzotint, aquatint, and lithography. These prints universally were printed and hand-watercolored by artisans as copies of an artist's work. These older book plate prints are usually quite expensive, and therefore should be purchased from a reputable book plate dealer or print dealer. Be sure to ask questions about the source of the print, the book's name and its history, and the provenance of the print you like before buying it.

> Secret: Characteristics of original color plate prints include paper deckles, plate marks, sewn edges, bright watercolors.

These vintage books were printed on handmade papers that are readily discernible if you notice the handmade paper's uneven edge, known as the *deckle*. Often, in these older pages from books, the viewer can see holes along one edge where the book was stitched. At one time, these marks were cut off, but now they are valued and left visible.

Look for plate marks. A smooth surface of one to three inches, providing margins around the painted image of flowers, tells you that this is an engraved print from an old book. The edge of the smooth surface is depressed by a plate mark. This provides a transition between the image and the rest of the page. The use of bright watercolors makes vintage color prints unique and charming. Hidden in books for decades, even centuries, these prints scintillate with fresh color, as if straight from the watercolorist's brush.

A century ago, color prints taken from books were produced by artists' and entrepreneurs' financial backers who wished to document a species of flora or fauna and raised the money to do so. At the time, there was rapid exploration of the world, which popularized cataloging every species and place. People with money, leisure, and wide interests and few distractions supported research and publications. The minds and purses responsible for these books were not artists, but they all had one quality in common: They were obsessed with a single subject and would do anything to document it completely, whether it was the life of a remote tribe of Indians or the characteristics of a particular plant.

Printing Book Plate Prints

Original book plate prints were printed by craftsmen and printers under the artist's supervision. They were either intaglio prints: copper engravings, aquatints, mezzotints, or stipple etchings; or lithographs drawn with crayon on lithographic stones in imitation of an artist's original watercolor of birds or botanicals drawn on the site, as in the case of Audubon prints. Money to pay for the printing was funded by those who pre-purchased books. Often, they were finished years later in a print workshop, where they were translated by hand onto copper plates or lithographic limestones to be reproduced in multiples, which later were colored by anonymous hands using brilliant watercolors.

As these plates were used over and over again, they changed. They wore down. Some printing marks became relatively invisible under the water-colored surface, or were reworked between different editions of a book with the result that copies of the same print from different editions are noticeably different.

Subjects of Book Plate Prints

Most old decorative prints originally come from books illustrating natural history, architecture, and world history. Sellers of decorative prints do not broadcast this fact because there is still a question of whether an old book should be kept intact.

Natural history books were made from 1700 until the late 19th century. From 1700–80, production of the earliest books was done from engravings drawn with sharp tools. From 1780–1830, book plate prints were characterized by the introduction of the mezzotint and aquatints. Mezzotints were made by systematically roughening plate areas that hold ink and create a rich tone when printed. Parts of the surfaces of these mezzotint plates were scraped or smoothed, until halftones were revealed when the plates were inked and printed. Aquatints were made from the roughened surfaces of a copper plate being accentuated by acid. They resemble watercolor washes when printed and introduced the best period for flowers and stipple engravings in France.

Death of President Lincoln, *a chromolithograph published by Currier & Ives. Courtesy of the Boston Public Library, Print Department.*

CHROMOLITHOGRAPHY

1830–60 was the beginning of the age of lithographs and chromolithography. In America, chromolithography introduced art assembly lines with people drawing and printing different color parts of images. Chromolithographs were used for drawing animals and landscapes, not for flowers.

The printing history of chromolithographs, such as Currier and Ives prints, is fascinating. The industrialization of printmaking arts came at the same time as The Shakers' mass production of the broom. With the advent of chromolithographs, art for the home became a commodity available to all.

Louis Prang of Boston was a leading chromolithographer during the late 19th century. The company, later known for their crayons, successfully translated into chromolithographs paintings such as Winslow Homer's *The North Woods* to hang over fireplaces nationwide, giving ordinary people the chance to buy and enjoy art inexpensively—for less than five dollars. When the Prang factory flourished, an assembly line of hand-operated lithographic presses produced valentines, playing cards, and menus, as well as romantic scenes of home and frontier. All were printed in many colors and were priced for the public from a nickel to five dollars.

The painter Thomas Moran was commissioned by Prang to produce watercolors of western scenery so his firm could produce chromolithographs of them. Moran was trained as a student to be a printmaker, making wood engravings, etchings, and lithographs before working as a painter. How well Moran succeeded is indicated by the fact that John Ruskin, British aesthetician, writer, and critic who disparaged chromolithographs, did purchase a set of Moran chromolithographs of Yellowstone National Park.

When reading about prints made from books, you will see prints referred to as *elephant folio*. This refers to book sizes—*folio, quarto,* and *octavo*. *Folio* was a sheet of handmade paper, folded once so it had two leaves and four numbered pages; *quarto* is a folio folded twice, so a quarto has four leaves and eight numbered pages; an *octavo* is a quarto folded again. It has eight leaves and sixteen pages. Both folio and octavo are tall books rather than wide. A quatro is square from a square book. An *elephant folio* is a giant folio; an atlas folio holds maps.

> Secret: Decorative prints from books were to inform, assemble, and collate information.

TYPES OF BOOK PLATE PRINTS

Flowers
Birds
Animals
Hunt
Nautical
Urban views
Architecture
Garden plans
Costumes
Coats of arms
Greek vases
Vue d'optique
American Indians
Moslems
Foreign cities
Americana
Airplanes
Shells
Maps
Fish
Insects

The authors, not the artists, are the names in the margins of these images from books. The printers and colorists are sometimes also indicated in the margins. Look for these renowned artists in your search for original book plate prints.

Maria Sybilla Merian and her daughter went from Holland to South America to document hundreds of insects; Jacob Van Huysum was another Dutch flower painter. Elizabeth Blackwell helped secure her husband's release from debtors' prison by drawing 500 hand-colored useful herbs published as *A Curious Herbal*. Thornton (mentioned earlier) was an English medical doctor whose *The Temple of Flora* is still unique, because all the colorful, larger than life flowers are set against lush, summery, romantic landscapes, filled with villas and palaces.

Pierre–Joseph Redouté from France is acclaimed the greatest of all flower artists, contributing to more than fifty books. From America came *Flora of North America*, by William Bartons. The Victorian age ushered in the chromolithographs of Mrs. London's ladies' flower garden series and the demise of brilliantly colored flower print books.

Bird Book Plate Prints

The earliest English bird book was printed and colored by Albin in 1731–38. In America, Catesby worked in 1712; in Germany, Frisch made 255 hand-colored etchings of birds; in Italy, Manetti did 600 hand-colored engravings; in France, the most famous bird books are by Martinet, with nine bird volumes in many editions. In America, Bonaparte and Wilson influenced John James Audubon, who, between 1827 and 1838 made *Birds of America* with 435 hand-colored aquatints, printed and colored by Haville in France.

Many of Audubon's paintings were done by others. Flowers and plants in fifty plates were the work of Joseph Mason, a thirteen-year-old pupil; flowers and insects by Maria Martin; landscapes by Audubon's sons. Seventy-six of 150 lithographs in Audubon's *Quadrupeds* (animals) were drawn on a lithographic stone by his son, John Woodhouse Audubon.

In England, the poet Edward Lear of "Owl and the Pussy Cat" fame, was renowned as an engraver and a naturalist bird artist, particularly of parrots.

Animal and Fish Book Plate Prints

Animal books made from 1700 to 1900 have always been less popular to collectors of natural history books and prints. One reason is that the art is not as decorative. In Audubon's book on animals, *The Viviparous Quadrupeds of North America*, I noted one color—brown—in almost all of the plates. In Edward Lear's animals, we note beautiful textures, but miss the brilliant watercolors of his parrots.

Mark Catesby, English naturalist, spent ten years in America researching, drawing, and writing the text for his monumental volume, *The Natural History of Carolina, Florida and the Bahama Islands* (1731–43). Half of his hand-watercolored etchings are of birds. Many are of brilliantly colored fish; colorful, well documented ducks; and botanical specimens, intertwined with snakes.

The prevailing influence on 19th century naturalists was Charles Darwin's travels, research, and the publication of his *Origin of Species*. His aptitude for observing and collating anything worthy in natural history inspired countless scientists to become artists.

Especially to be noted is Professor David Low's *The Breeds of the Domestic Animals of the British Islands,* a two-volume folio with fifty-six watercolored aquatint plates, which you will recognize for their charm and uniqueness, because the cows and other animals are shown against softly colored rural English country scenes, portrayed in the best of the English tradition of landscape painting.

Shells in Book Plate Prints

Shell collecting and annotating shells in their variations obsessed aristocrats and scientists during the 17th and 18th centuries. The shell books were intended as aids to identification.

British naturalist Thomas Martyn's *The Universal Conchologist* is considered the greatest of all books on shells. In four volumes, it has 160 hand-colored copper engravings. The shells illustrated were bought in 1780 from Captain Cook. Because the shells were drawn and colored by his school of young artists, some of the shells illustrated are embellished with gold; some have decorative margins; some are flat and dull.

Indians in Book Plate Prints

Among the more obsessed visual collectors of data about North America were the four giants who wrote about and painted the vanishing North American Indian tribes. They were Theodore DeBry, 16th century engraver of Florida Indians; Prince Maximillian of Wied, who in 1883 brought Karl Bodmer, twenty-three-year-old Swiss artist to paint Western scenery and Plains Indians; Colonel Thomas McKenney, government official, who commissioned portraits of Indian leaders and later produced *The History of the Indian Tribes of North America*—lithographs of Indian chiefs in full regalia; and George Catlin, a lawyer and oil painter who, in the 19th century, painted Indians on their reservations and in his *Letters and Notes on the North American Indians* became their historian and advocate.

Looking at examples of these artists' works, we gather an impression of verified and idealized Indian life in every facet, from heroic garbs and noble battle scenes to humble games and domestic vignettes. These artists began a proud American art focus that you will find echoed today in prints produced and sold popularly, particularly in posters and reproductions of contemporary paintings of Indians. Unfortunately, the works of DeBry, Catlin, Bodmer, and McKenney have not been reproduced as popular commodities and decorative prints as frequently as the flower and bird book plates have been. But I feel it is of interest to look briefly at the work of these recorders of North American Indian life, in order to make comparisons as you shop for Indian art today. Also, the prints made by these artists present an informal interesting survey of printmaking methods used in Europe and America from the 16th through the 20th century. All of the prints discussed, although in book form, were impressed on paper by hand from engraved, etched, or aquatinted copper plates or from hand-drawn lithographed stones, and later, if in color, were watercolored by anonymous craftsmen.

Theodore DeBry. A 16th century Flemish goldsmith and engraver, DeBry was passionate about recording the success of the Protestant settlements in North America because he himself had fled from the onslaughts of the Catholic rulers in Flanders. DeBry's engravings were the basis of the work of two other artists, John White, who depicted colonizing expeditions to the southeastern United States, and Jacques LeMoyne DeMorgues, watercolor painter of Florida Indians. DeBry's line engravings of the American Indians show the same idealized, genial, over-dignified personages we find in contemporary reproductions of heroic Indian paintings today. Here is the beginning of our tradition of romantic idealization of Indian life that has become confirmed in the arts over the centuries, but not in our nation's real relationships with Indian tribes.

Thomas McKenney. Superintendent of Indian Trade from 1816–20 and head of the Bureau of Indian Affairs from 1822–30, Colonel McKenney was not an artist. He commissioned lavish and heroic portraits by Charles Bird King, painter of statesmen and Indian chiefs, and worked with writer James Hall to produce *The History of American Tribes of North America*, remarkable for its forty-eight lithographic plates. This volume was printed from 1829 until completion in 1844 by lithographer Albert Newsam in the Philadelphia firm of Cephas G. Childs and later by John T. Bowen, who also printed Audubon's lithographs.

George Catlin. Catlin devoted his life (1796–1872) as artist, portraitist, and showman to recording for posterity the life and customs of Indian tribes. He took numerous trips to territories hitherto known only to fur traders. General William Clark introduced him to tribal delegates and took him to Indian councils in remote areas, where he depicted brutal initiation rites and tribal games. He focused particularly on the Mandan tribe, later wiped out by the ravages of smallpox.

Catlin opened a display of 470 oil paintings and Indian artifacts and toured New York, Washington, and Philadelphia. After Congress failed to buy his gallery, Catlin opened his show in London, even bringing troupes of Iowa Indians in to perform.

The result of Catlin's long-term association with the Indian peoples was *Catlin's North American Indian Portfolio*, a series of twenty-five lithographs adapted from his paintings by the English firm of Thomas McGahey, which was later lithographed by James Acherman in New York. These show heroic but sympathetic portraits of North American buffalo hunts and Indian games set in the North American plains, in subtle colors, all hand colored under Catlin's supervision. Some originals of these color plates are still available for the buyer of Americana.

Karl Bodmer. Bodmer, as a twenty-three-year-old Swiss artist, was brought to St. Louis by naturalist Prince Maximillian of Wied, Germany, after the scientist's own drawings of the native peoples of North America dissatisfied him. Delicately hand-colored aquatints were produced in their joint effort. *Travels in the Interior of North America* provides the most detailed and comprehensive record of Indian domestic life and tribal ritual including scalp dances, dances of Indian women, and horse racing, as well as heroic portraits in traditional Indian garb. Still available today, Bodmer's lively and richly colored book plate prints are prototypes of Indian prints found today in many southwestern galleries. Even the details of Indian dress—beaded moccasins, elaborate headgear, and beaded coats—inspire contemporary buyers of Indian artifacts.

The American Landscape

When illustrator Thomas Moran was asked by *Scribners Monthly* in 1870 to illustrate an article on Yellowstone Park, he resolved to paint the wilderness first hand, and borrowed money from an editor at *Scribners* and the owner of the Northern Pacific Railroad.

Subsequently, Morán sold several paintings of the West and accepted the offer of Boston chromolithographer Louis Prang to reproduce his watercolors for sale. Fifteen of these were later published in a book, F.V. Hayden's *The Yellowstone National Park and The Mountainous Regions of Portions of Idaho, Nevada, Colorado and Utah* in 1876. Many critics have placed these delicately colored and well composed prints as the finest examples of American chromolithography because most chromolithographs were printed in jarring color combinations. Moran's chromolithography exaggerated natural phenomena in scale and color; one of his trademarks was mauve sky and land forms.

COPIES OF BOOK PLATE PRINTS

New copies of color plate prints are being reprinted today photomechanically in Europe. You should find these reproductions in framers' shops and department stores, as well as museum catalogs, at a low price. Some of the characteristics of these natural history reproductions are: smooth papers that readily accept printing inks, and overall surface slickness that sometimes resembles a good poster. They are printed with soft, not brilliant, colors which often seem somewhat dull when compared to the watercolors on original book plate prints. Some contemporary reproductions are hand-watercolored today when they are printed in Europe.

NOTES FROM A JOURNAL

Yesterday, I saw a reproduction of a painting that reaffirmed my life in a special way. It was a large print of a dusty studio with all the tools of printmaking, easels, tables, quiet gray walls. In the middle of the image was a woman reading. Behind her were buildings of any city, quietly laid in warm colors. There was something about the way her head was tilted that made me pause and feel pleasure. But this same print did not do anything for my husband. I bought it anyway.

CONNOISSEURSHIP
Developing an Expert's Eye
3

When we were thinking about this book, I became obsessed with the question: "What should we recommend to readers that would have lasting importance?" We addressed this same question to the director of one of America's oldest print galleries, Associated American Artists in New York, where prints have been exhibited for half a century and sold from simple black and white four page catalogs during the 1940s and '50s, by mail for five to fifteen dollars. The director, who looked like a country doctor in his brown tweed jacket and striped tie, gazed rather intently at me and said, "The core task will be for your book to teach readers how to become print connoisseurs. If you can share the basic principles of connoisseurship, you will have done something of lasting value."

To be a connoisseur is not as difficult as this bit of art-speak, "connoisseur," implies. You have been learning about it in the previous two chapters. This chapter sums it up for you.

A TRAINED EYE

When you buy a print you buy what you like. The goal is to be a discriminating buyer and know *why* you like it and exactly *what* it is. This chapter will help you become a connoisseur, a person with a trained eye who is able to know what he or she sees and whether it is technically, as well as aesthetically, worthy of consideration.

A print connoisseur is a person who has trained himself by looking, looking, and more looking at many prints from many sources; who reads constantly about print and printmakers; who talks about prints to gallery personnel and printmakers,

gathering facts and perceptions that lead to a well grounded intuition about prints, seen even at a glance; and who makes informed print purchases that might prove to be sound investments.

One of our clients who is a collector focusing on prints told me that he can drive past a gallery and discern the quality of a half-seen print. A psychiatrist, he claims that he has trained himself to remember print characteristics as carefully and thoroughly as he stores client information. Recently, he made an educated guess about a print that he found in a London bookstore for $250. He sent a photograph of it to various auction houses with a question about the signature and a guess about whose work it was. He heard from Sotheby's that he would be unhappy on one count and happy on another. The unhappy news was that the signature was a fake; the happy fact was that the print had been authenticated as genuine and they had sold it for $16,000. It is definitely worth it to become a connoisseur!

THE QUALITY OF AN IMPRESSION IS IMPORTANT

Begin by learning to differentiate between state, condition, and quality. These are different variables to note or ask about when looking at a print. Every change made by the printmaker on the plate, block, stone, or screen of the print matrix or subsurface will result in a different state in the print pulled by the printmaker. This might be indicated on the print with the words *state proof,* but generally it is not. The changes made by the wearing down over many printings of the incised or drawn lines on the sub-surface do not make a difference in state. But they do make a difference in the *quality* of the impression or print.

Quality can be affected by soft etching ink being rubbed into the lines of an etching, drypoint, or mezzotint, which results in some lines printing in a slightly smeared way. Another change in the quality of impression is due to the lines or areas being printed repeatedly so that later impressions are not as clear or crisp as earlier impressions.

But too great an emphasis on quality of impression turns prints into precious gems. And what is fine quality for one printmaker would not be to another because the artist's imagination and vision determine the length of time the plate is left in the acid or the stone is drawn upon. Dark, rich lines are not done for their own sake but for the sake of the image, the artist's vision, and his draftsmanship. I've seen plates drawn by dipping a stick into etching blockout or resist that sang with a brighter song than those laboriously drawn and etched. And fine impressions of early prints (15th to 18th century) might be so difficult to obtain that the buyer feels gratified to find or afford a poor impression. Whether a particular print is a good impression is decided by looking at many prints and developing an eye for what to expect, or by direct comparison with other impressions of the same print.

Condition is a matter solely of the physical condition of the paper on which the print is printed. Early prints, which were often pinned on the wall, were pricked all over. Such prints might be superb impressions but of poor quality. Auction catalogs always note the condition of a print, but such verbal representations do not replace first-hand examination. So when considering buying by telephone, ask to see the print on approval.

Secret: Artists printing original prints usually select handmade or 100% rag papers.

EXAMINE PAPER QUALITY

The quality of the paper should be examined first of all. The paper printmakers use is usually manufactured in Europe and shipped worldwide by distributors. When you examine a print, you should hold it so it is observed in a raking white light, preferably daylight. Face away from the light, not into it. In this way, the texture of the paper and the inking on the face of a print make their clearest statement. The lines of an intaglio stand up from the surrounding surface. The lines of a relief print such as a woodcut are sunk into the paper so they lie below the surrounding space. Viewing a print in strong raking light is the best way to note a repaired or restored print. Even the insertion of a patch is noticeable. A print that has been washed or cleaned too much and subjected to very strong pressure while damp is apt to have lost the relief of lines and surfaces.

Print connoisseurs recognize rag paper by its heavy, luxurious feel. It might be tan or buff, cream, white, or blue, but there is usually an unmistakable feeling of density and quality to it that one can liken to the texture of a good cotton sheet or a linen table cloth.

Some of the characteristics of intaglio printmaking papers to look for include: grid marks, watermarks, softness, pliability, and in the case of papers for lithographs and silkscreens, a crisp surface. Relief prints are characterized by fine, thin, handmade Japanese papers. The grid simulates a look of the wires on the top of the screen used in making handmade papers. Watermarks are shaped spaces in the paper that form the symbol of the paper's maker.

A lack of the paper manufacturer's watermarks can be important to note in order to determine fakes or re-strikes of early original prints. Encyclopedias of watermarks are available in major public libraries and can be helpful in pinpointing the age of a print. Hold the paper up to the light to locate the watermark. This is not fail-safe, however, because on a small print using a quarter or half sheet of paper, the printmaker may have used the paper part without a watermark. Reproductions are sometimes printed on high quality paper, such as 80 or 100 pound coated cover stock, which is stiff and impregnable.

A print connoisseur should be concerned with a print's sub-surface, i.e., the paper, particularly

Examine the quality of the paper. It will have a soft feel and a ragged edge.

when authenticating a very old print. Many Rembrandts are true etchings, but are distinguished as reproductions because they were printed on a modern wove paper that did not exist at the time Rembrandt worked. In Europe the earliest examples of handmade paper were *laid,* rather than *wove,* a help when we need to authenticate master prints. Laid papers were the oldest papers, although laid papers are still made today by hand papermakers. When held up to a light, laid papers reveal translucent lines created by the wires and the chained lines of stitching that held the wire lines in place. Wove paper, which did not exist until after 1750, is made on a woven wire cloth, hence reveals no structure when held to the light.

> Secret: Indented plate marks are a sign of an intaglio print.

LOOK FOR PLATE MARKS

All intaglio prints, aquatints, etchings, engravings, drypoints, and mezzotints, and sometimes lithographs, have slightly raised borders where the

press has indented the paper at the edge of the plate or stone. Be careful though, because these plate marks can be faked by pressing a blank plate over a reproduction.

> Secret: The editioning of original prints by the artist is a fairly recent practice.

Clues to look for in an original print: the raised edge of the plate mark at the edge of the image, the quality of the deckle-edged paper, the artist's signature in pencil on the bottom margin, and the limited edition size. Wisteria, collagraph by Mary Ann Wenniger.

THE SIGNIFICANCE OF EDITION NUMBERS

Edition numbers are written as a fraction, such as 3/120, and written in pencil so as not to fade or bleed if dampened. The bottom (right-hand) figure is the total edition size. The top (left-hand) figure is the print number as it came off the press or was numbered by the printmaker when he or she signed the print. A low print number is usually a significant attribute with drypoints and mezzotints, since the raised burr of the incised line on the plate, which is unique to them, can be flattened after repeated printings. A later print in the edition will not have the same velvety quality to the inking as a low numbered drypoint.

A low versus high numbered print in the edition is not particularly significant in other printmaking techniques. In fact, some printmakers number the prints in reverse order as they come off the pile after printing!

> Secret: What is important to the print buyer is the *size* of the edition.

Hand-pulled original prints usually have limited edition sizes of 100 to 300. Any number larger than 300 makes one suspect that some photomechanical reproduction process was involved. The sheer work of hand-pulling a print usually limits the number an artist will produce, either from boredom, or fatigue, or both. Many printmakers who pull their own prints can be discovered because their total editions are between ten and 100.

On the other hand, once the photomechanical press is running, it makes very little difference to the expense, except in terms of paper cost, to run 500 or 5000 reproductions. It should be noted that publishers of both limited edition prints and original prints have been known to keep a press run low deliberately, so as to be able to charge more, by using the ploy of scarcity.

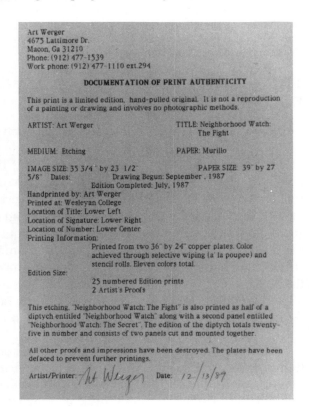

A Certificate of Authenticity prepared by the artist/printer and given to the gallery for presentation to a future buyer.

ASK FOR DOCUMENTATION

Upon request, some printmakers will provide the art dealer, gallery, or publisher with documentation, a certificate of authenticity, especially if the work is printed in collaboration with a master printer. Printmakers routinely provide information on edition size, paper used, date of printing, and status of the original plate. As a buyer, you should ask for a copy of print documentation, if available, especially if the print is an expensive original and was printed in a print workshop.

SIGNED WORK

It has been a common practice since the 1950s for printmakers to pencil sign their work indicating title, edition information, and adding their name under the image. In reproductions of paintings the signature is *inside* the image itself because the artist signed the original painting on the canvas.

> Secret: An artist's signature is not common in older prints.

Not until the 20th century, during the 1950s, did it become common practice for the artist to sign his original print, usually an etching or engraving, in the bottom margin in pencil. Often, only the initials are seen as scribed on the original plate or wood block.

Using a magnifying glass, inspect the pencilled signature. The pencil mark should leave a slight indentation and should shine in reflected light if it is an original. The signature on a photogravure reproduction will appear slightly fuzzy and may even show a halftone dot screen pattern. As a final check, compare the signature to other known examples of the artist's work.

Further assurance of authenticity can be supported by the stamp or chop mark of the printmaking workshop where the artist had his edition printed. Certain printmaking processes, such as lithography, are so technically demanding and complicated that an artist will make use of a qualified printer's workshop to do the work under his supervision and approval. The artist will sign and number the completed prints and the printer may

Typical chop marks. To the right of the signature is Sally Morgan's own mark, and at the bottom right-hand corner of the paper is that of the printmaking workshop. Detail of silkscreen print by Australian artist Sally Morgan.

also sign them or add his chop as an authentic record of his part in the process.

DETECTING A PHOTOMECHANICAL REPRODUCTION

Photomechanical reproductions are similar to photographs reproduced in a newspaper or magazine. Use a magnifying glass to examine the image for a halftone dot screen. Lack of such a screen is not proof of the work's originality, however. New reproduction techniques such as photogravure and heliogravure can create prints without the telltale halftone dot screens.

If lines appear coarse or blunt-ended, the print could be a photomechanical reproduction. The magnifying glass will also disclose the quality of the lines in an original etching, drypoint, or engraving. A hand-drawn incised line is generally sharp and comes to a gradual point.

Photoengraved reproductions appear flat and evenly inked, compared to an original etching print. The originals have a three-dimensional look and rough feel. The inked areas have embossed or raised surfaces where the paper was forced into

incised lines by the press. Also, original woodcuts or linocuts have raised areas on the back of the paper where the image carved on the block of wood or linoleum was pressed into the paper's surface. Silkscreen prints usually have a visibly thick layer of ink with a shiny or matte finish.

Photographically reproduced lines appear rough and grainy when examined closely. Heliogravure reproductions, which also use photographic techniques, have a raised area in the surface of the paper because the matrix used is similar to the artist's original. Their general effect is coarse compared to the sharpness of an original print.

AVOIDING A FAKE

How do you avoid being deceived when buying art? Remember, first of all, that art is a visual medium and cannot be responded to or evaluated as to quality, state, condition, and most important, aesthetics over the telephone. A few tips: Beware of print sales pitches made by people or places guaranteeing that "Your money will be doubled by this purchase." If there is so much quick money to be made buying and reselling prints, the sellers should be so rich by now, they wouldn't need to be pitching prints.

Beware when "rare" and "investment" are the focus of a sales pitch rather than assessments of the quality and the artist.

Beware of prints with endless documentation and guarantees. I think some certificates of authentication took longer to create than the prints they are attached to!

Remember that limited edition prints are reproductions. This does not mean that they are fakes, nor does it mean that they are original prints.

> Secret: The ink on art reproductions appears dull and flat.

The overall quality of the print's inking is important to note. The surfaces of original prints have rich silky luster, which will vary from shiny to matte. The reason the ink on art reproductions is dull and flat is partly due to the technical requirements of high speed presses using thinned inks and also to the fact that reproductions are printed by four-color plates printed one right after the other, wet ink over wet.

> Secret: Prints may be purchased from a number of sources.

If you are a new buyer of prints, there are many places to find prints, some better than others in terms of protecting you from frauds and ill-advised print promoters.
• retail galleries and specialist dealers
• auction houses
• mail order companies
• art lending services
• print publishers
• print collectors
• artists' studios
• catalogs

GALLERIES

Your best bet in becoming a print connoisseur is to develop a good working relationship with at least two art dealers, who agree formally or informally to act as your print advisors. These dealers will act as your support system. Your art advisors, in this instance, are best qualified if they specialize in prints.

Galleries are an important part of our art world: frequent changing exhibitions, researched, arranged, and installed by devoted gallery people working long hours, often on lower than marketplace wages—these are a vital part of the process by which an artist's work is seen in a contemporary context.

Although there is academic training in arts administration offered to art history students, most gallery owners and personnel learn by doing, and become known for their integrity, impeccable taste, and service to their community in finding worthy and significant exhibitors. Unfortunately, in the art industry (which is indeed an industry, with all that implies), there are promoters and hustlers.

One way to find reputable galleries specializing in original and reliable prints is to call a museum print curator or the print room of a city library. Library and museum curators have long-established buying relationships with print galleries.

If you are in Montana early on a Friday afternoon deciding which city you might fly to on Saturday for a little print shopping, you can get shopping advice from a print curator in Brooklyn, or Santa Fe, or at the Ringling Museum in Florida. Or you can pick a city and start walking on gallery row, asking which gallery specializes in original prints.

The New York Public Library's print room would help narrow your selection from the hundreds of New York galleries, to recommend fewer than twenty galleries which have been in business selling prints for more than five years.

> Secret: The world of print dealers is relatively small.

Galleries specializing in original prints are limited in number and known to each other. Often parts of gallery exhibitions are borrowed from another gallery or from clients. Prints are found and checked out for customers through hours of gallery telephone shopping. Hence, warm relationships develop between print galleries, and reputations of print expertise become known and respected in the print field and lost or stolen prints that surface can be quickly returned.

Part of the American art tradition is that printmakers gravitate to resorts. I think of Edward Hopper on Cape Ann; Blanche Lazell and Robert Motherwell in Provincetown. You can find print galleries in resorts as well as in cities. Part of the evening's entertainment in resorts is to check the galleries after dinner, as you stroll. This is not usually a time to buy; that comes later, if an image stays with you. You can telephone and have the gallery ship work to you on approval.

There are usually art associations in resort areas as well, promoting the activities of local artists, where you can get recommendations for reliable print shopping. At resorts, there are also many reproduction galleries providing lively and decorative reproductions of local artists' work and copies of paintings of local scenes. Since the prices of reproductions can be the same as original prints, be sure that you use the tips of connoisseurship to evaluate what you are viewing. Reread Chapter 2 to review the questions to ask about reproductions before you buy.

> Secret: Print dealers will spend time educating you.

DEVELOPING A RELATIONSHIP WITH PRINT EXPERTS

It is important to develop a good relationship with at least two print dealers who are willing to share their enthusiasm about their field of expertise and stories about their artists. You will quickly learn if their advice is congruent. A friend of mine who is frightened of galleries talks about one print dealer who impressed her when picking prints for a hospital installation because the dealer picked the least expensive print for one site.

Most dealers are willing to share their knowledge and taste and will give you an honest opinion of the quality, condition, and lasting value of the prints they sell. Most dealers will take inordinate amounts of time talking to novice buyers about prints. After all, these prints and collecting them are often their passion as well as their livelihood. Most print dealers and personnel will offer friendly advice about purchases and tell stories about their own purchases and those of others, on the theory that well-guided customers will become better customers in the long run.

> Secret: Novice print buyers should gallery hop.

Visit several print dealers before making your first purchase. This enables you to do comparables. As in real estate, compare what is out there to buy. Not only comparisons of prices should be made, but also of quality. Develop an eye for prints by looking and looking. Within a short time, you will be able to note artists' styles and even pick up on the criteria of a print connoisseur. A brief chat with various gallery owners will reveal which ones are responsible print lovers and which ones are fast buck promoters.

Good print dealers can talk about their printmakers in terms of:
• their artist's aesthetic concerns
• their artist's printmaking techniques
• their artist's place, or unknown status, in art history
• the truth about the quality and condition of the print you like
• where this print stands in terms of all the artist's work
• getting confirmation from the artist or his publisher about a particular impression; i.e., the paper it is printed on, its condition, the size of the edition, the number of artist's proofs

AUCTIONS

Until you become well versed in recognizing good quality prints and can distinguish bargains from overbid and overpriced junk, auctions are not recommended places to make your first print purchases.

However, it is a good idea as a novice to attend one or two auctions and auction previews as a learning experience. Auction previews held by reputable auction houses, one to three days before an auction, will give you an opportunity to inspect and compare a large number of original prints.

Better auction houses employ a staff of experts to assess the quality, authenticity, and condition of prints brought in to be sold, so forgeries seldom get by.

> Secret: Estimated price ranges in catalogs are generally accurate assessments of true market value.

Auction catalogs, if available, can be purchased even if you do not intend to bid. They provide valuable information on the artist, the date the print was made, the edition size, the type of paper, the condition of the print.

Most auction lots are subject to a *reserve*, which is a minimum price agreed upon by the seller and the auction house. The reserve price is not revealed to the buying public, but it is usually set slightly below the low end of the estimated price range given in the catalog. So even if you are the only bidder on that lot, it will be impossible to acquire it for much less than the pre-auction estimate.

If you decide to bid on a print, mark your catalog with a firm bidding limit, over which you will not go. This is the next step after you have inspected prints you intend to bid on at an auction preview. Keep in mind that you will have to pay a buyer's premium to the auction firm (usually 10% of the final selling price). The auction firm will collect a similar commission from the seller.

To bid, you will also have to register with the auction firm and obtain a bidding number. You show this number to the auctioneer when you make your bids. You also should complete a credit reference several days before an auction, or make other payment arrangements beforehand.

> Secret: You can bid at auctions by telephone or by mail.

Most firms will accept the first telephone or mail bid received, in case of identical bids, and ignore the others. To bid by mail, submit the top bid you would be prepared to make if you were attending the auction in person. An agent or the auctioneer himself will bid on your behalf against bids from the floor, up to the maximum price you have authorized. However, the auction firm will always attempt to secure the print for you at the lowest possible price. For instance, if bidding stops at $100 less than your top price, you will get it at that lower price.

> Secret: Pay special attention to prints selling outside their geographic market.

It is possible to pick bargains at auctions held in countries or localities where a particular artist's work or style of art is relatively unknown. Prints by American artists often sell for less than their American market value when offered in European auction houses and vice versa.

BUY THE BEST

Whether buying a known or unknown artist, you should try to discover the artist's best period and most remarkable body of work. Etchings of Jim Dine's clothing are more typical of his work as a leading pop artist than is the series of prints of his wife. Some experts recommend buying the work that is most valued, but you might find that you like an unknown artist. With an unknown or relatively unknown artist, such a distinction may not have been made. In that case, buy the print you like the best, the print that you cannot *not* buy.

> Secret: Don't put off a gallery owner by trying to bargain.

DISCRIMINATE, BUT DON'T BARGAIN

One of the ways to tell your age is if you attempt to bargain when buying prints. Back in the 1950s, before print dealing became a major part of the art industry, it was commonplace and admirable to try to strike a great bargain for your art finds. Maybe prints were devalued then, or perhaps they were thought not worthy of ever selling for more than a few dollars. This was the case during the Depression years, when artists I know signed their mothers' maiden names on etchings, so they could sell them for a penny without artistic loss of face. Or maybe dealers were known to mark up prices so they could come down after a brief skirmish.

Now that the print industry has stabilized and print prices by contemporary printmakers are required to be uniform wherever their works are shown, print dealers are working on consignment, with only a 50% markup, which in most business settings would be untenable. When you add the slim markup to high rents in gallery rows, you realize why print dealers look insulted if you start to bargain. There are four exceptions to this.

• If you are making a purchase as a decorator holding a tax number, a courtesy discount of 5% to 10% can be expected.

• If you are buying many prints at the same time, some dealers might give you a small discount.

• If you are buying an expensive print for thousands of dollars, some room for movement might be built into the price.

• If you are buying from the artist directly, you might be able to strike a lower price.

If there is room for a price adjustment, wait for the art dealer or artist to offer it. They generally will, if they can, in order to secure your confidence and return business.

AUTHENTICATING A PRINT

A commonplace question that is addressed to paper specialists in a museum's print laboratory is whether a print is an original or a reproduction. Some prints are easy to distinguish visually. The lay person can learn by looking at other prints and books. Ask a print curator in your museum's print department to show you a variety of original prints in order to develop an eye for different media and to discern the difference between an original and a reproduction. A book helpful in this regard is William Ivins' *How Prints Look*, available from The Boston Museum of Fine Arts.

Many museums have clinic days when you can make an appointment to discuss a print. This is an opportunity to determine what you have, and ask if yours is a good impression—an early or late impression—even to help with the decision to buy or not. What a museum will not do is make a written statement about authenticity or give valuations. But a print curator will give you a written recommendation of galleries that can give appraisals or valuations of a print under consideration.

Technologies are available in museum print and paper conservation departments, when higher magnification might help you determine authenticity. A stereo microscope magnifies the surface of a print in three dimensions. It reveals how the ink acts—if it lies on the surface of the paper fiber or penetrates it.

Ultraviolet light can determine the prior history of a piece of paper, which will tell you a great deal about your print. It reveals stains, repairs, corrections, and any additions to the medium used. It reveals if a paper was stained and then bleached and tells if mold has been there and removed. Beta radiography involves the X-rays that reveal watermarks of the paper—a clue to the identification of a print.

Paper is one of the most important parts of a print detection system. Since wove paper didn't exist until after 1750, if the print in question has been printed on a wove paper instead of a laid paper (paper without obvious grid marks, or impressions of the wire lines of the ancient paper mold), a print purported to be printed before 1750 could not be genuine.

To become a happy print connoisseur, you must look at prints relentlessly, read about them extensively, and buy them when you see them. This is the only way you will build your confidence to make comfortable, satisfying decisions about prints by yourself.

ONE PRINT BUYER'S STORY

Marci only wanted to spend $150 on a particular shopping excursion, so she bought a small Whitney Hanson woodcut for that price, not permitting herself to buy the Hanson woodcut *Pears* at $300, which she liked best. Three months later she telephoned that she had dreamt of the *Pears* and asked if she could exchange the print she bought and buy the *Pears*. We thought it had sold because it had been misplaced. We ordered another *Pears* from Hanson. When it came, it was slightly different in color from the first since it was a hand-pulled print made from three color blocks. Marci was so disappointed, she cried. After a few months, the story had a happy ending because the first *Pears* turned up in a drawer. We were all relieved, especially Marci, who vowed never to compromise her taste again.

TIPS
How to Work with Galleries
4

Betsy in a tweed skirt, cashmere sweater, and a smile; George in blue jeans, button-down shirt, and cowlick, were visiting the galleries. A tax refund, a raise, and a new house in the suburbs made their usual weekend gallery prowl more purposeful. They were accustomed to comparing new cars and bargaining for them, but they did not know how to find or settle on the art that they wanted. And they were afraid of buying a worthless piece, even a fake. Although they had been in many galleries, the gallery scene still seemed mysterious. And how should they cope with gallery people? And how can they decide what to buy?

Betsy and George have different tastes stemming from their different backgrounds and aspirations. Betsy, a banker, had a comfortable childhood with participation in all of the arts—music and ballet lessons and watercolor classes. Her mother bought expensive Oriental rugs but only purchased art that coordinated with her furnishings. Like her mother, Betsy has decorated each room carefully with period antiques. George, trained as a physicist, was brought up in the post-Depression era when art was considered wonderful when seen in museums but not for an ordinary family to possess. George's college treasures, M. C. Escher posters, were banned from their newly furnished Georgian living room.

This could be you: Both Betsy and George were hungry for art and beauty to be part of their lives, but they did not know how to get started. They only knew what they did not like. When I talked to them briefly, as they did a quick turn in my print gallery, I suggested that they start by making their goal a *coup de cœur* which, loosely translated, means an affair of the heart, a purchase made out of delight. If they saw a small piece that delighted either of them, they should just buy it as they would a necktie. He said, "No way. She has only let me pick one necktie so far."

They further confided that they did not mind our prices, although they wondered how they would know if a price was fair. They never bought because they were not sure that the prints they liked were worth the prices asked. They had heard so many rumors about faked art and the quirks of the art industry. How could they get fair treatment and buy art that would please both of their tastes?

In this chapter we will answer all these questions and give you ideas on how to get the most help in a gallery that handles works of art on paper: original prints, drawings, and watercolors. The principles discussed can be equally applied to other types of galleries.

LEARN HOW GALLERIES OPERATE

> Secret: Look for a print dealer with artistic tastes that are compatible with yours.

Print dealers with your taste are recognized by the type of prints they sell. If you prefer decorative prints, seek the galleries that specialize in colorful, trendy work. If you want avant garde prints, look for galleries where the dealers will defend their selection in terms of aesthetic and long-term value. And if you want master prints, seek galleries with personnel who will explain the historic relevance and rarity of these prints. If you want vintage

American prints you will find galleries devoted to them. There are also galleries with only Japanese prints or local printmakers. And many galleries are eclectic with a bit of everything. Don't decide on a gallery by their ongoing installation. Ask what kind of printmakers they represent.

Some print galleries show academic printmakers, teachers who print editions of their own prints and sell them in a low key manner nationwide. Other print galleries show the more recognized printmakers whose prints are made in print workshops and advertised in national publications. Still others are a combination of all of the above. It all depends on the enthusiasm and creativity of the owner and the time and captial that he or she can invest.

It is an important moment when you look at a gallery wall and decide that, at last, you are going to buy a print if you can find one that you like and can afford.

You should find not one but several galleries that look attractive. Set aside a day for visiting them. Wear shoes and clothes that you will be comfortable in.

Decide to be yourself when you visit print galleries. Never allow yourself to feel inferior even in the most elegant of galleries. They are not sacrosanct but are there to serve people who love art.

Engage a gallery person in conversation. Consider him a resource of valuable information and guidance and ply him with questions. If you cannot get personal information about the printmaker's background, or you sense confusion about the print medium used, or hear double talk about pricing or aesthetics, think about leaving. Do not be put off by coldness affected by owners. This coldness can be a manipulating trick designed to shut down your inquiries and make the gallery person seem superior.

Ask if there are print drawers in which you might browse. Do not assume that the best art galleries should look like museums. Work sparsely spaced on the walls with appropriately typed labels is not worth more than prints in drawers or in bins. In some galleries there are contrivances such as adjustable lighting, soft couches, Oriental rugs, wine serving that subtly make the visitor feel like a privileged guest and not a customer. These can be lovely, soothing marketing devices. But be aware that galleries can carry wonderful prints, even if they are plain and simple.

Secret: A gallery is a business.

No matter how a gallery looks, it has to be a business to survive, unless it is a tax write-off, which cannot last longer than three years. Galleries are stores with obligations and responsibilities to clients. They have to sell their wares just as any other retail outlet does in order to stay in business.

Our gallery, and every other gallery, is a store; anybody with space has to sell to stay there as well as put on exhibitions. Every gallery is a store, no matter how elitist, spare, funky, or crowded it is. It is set up to show and sell artwork. We own three fine galleries which are art stores. People buy the prints we have borrowed from printmakers on consignment who are academicians teaching printmaking in Europe, Japan, Korea, China, New Zealand, Australia, and all over the United States.

GALLERY OWNERS VS. ART DEALERS

Gallery owners locate art and assemble collections and exhibitions which reflect their personal tastes and interests. We are both printmakers, so our gallery specializes in contemporary original prints. One young gallery owner I know specializes in artists of the 1930s, a period that has interested him since his college days, when he helped uncover boxes of WPA prints made during the Depression.

An art dealer is actually different from an art gallery owner. An art dealer tries to present new trends and to discover and rediscover artists. But an art dealer is also someone who deals with art speculatively. He searches for and sells art to and for clients and institutions, as well as organizing exhibitions.

An art gallery owner is something of a show person, similar to a circus manager—always looking for new animals with outrageous tricks or lovable animals that people will admire. He presents prints that represent new trends or new work of established printmakers or newly discovered printmakers in order to stimulate the interest of the public. He takes work on consignment or purchases it outright in order to make it available to sell to the public through his gallery. A gallery owner can be an art dealer too. I sometimes purchase work on speculation, with the idea that I will make money eventually on what I buy because the work will escalate in value. When I purchase work outright it is for convenience or because it is rare. For example, a client offered to sell us a folio of Ben Shahn lithographs at what seemed to be a reasonable price. We bought it and thus have enabled many people to purchase a single Shahn lithograph, and we have made a profit from it as well. On occasion, when we know that certain work definitely will sell, we pay the artist for many prints at one time and thus sidestep the hassle of making a payment after each sale.

Gallery professionals are sometimes artists and often art historians, writers, psychologists, and anthropologists. They are romantics and ecstatic personality types characterized by enthusiasm and persistence in the face of hard odds. They generally love art more than is sensible because the art world is a tough, competitive one, not the gentle and refined arena you might think.

The questions for most people are: What is an art gallery? How should I act there? Who is the person selling art there, and how useful can that person be to me? Is a gallery like an art museum? If not, how is it different? Is it actually more like a shop, or is commerce considered a vulgar association?

Translated from the Latin, *galleria* is a corridor in which objects have been arranged for the public to view and to buy. An art gallery is a space designed to display works of art for sale to the public. An art gallery has private rather than public ownership.

A museum collects, preserves, and presents works of art for the edification and enjoyment of the public and art historians and other scholars. An art gallery exhibits art for the purpose of presenting it publicly, supporting it enthusiastically, and selling it; and characteristically specializes in a particular type of art reflecting the interests of the gallery owner rather than presenting different periods and styles within a historical context, as museums do.

Among the types of art you are likely to find in a gallery are: work by established avant garde printmakers; portraits and landscapes; early American prints; folk art; the work of young, unknown artists, as well as that of recognized, "blue chip" artists. There are galleries in cities and resort areas that specialize in paintings, book plate prints, original prints, fiber works, sculpture, and some galleries that mix pastels, watercolors, prints, and other works of art on paper. Galleries arrange periodic exhibitions, featuring either the work of a single artists or of a group of artists. Advertisements for these shows can generally be found in newspapers and art journals. There are other galleries that focus on artists' reproductions and posters. They are often found in malls and department stores.

Sometimes a gallery's strongest pieces are not its greatest source of income. A gallery owner I know, who is recognized internationally as an important source of early 20th century prints, earns his living with summer exhibitions where he sells quantities of seascape prints.

HOW THE PRINT GALLERY BUSINESS WORKS

Prints are either taken on consignment or are bought outright from artist printmakers or their publishers. Prints are chosen for consignment after printmakers submit slides for the galleries to review. The criteria by which they are selected are inexact; the process often boils down to how their images fill an existing need in the gallery's stock of printmakers' work. When work is consigned, the artist sets the retail price, which should be uniform wherever you find his work, even in his studio. He is paid from 70 to 50% of the retail price within a month or two after a sale is made.

Prints are also bought at 50% of retail from a print publisher, the person or company who puts up the money that pays the printmaker or his printer for an edition of prints to be printed. Our daughter worked for one year laboriously printing separate parts of the pochoir prints of Sol de Witt when she worked at Solo Press in New York. Hence when these prints were purchased by galleries they were not inexpensive.

Many prints are purchased from the printmakers directly. Often the printmaker receives only 20 to 25% of the retail price, but the payment is immediate and often the order is for a number of prints in the edition.

Many galleries are supplied by print wholesalers who carry print samples with them to galleries. When they are ordered, the artist is paid 25%. The printmaker/artist often seems to get the short end but since the art business depends on galleries sustaining themselves, they find out which galleries pay regularly. And the more savvy artists help their galleries with suggestions for exhibitions and contacts with the press and clients.

> Secret: Buy it when you see it.

The inventory of galleries fluctuates according to exhibitions, seasons, cash flow, the good will of the artists, and the energy of gallery keepers. Although prints are multiples, do not assume that a print will be there when you return next year. Editions and follow-throughs are limited. I have seen too many disappointed people—I insist that prints are but fragments on paper, transitory at best.

> Secret: Print galleries either consign or buy their prints.

Galleries generally acquire prints slowly and carefully, piece by piece, artist by artist, sometimes purchasing outright from the printmaker or his representative, usually taking work on a consignment basis. The gallery owner or manager assesses the artistic merit and the beauty of each print when he accepts or rejects it. He looks at the technique used to create it and judges the craftsmanship, as well as the concept behind the work. Auctions are an important source of art for the gallery owner; prints sold at auction have been pur-

chased before and are once again in circulation.

Galleries, collectors, museums, and art dealers help one another with special exhibitions, supplementing each others' collections and, when selling, split the commissions. Even museums sell art. This is called *deaccessioning*. Today, there are art fairs throughout the country acting as national clearinghouses for prints. Even junk shops are sources of prints. The best sources are the artists themselves, and thus, many stairs are climbed to artists' studios by gallery people, and many client suggestions are followed by letters and gallery staff traveling to remote places in order to track down unknown printmakers.

HOW CONSIGNMENT WORKS

Most galleries will take a piece of the artist's work on consignment. Consignment means that when work is sold by a gallery, the retail price is set by the artist, not the gallery. When sold, a certain percentage of the retail price goes to the gallery, and a certain percentage is paid by the gallery to the artist. This can vary from 33⅓% to 60% kept by the gallery, and depends largely on the gallery's location. If the gallery is located in a high rent part of a city, they will take a higher percentage as their commission. I have been told that in major cities today, no gallery can afford to sell anything for under $500; their overhead is too high. A sale involves personnel, payments, and bookkeeping, each of which involves a high cost plus rent, advertising, and other overhead.

The big advantage of working on consignment is that work that does not sell can be returned to the artists. Since a gallery is expected to be a showplace with new pieces on the walls, the consignment practice helps limit storage and inventory. Therefore, it is important to buy what you like at the time you see it, because it might soon be returned to the artist or the gallery that lent it.

Although some prints are bought from print publishers and some from artists or artists' estates (usually at a price far less than the 50% wholesale price), most galleries operate on a tight margin, taking prints *on consignment* from printmakers. Stores carrying reproductions of paintings, limited edition prints, and posters, on the other hand, are operated more like furniture stores, with outright purchases made based on speculations about decorating trends. The store then marks them up 100% or more.

When print galleries consign works, an arrangement is worked out whereby the consignee is paid from 30% to 60% of the selling price within two months of the sale of the print. Keep in mind that if the gallery lets you pay for your print purchase slowly, both the gallery and the unpaid artist are financing your purchase.

Some galleries purchase artwork outright from an artist or an agent. When a gallery purchases a work outright, it is usually at 50% of the retail price. If many works are bought wholesale from an artist, the payment to the artist might be as low as 25% of retail. An advantage of purchasing artwork is that, if the gallery owner's eye is trained, he can buy low and sell high.

Some galleries prefer to purchase their prints outright from the artist because it eliminates the bookkeeping problems and administrative tasks attendant on consignment acquisitions. However, many galleries cannot afford to do this, due to the financial outlay involved, and the limitations of storage space.

In order to ensure a continuous stream of visitors, a gallery must change its exhibits frequently. To do this with work purchased outright would require financial resources that most galleries do not have. And showing the consigned work of up-and-coming, innovative, unknown printmakers is far less risky than buying established expensive prints that might fall on the ever so fickle marketplace.

USE YOUR PRINT DEALER'S RESOURCES

Good print dealers offer backup steps which can be written on the bill of sale to assure you that your print purchase is a safe one:
• referrals to their reference libraries, books, or public libraries in order to help you check on your artist; or information in a catalog to verify the worth of your print purchase
• offer to send an artist's checklist of work avail-

able with Polaroids® of the work so that you can shop from home
• offer "on approval" service to customers whereby you phone or write in with a credit card or check to hold a print which can be sent to you, insured, for a stated, limited amount of time
• arrangements whereby, within a prescribed time, the print purchased can be exchanged or sold by the gallery on consignment if you want to upgrade or liquidate your purchases
• refunds—should a print's authenticity be questioned later

SECRETS TO VISITING GALLERIES

• Do not apologize for a lack of knowledge or taste.
• Do not hesitate to explain what you like and need if it is not what the gallery owner is exhibiting.
• Give the gallery person the scope of your budget and taste. And if there is a possible taste conflict between you and your partner, be up front about it.
• Ask for information. The gallery person can help your perception deepen and clarify your understanding and appreciation. Historic and artistic implications of a print or a style are fun and challenging for a member of the gallery staff to try to explain to you. For example, art from the 1940s has a rounded look that needs certain tutoring to appreciate, I find, and minimalist work needs explaining.
• Ask about prices. Why is this print priced more or less than others in the gallery? Ask to be shown comparables. I borrow this term from real estate because similar work is often priced in the same price range. Printmakers keep up with the marketplace and know who is charging what. Remember that there will be a great difference in prices asked for rare master prints, blue chip prints created in conjunction with a master printer, and prints pulled by academics and professional printmakers, which are usually less expensive than the others.
• Expect frank disclosure about the print: its provenance—where it came from and how it got to the gallery; information about the printmaker—where he works and exhibits; the artist's track record; the number of prints in the edition; the print-

maker's professional affiliations and museum assosociations; and whose collections include his prints.

PRICING OF PRINTS

> Secret: Print prices will be from $10 to $10,000.

If you buy a really good print at a yard sale, as my sister once did, you are lucky! Most original prints sell for $50 for small prints, to $800 for academic and professional prints, and up to $3000 for blue chip and popular printmakers. Master prints cost thousands of dollars depending on the condition and the quality of impression.

Reproduction and limited edition prints are in a different league. They are priced as the market will bear. They are all made photographically and mechanically on an offset press, not by hand as are original prints. Thus pricing is quixotic and idiosyncratic. If the image is popular, the price might be as high as $1200. Some reproductions cost only $30. The variables in the equation, which the wholesaler or retailer considers when setting the price, are the fame of the artist, the popularity and often the sentimentality of the image, and printing and marketing costs. We think that a fair price for a good reproduction well printed on fine paper should be around $200 to $300, and posters should be $10 to $20.

> Secret: Reticence on the part of the gallery owner can be expected.

Many galleries are owner operated, so the person on the floor might be the name on the gallery sign. If that person is reserved, this is why: Gallery personnel are torn between conflicting energies—being suspicious about possible thefts or intrusions and providing a cordial welcome to visitors and prospective clients. Remember, they are working with all of the art-loving public—art students with their demands for help; artists with their unflagging egos that need to be stroked or held in check; academics and amateurs, who need to be informed; collectors and curators who need

in-depth help; and thieves, who try to distract gallery personnel with conversation, so an accomplice can slip a print inside a raincoat or paper bag. After years of dealing with the walk-in public, many galleries go private and cease to provide public exhibitions, showing by appointment only.

I have had customers whom I remember gratefully because they brought me a small bouquet of flowers or a cup of coffee or thanked me for arranging an exhibition. I remember especially, one young woman who mused perceptively, as she stood holding the two $300 Chinese wood-block prints she was buying, "This is a glorious exhibition of prints, but why did you arrange it? There isn't much money in it for you."

GALLERY PEOPLE ARE THERE TO HELP

Galleries offer services as well as products. In addition to exhibiting and selling art, gallery owners also act as consultants. They educate clients about art trends and the backgrounds of their artists and, for an hourly consulting fee, they often will produce artwork for collectors, decorators, and architects.

Every gallery operator is different. Some are artists; some are confirmed art collectors who are so addicted to amassing works of art that they open a gallery. Others champion up-and-coming artists they have found. Still others are retirees who like art. I find that the more firmly established gallery people are, the more gracious they will be. Leo Castelli, the famous New York art dealer, greeted me like a long-lost friend when I wandered into his showroom, unknown and shy.

Art gallery persons should be able to talk to you in detail about the particular works you are interested in. They should be able to reassure the buyer that a work is a genuine original print and not a reproduction. If the print is a reproduction, that is all right, as long as you know it!

The ways gallery people can be helpful include:
• Information about the print's source, where the gallery got the print: from the artist directly, from his family or estate, from an auction, or from a print publisher.

• The medium used by the artist and the quality of the print impression.

• Documents surrounding the choice, including the artist's biography. The condition of the work should be discussed. Is it perfect or not? If not, does it have problems that a conservator can take care of?

The gallery person should let you examine the print. A photo reproduction looks and feels machine printed. The layer of ink is thin. The surface is slick. Sometimes there is a photographic dot screen. An original etching is rough to the touch and has an indentation from the plate being pushed into the paper during the printing process; a silkscreen has a discernible skin of color; a lithograph is harder to identify because its quality is closer to photo offset, but it often has intensity of color and range of tones that make you feel the difference. Woodcuts evidence the wood used and are slightly pressed into the paper. The gallery person should talk about how and where the artist works, whether he is still alive, and if and how you could meet him.

People working in galleries have studied art all their lives and have asked their artist enough about their work to be able to speak knowledgeably about them, their histories, their techniques, and their aesthetic intentions.

The gallery person is a go between, a marriage broker between the printmaker and you. His main obligation is to you, the customer, to help you understand and appreciate what you are seeing. But no gallery is perfect and each has its own individual character and focus. Chances are you will find a gallery where you are comfortable. That gallery is the best place to look for prints when you become serious enough to purchase.

GALLERY PEOPLE, DECORATORS, AND ARCHITECTS CAN HELP YOU FIND PRINTS YOU LIKE

It is most important that you tell the gallery associate with whom you are dealing as much as possible about your wants, regardless of whether the prints you see displayed bear any similarity to them. There may be a hidden cache in the back room that you will never see unless you tell the gallery owner what it is you like. One day in our Rockport gallery, I remember showing a variety of handmade papers to a customer who told me that he collected mezzotints. I invited him to meet me the next day to see our superb collection of mezzotints in the Boston gallery, an invitation he appreciated and consummated with two serious purchases. It would not have occurred to me to mention them had he not expressed a specific interest.

Most gallery associates are delighted when they receive a thank-you note from a customer or some flowers at an opening. Praise for an appreciated show is well received. The truth is, galleries can be lonely places. Bring in warmth and enthusiasm and you will not regret it.

Getting back to George and Betsy, I advised them to return with an agreement before our appointment that they would let each other have three art choices. They would take turns eliminating them one by one until they reached their final choice on which they both could agree.

If you, as Betsy and George did, want to search for a picture for a certain place in your home, this is a legitimate strategy. Ask for assistance. Define your taste and specify details of size, mood, even colors, as much as you can. It is important to tell the gallery person exactly what in the gallery does attract or repel you.

If George and Betsy are still hesitant about their final choices, an excellent solution is to ask the gallery person to let them take a few prints home on approval for a week. This would let them see the art in their home setting before making a final purchase.

Another way individuals or couples can arrive at a good choice when decorating is to bring the gallery keeper and decorator together and have all three parties, including the buyer, work out the choices. After all, gallery people and decorators experience this situation on a daily basis. Put your trust in them.

From my own experience I can suggest what an art gallery person can do for you. I have been glad to answer questions about the artists whose work I display. I would fill in information about where they fit into the history of American prints and art history. For example, I offered information about one of our silkscreen artists, comparing his work to constructionist artists Edward Hopper and George Sheeler. In doing so, I told my client about the American narrative art style and placed my artist in perspective in American art history.

MAKE FRIENDS WITH GALLERY PEOPLE

> Secret: Let a reputable gallery person guide you to smart art buying.

A gallery person can educate you. Do not forget that he or she can learn from you as well. Your fresh perception and enthusiasm help gallery owners realize that their print finds are as wonderful as they hope they are. Gallery owners get so bogged down with arranging exhibitions, framing, and making payments to artists that they need all the strokes they can get. If encouraged, people at a gallery can discuss all the variables that might influence your decision to buy or not.

Why are you so intimidated about art-buying decisions? Do you think your image is directly related to the types of art you hang? Have decorating magazines inhibited you by too many prohibitions, or is it that the work you think you can afford is not sufficiently expensive looking to show how classy you are? Is the bottom line your own responses to art?

> Secret: Trust gallery people.

Most gallery personnel are eager to learn all that you can tell them about your tastes. Do not be timid about your goals, ideas, and art needs even if you cannot articulate them precisely.

Search for an art gallery person with integrity who will encourage you. They are, after all, truly dedicated people. Art is their perk: to help you is everything. I relish the young couples who hug each other when they decide on a print for over their couch; who celebrate an anniversary with a print. I love the person who looks at my prints and becomes so involved that my presence fades.

Gallery people can smooth the way for you as you buy. They are mostly dedicated people slavishly driven to bringing art to their small worlds. They put up with snide remarks such as, "Is that $2.00? It couldn't be $200." They work weekends, evenings, six days a week, even if they are doing it as a hobby or retirement business. They interview artists, screen slides, find artists' studios, post bonds to get prints into the United States, invite and cajole people to share the pleasure of owning a beautiful work of art.

> Secret: Galleries are not flea markets.

When you buy art at a street fair, rummage sale, junk shop, or any casual atmosphere, it is legitimate to try to strike a bargain. We all do it and enjoy our victories. However, realize that galleries are stores with fixed costs. Do not offend gallery keepers by asking for a discount. Many will shrug and walk away. I stand up straighter and look as offended as I feel, while I restate the price and explain why it is not negotiable.

Art prices are firmly fixed in most galleries. The artist, gallery owner, gallery staff, and all intermediaries, as well as gallery upkeep, must be paid. Besides, it takes too much of a gallery person's energy and time to bargain. The only exception to this anti-bargaining stance is that there sometimes is room for movement when a print is priced in the thousands of dollars range.

> Secret: Gallery grouches are pushovers.

Let us examine that person behind the desk, shuffling a card file ever so quietly or talking on the telephone. He is taking care of countless duties and emergencies: finding artwork for clients; shipping; insuring; returning; responding to requests for special prints; organizing exhibitions; doing public relations; and making follow-up calls to clients. The list goes on and on.

However, beyond these tasks, recognize that coolness protects gallery personnel from the time-eating invasions of customers. Gallery owners are human. The pressures of their jobs are high; survival is at stake. When they spot a "lover and looker," as we call the hangers on, they back away. Do not monopolize gallery people's time with stories about every art purchase you ever made. Use time in the gallery to ask questions and interact sincerely with people there about their artists. But after a period of many polite interactions of your questions and their answers, gallery people might legitimately become grouches if you do not buy. They want you to begin to make a commitment before offering more education.

DEFINE YOUR REASONS FOR BEING IN THE GALLERY

There is no shame attached to going into galleries just for a look. That is how Betsy and George came into our gallery. It is wordless looking that results in enjoyment and eventual commitment.

There is no shame in going in with no intention to buy. Be up front and tell gallery people you are there to look. They will respect your privacy.

Remember that gallery people get tired and confused with too many questions or too much talk for too long a time. They start to flag, giving shorter answers. Gallery people serve with little immediate gratification. Sales often happen after a time lapse or after several visits.

Be friendly to gallery people. Let them tell you about the prints they represent. Their enthusiasm will help you appreciate what you are seeing. Our own perceptions can be enlarged by other perceptions.

On the other hand, it is fair to point out that calculated coolness is a well-tried selling device. Many a sale has been made by being snooty. By being remote, art dealers might try to negative-sell you into the elite art world.

It is all right for you as a visitor to a gallery to say, "I do not know anything about art, I only know what I like," and then ask to be left alone. You can expect to be filled in with information about an artist's background. Anyone can detect a person who is manipulating them in order to sell, rather than helping fill in with facts about the artist and reasons why they respect these prints.

INVESTMENT ARGUMENTS ARE SUSPECT

> Secret: The art business has grown into a tremendous industry with its own merchandising skills.

Suspect a hard sell and move away when a gallery person emphasizes investments. In general, I can only say that if you want to put money into predictable investments, try gold bullion. Do not let a skillful art merchandiser convince you to buy or make you feel guilty about not buying just because a work of art will go up in price next month. Suspect that you are being manipulated.

But if your eye is good, your source of advice is sound, the price of the print is low, and your timing is right, you might make a good investment, but do not expect this to happen. Buying art as an investment is always dubious. There is honestly no way to tell if a young artist's success will continue. Go back to the old saying, "I buy what I like."

> Secret: Do not purchase art because it is expensive and, conversely, do not overlook prints because they are inexpensive.

Buy what you like for its inherent beauty or because it interests you, not for its price. In a consignment print gallery, the artists set the prices. Often the more productive and creative the artists, the fairer the prices they set. They know that each creation is not the last. In fact, they are often delighted when their work turns over quickly. I find that the more amateur artist sets a higher price than the professional. Another observation is that the public senses when a price is too high; they have an inherent sensitivity about what is a just price.

On the other hand, do not suspect low prices if you like the work. A person asked me, "If that printmaker's work is so good, how come his prices are so reasonable?" This is unfair. Maybe the printmaker needs both encouragement and sales money in order to continue this odd way of life called printmaking.

> Secret: Take your time.

Art buying can be a drawn-out process. We want you to buy on a love at first sight basis. But often it is more like a dance—back and forth, checking other works, getting information along the way, making comparisons until you know it is the right decision. This can mean a number of visits to a gallery for your own information and education before you decide to buy.

The art selecting process generally works like this.

1. Establish a preference if you are attracted to a body of work. Take this seriously; keep in mind the young man who returned to my gallery and was frustrated because, "I cannot seem to forget the work by that Alaskan artist you showed me three years ago." The prints had long since been returned to Alaska!

2. Gather information about the artist, the medium, and his other works.

3. Think about how the art will work in your life. Your goal is to be persuaded of its contribution.

4. Having done enough homework about a print of your choice, the result is satisfaction and delectation because you can now make a sound decision to buy a print.

PAYING FOR YOUR PRINTS

> Secret: Buy artwork for pleasure. Buy as a *coup de cœur*, because you cannot *not* buy, and then ask about payment plans.

What options, besides paying all at once, do you have if you think you want to purchase a work of art? Do not be afraid to ask for a slow payment plan. Galleries can work this out with you more easily than you might think.

Often galleries and auction houses will finance a work of art so you can acquire it gradually. Galleries let you take the piece home after a partial payment and a plan for other payments has been arranged, or they can hold the artwork while payments are being made. Often a contract is drawn up and signed between the buyer and the gallery which defines, for both parties, how soon and how regularly payments will be made. Such a financial arrangement helps a gallery, and the buyers become grateful customers. They bring their friends. The gallery becomes their gallery.

You can borrow money from a bank or a friend in order to buy art. In fact, among clients I have interviewed, it is the piece that they borrowed money to acquire and struggled to buy that they love the most.

BUY IT WHEN YOU SEE IT

Marvin Jules is one of our vintage artists. He is in his seventies and has watched the art scene as an artist in New York and as an aesthetics teacher. He sat in his wheelchair on the bayside deck of his Provincetown cottage and told me this story, which I think illustrates the pleasures attendant to "buying it when you see it."

When he taught his aesthetics courses at a Massachusetts museum, he always told his students that they would not understand a print unless they made a commitment to shopping for prints and purchasing at least one piece. "During the 1940s one of my students, a young bachelor," he mused, "made me come to his apartment ten miles away to see what he had fallen in love with and had purchased during the previous weekend in New York. He borrowed money from the president of the company he worked for and bought it. There it was, a woodcut by Edvard Munch," Marvin Jules laughed. His student eventually became a renowned print collector as well as the president of that company and others, and even married a lady he met in one of the galleries he frequented. Art had an ennobling influence on his life and can exercise the same charm on yours. The most important secret in this book is to tell you that you will be happy if you act on this buying impulse; if you love a print you will not be sorry if you buy it.

BROWSING
Practical Steps to Smart Print Buying
5

Visit print rooms in libraries and museums to become informed. Recently, a Japanese artist spoke to me as I was working on a handmade paper piece. She suggested, "Keep a quiet place." She said that she always preserves an unworked area in each piece that she creates, which reflects a quiet place inside herself.

I have gravitated towards a way to nurture this quietness. I find that I can quiet myself by becoming an art junkie. As I concentrate on an outstanding collection of contemporary American prints, I feel a sort of relaxation.

Will Barnet's early lithographs and etchings enthrall me in their expansiveness and beautiful composition. Raphael Soyer's lithographs inspire me with his ability to convey mood and feeling.

Early etching by Will Barnet, At the Seashore, *1939.*

> Secret: Prints should be sought as pleasure.

The purpose of the thoughts in this chapter is to introduce you to the joy of choosing and collecting prints. I want to help you start your art buying without always having to mix and match. I want you to be able to enter an art gallery or art museum feeling confident. I want you to try to be completely relaxed when you approach and visit art galleries. Being in a relaxed frame of mind is especially important, because you will be a thousand times more receptive to the art you see. When you are relaxed, the receptive, not the cognitive, part of your brain plays a major role. Instead of trying to find a certain predetermined type of print, whether it is Art Nouveau or an English landscape, try to adopt an open, interested, non-judgmental attitude. I hope you will feel at home in an artist's studio, art gallery, or art museum. Ask questions; invite the artist, art dealer, or museum curator to talk to you. You probably will not like everything they say or everything you see, but you will learn gradually what it is that you *do* like.

LOOK AT ART FOR FUN

Let art come into your consciousness. Perhaps as you walk through a museum or art gallery, something will affect you. The 20th century woman is mind-washed by the plethora of magazines that lie in our coordinated rooms. Month after month these appear with their rules of how to assemble furniture; how to match color schemes; how to create formal or informal, modern or traditional living spaces. So women, more often than men, tend to buy art analytically, as they would buy wallpaper. As an art buyer, you need to let go of the formal conventions of decorating and allow yourself to buy prints purely for the fun of it; for the pleasure you will experience each time you see the print hanging on your wall.

What bothers me, as a seller of artwork, is that art is somehow drastically diminished by this process of buying it to mix and match color schemes. Selecting prints for pleasure should not be a problem, if you elect to spend some time looking at art for fun, as an indoor sport. The more you do it, the easier it will become. Try exploring various art galleries and exhibits once every month or two. By taking the time to permit the artwork to interact with your spirit and intertwine with your moods, you will find that you develop a confidence in your ability to make choices, and the act of purchasing a print will become a pleasure, not a chore. It is an alternative to running in and out of art galleries once every two years, looking for a certain color and size, feeling hopelessly inadequate.

LEARN HOW TO SEE

Soon you will be "seeing" and not just looking. Seeing is a cognitive process. It is a willingness to open up your mind and recognize what is there to be seen. Some people return many times to a gallery to drink in a work of art before they eventually purchase it. Ask questions; if you do not have any at first, the more you visit galleries, the more questions will pop into mind.

TAKE TIME

Take the time to look at your leisure. I think that movies, television, and photographic images have confused us about the nature of looking at anything. *Seeing* cannot be accomplished in ten second takes. I can assure you that before an artist paints or prints an image, he is thinking about it, looking at it mentally for a long time. In working with any medium, it takes an artist a long time to

The first print ever bought by the author. Artist unknown.

realize his concept. So the work is not intended to be perceived in just a few seconds.

Try two minutes, then five minutes, then half an hour. Find something in the work that interests you intensely and let that lead your eye to other things in it. Pretty soon you will begin to get into the piece, and you will begin a dialogue with it.

Try to empathize with the intentions of the artist. Let yourself experience the energy and spirit of the art. In other words, enter into the artist's experience—get yourself past yourself, by creatively allowing his or her point of view to be yours, for just a few moments. Allow yourself to move beyond your own life experience and participate in the artist's compelling drive to share his insights, as perfectly and as completely as he can.

I think of Monet's lovely garden at Giverny as I write this—how he created a lovely water lily-filled pond, flowered paths, and Oriental bridges covered with white wisteria. There he worked relentlessly to share with us how the pond and the lilies appeared in the changing light at various times during the day. His joy in his beloved garden and in the light playing on the water lilies is a gift to humanity, readily available to those who take a moment to look and feel creatively.

> Secret: Print viewing can be an alternative to other indoor sports.

To feel at home and confident when you are in a gallery, a studio, or an art museum, you have to let go of some of the time you devote to other things. Instead of attending every sports event, decide to let art become part of your life by regularly visiting museums, art galleries, and art studios.

You do not need to take a great amount of time to do this. My husband and I stole away to a museum last winter for a lunch and a quick viewing of the Fairfield Porter exhibition. In the middle of February, it cheered me immeasurably to look at his sun-filled landscapes of the Maine coast, his flower garden, and his old white shingled house.

BROWSE ALONE

A gallery really is a type of store. I've made that point many times in order to demystify galleries and help you feel comfortable in any gallery. However, as an artist, and for all the printmaker artists I represent, I must also protest that most galleries go beyond stores. They are repositories of the warmest, most beautiful, and most insightful statements human beings can wring from their souls. Please give them time and space in your life. Experience the pleasures of art shopping.

> Secret: Just browse; decide not to buy art today.

The first step in becoming an art buyer is to make a decision that you will not buy art, at least not immediately. Don't let art become just another commodity. Decide not to buy art now. Decide that first you will experience art as gradually and as fully as possible. And enjoy doing it. Let art surprise you. It might not all be pretty. It might be moving, disturbing, even vulgar.

This step is crucial. Let go of your urge to search for art you need: the pink or mauve flower pictures under ten inches tall; a sailing print in strong blues; the bright abstract in your couch colors, 32 inches wide; the Chinese dragons to match your draperies; the pale statements large enough to cover cracks; the small print to fit a secondhand frame in your hall. I could list thousands of such art orders that filter through our gallery.

> Secret: Images move us when we browse.

Art *should* disturb you; shock you, grip you; be unforgettable. The experience that a work of art provides changes your life. It's a sort of epiphany, a tender visit by grace, tantamount to a religious experience, when a piece of art truly affects you, but to let it in is the challenge, to get past the wallpaper approach to browsing. Paradoxically, one searches in too narrow a way when one is most hungry for the experiences that art provides. Hence, you will come away from such a search emptier than ever with no art, or meaningless art. The secret is to let go of preconceived notions of art as an object and substitute art as an experience.

> Secret: You will know it when you see it.

Many works of art will speak to you if you go to art galleries with a simple goal: to be a creative browser. It is not without truth that the old saying, "I'll know it when I see it," comes to the buyer's mind when browsing in an art gallery. But what this really means is, "I will love it when I experience it."

When I hear these words, "I'll know it when I see it," in our gallery, it is a signal that people are beginning to be out of words, and that they are starting to experience art. They leave their verbalizing state (often called left brain) and travel to the nonverbal right side of the brain, a creative, intuitive state, which leads them to experience becoming involved with the art that gives them pause; appreciating, possibly taking steps towards buying art, with appreciation and understanding as the result.

In this creative state of mind, it is easier to enjoy art, to understand intuitively the artist's intentions, to respond to colors, forms. This absorption in the art will lead you to artwork that seems to have been waiting for you.

EXPERIENCING ART

> Secret: When browsing, let yourself drift into a quiet state.

When you start to experience art, it is hard indeed not to talk about what is going on. People tend to grunt, laugh, wheeze, breathe hard, and not speak in full sentences. They concentrate. When I am deeply involved in my own printmaking, or looking at art in a gallery or museum, I am unable to carry on a conversation. And this is a pleasure. I liken this to channeling, intuitively realizing the artist's quest. In the course of life with its stresses, this is a wonderful gift to give to oneself: time to be alone with someone else's essence, which is what art is.

Recently, I was sketching the view from the porch at twilight with others in the family nearby, including my son, who was describing an incident to me. I couldn't follow his point and, consequently, kept asking him to repeat what he had said until he muttered he would give up until after I had finished my drawing. You can see that this state of mind has some disadvantages, but for becoming centered to art, it is worth cultivating. Getting into a artistic mode of right-brain activity will lead to a genuine enjoyment of art and often to purchasing art.

Try to look at artwork with the right side of the brain, the more relaxed part of yourself, the affective, emotional part of your being. Let each work that interests you speak to you, even for a moment.

The first print I bought was the result of a casual glance into a student's rooms as I passed them at the University of Chicago dorm during a conference I was attending. I fell in love with it and finally bought it off the young student's wall, although I had no apartment of my own at that time. It was an image of a mother and child, sitting in a meadow, touching flowers. Maybe it was a projection of my own dreams of having children. I still cherish this work of art, bought because I couldn't *not* have it.

USING RIGHT-BRAIN BROWSING

The trick to right-brain browsing is to turn on your creative self, your right brain, in an art gallery. In this chapter, I will suggest ways for you to work through the three stages of creativity when you are looking at art. This will invite art to involve and entertain you on many levels, as well as cover and decorate your walls.

The three stages of browsing are *saturation, incubation,* and *illumination.* These terms have been borrowed from the book, *Drawing on the Artist Within,* by Betty Edwards (Simon & Schuster, 1986). I have asked her permission to use these terms in the context of this book.

STAGE ONE: SATURATION

> Secret: Saturate yourself in prints.

In order to find original prints, old and new, you should travel to artists' studios, mall art shops, antique shops, art galleries, art auctions and regular auctions, outdoor art exhibits, both in resort areas and in near and far cities. Look at everything quickly until your taste forms and you find how you react to art. Do you like abstract, realistic, textured or slick, lithographs, intaglio, silkscreens, or woodcut prints? Interact with the gallery people; ask what the difference is between types of prints and reproductions, master prints and academic prints. But most important, tell yourself to keep moving. It is like aerobics: If you keep moving and looking hard, your art-looking muscles will form into certain likes and dislikes that you can easily articulate to anyone interested, like a helpful gallery person.

If you are going to saturate yourself in art and eventually start to fill your walls and shelves, rather than turning this task over to a decorator, recognize that a sense of vagueness and unease will be part of this art experience. It is important to recognize that anxiety is one of the factors of any creative activity. This certainly applies to the act of experiencing art and deciding what prints to buy.

It takes time to saturate yourself in works of art. You need to be open to creative possibilities. Also, immerse yourself in experiences that relate to art such as reading about prints, doing research about artists, visiting artists' studios, and taking museum trips.

Etching by Art Werger, Neighborhood Watch—The Fight.

Tricks to Increase Art Saturation

The aim of this exercise is to encourage you to become totally involved in art you like. This means that you have to start to decide what interests you. If nothing in a gallery interests you at all, walk away. Find a work of art that is compelling to you; sit or walk about in front of it, if possible. Drift with it.

Make up games about the art. If it is a figurative landscape, what do various pieces remind you of: trips that you made, vistas of beaches, celebrations? Be in touch with your feelings: Does a piece make you laugh, cry, wince? Associate freely with the art. Chat about it. Prop it somewhere and keep coming back to it as you do other things.

Playfulness. Make believe that this is not a print-buying expedition; you are there to browse. You are going to galleries to learn, to experience the artist's feelings, to be alone with art and enjoy the artist's interpretations of life.

Most of us hope that some artist somewhere has the same feelings about nature as we do: wide landscapes, skies that are full of stars giving a sense of the eternal; reflections on humanity which pinpoint our own agonies and joys; warm home scenes that capture and celebrate intimate passing moments that are precious in all of our lives. One of my favorite ways of buying art is to have a picture remind me of something I have loved or could empathize with. For example, my favorite wood engraving by Rockwell Kent is a black and white silhouette of a man astride the bow of a boat, reaching out to a patch of white on a far horizon. It is obvious that I haven't been there, but the taut moment is an ecstatic one which I share when I look at the small piece on my wall.

Inside Out. When you've found a print that works on you, focus in a different way. Concentrate on inner details. Abstract or realistic, there are tensions of lines and forms; shapes working against shapes. In a figurative work, details tell a story; stories pile up to convey more dramatically the central drama of the piece. (See the illustrated etching by Art Werger.) What do the small pictures inside the image mean?

Negative Shapes. The most important hidden part of an image that artists struggle with are negative spaces. To see these, concentrate first on looking at the positive shapes—realistic or abstract. Every work of art, including sculpture, has positive shapes. These are what are most readily apparent. They tell the story. They provide the arrangement

Wood engraving by Rockwell Kent.

that you see as you run through a gallery or shuffle through a bin.

The negative shapes, seen by shifting to the edges and looking *between* apparent described forms, provide drama. They juxtapose dramatically and make the piece work in the abstract. You are really getting into a picture when you can appreciate its negative shapes.

Turn the Work Upside Down. If you do this, the underlying drama of the work, less obvious, emerges with great force. For example, a seemingly quiet landscape of an ocean with clouds, turned upside down may jump up and down with contained activity or it might become oppressive to the viewer depending on how the clouds are printed. Perhaps you focused on the horizon and the water when the print was looked at right side up. The strength of the composition becomes evident when an artwork is turned upside down. If it is a semi-realistic piece, it becomes more abstract. Squint your eyes. How does it work?

Note the tension of forms—when strong shapes are juxtaposed one feels the mood that the artist wants to convey. In prints, notice also the abstract disposition of colors. Artists often arrange colors so that there is a pattern or arrangement which strengthens the composition of the print.

Get Into a Picture. The goal here is to feel as intensely as possible the print you respond to, after letting go of the useful ends of filling blank walls, status, cultivation that art might serve for you.

What is the dominant tone: Even an abstract piece has a prevailing mood. Is it lyrical, dramatic, spontaneous, angry, ecstatic, playful, erotic? Tell yourself about it.

Edges. Edges bring us back to concentrating on details in the work you like. In a work of art, edges work upon edges. The tension of edges barely touching and shapes between edges elicits a whole new appreciation of what the artist is trying to do.

Search for Symbols. There are elements in artworks that convey more than the total image. A whole vocabulary of symbols exists and lies ready to jump out and talk to you, if you allow yourself to become open and sensitive to them.

Note Meaning of Shapes and Sizes. Because most still lifes use a horizontal format, a vertical still life seems monumental. A face that fills a canvas produces a different effect than a small face of the same size in a large format.

Go for a Walk with a Line. Look at lines. The content of a work of art is conveyed in the language of the art. Are the lines broken or unbroken, thick or thin, long or short? Paul Klee spoke of the mind's ability to follow a line's movement and emotional content: A line moves quickly or slowly, assertively or tentatively.

Look at Surfaces. Is the presence of the printmaker obvious in strong textures, or is the surface

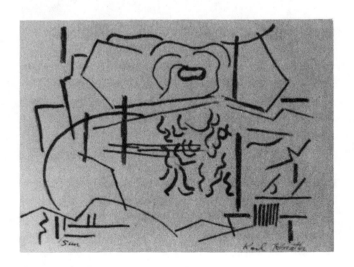

Drawing by Karl Knaths, Sun. Example of a strong composition that works equally well if turned upside down.

machine-clean and artist-anonymous as found in reproductions?

Find Meaning that Relates to You. Content is not just subject matter. You can find emotional meaning in the way a subject is handled. Printmaking is not an exercise in dexterity, but above all, a means of expressing intimate feelings and moods. Even abstract or non-objective art reveals an artist's feelings.

> Secret: Give up and let the art come to you.

I see art best in a museum when I am utterly exhausted and collapse on a bench, barely looking at the art around me because I am so tired. Suddenly, something comes off the wall towards me. It speaks to my satiated eyes. My appreciating self is suddenly tasting the sweetness of really feeling what the artist intended. I remember realizing the light in a Rembrandt print from across the room, or the intensity of a small etching as I glanced at it over someone's shoulder.

This happens to art buyers. I have had many a purchase happen when a customer collapses into a chair and starts to relax and then finally wants to check on something seen out of the corner of one eye.

Wood engraving by Claire Leighton, Maple Sugar. *Note how the artist has emphasized juxtaposition of strong shapes to create mood.*

Illustration of interplay of edges. Note the tension of strong diagonals created by railroad tracks and roof edges. Collagraph by Mary Ann Wenniger, Waiting for the 6:05.

Now Define Your Art Needs

Be ready to define your perceptions, along with your needs and limits, to gallery associates. It will help them know what further to show you. Is a certain wall really the most important in your house and is there only one way to put art on it? Think creatively about prints you like; consider them. When you budget for your art, I suggest that you budget just as you would for a washer and dryer or even a car which, of course, will be obsolete within five years.

I really enjoy art-buying people who give art to themselves as a personal gift, who love themselves enough to search for something that triggers an emotion, sufficient to make them choose art in a free way, not defined by wall needs, nor circumscribed by colors. This is the time to elect to buy art instead of clothing! Art is often less expensive than clothing; but in America, clothing is bought more readily because clothing is considered a necessity and art is not.

STAGE TWO: INCUBATION

> Secret: Walk away to incubate, let it all go.

You've made your search for art information. You have immersed yourself by looking at prints in dramatically different ways: upside down, at the edges, with a gestalt in mind, negatively, inside out, out of and in proportion. The recommended next step is to go home and let it all go. Do not try to decide on a print at this stage. Let what you saw work on you. Many art dealers tell me that they will not sell a piece when someone is in the saturation stage unless they show that they are faster than most and have gone through incubation then and there. They send them home with directions to think about what they have seen and experienced. In other words, it is suggested that they "incubate" and *then* come to a decision.

> Secret: Find art you cannot *not* buy.

Looking at images in such a relaxed way inevitably leads to purchasing something. If you go through galleries and artists' studios just to look at and enjoy art, something will speak to you.

The incubation stage of buying art is mostly unconscious activity. No one can tell you what really delights and intrigues you. That is something that you have to learn from yourself. It is a time to rest or think. It is time for you to do something else. Go eat lunch; read; go back to work. Let the art act on you. If anything is really for you, it will grow in your awareness. It will bring a sweetness to your mouth and tingling to your fingertips because you are entertaining the possibility of buying this wonderful work of art.

Try to Visualize Your Needs. Try color sketches expressing the feelings you want in a room. When I do commissions, I delight in involving my custom clients. I ask them to try to make small sketches with crayons, even if they can't draw, and they often delight and surprise themselves that this is not beyond them. This returns them to the common vocabulary of art. It helps them define their wants and show me what they have in mind.

Go Out of Proportion. Have you ever found that when you are in one place a long time everything becomes bigger, larger, much more important? A print acts on me best when I am lying on my stomach half asleep, only glancing at it. I barely squint at it out of a sleepy eye, then the forms play against each other abstractly. It all comes forward

Wood engraving by Fritz Eichenberg, Mary.

to me as the most important, dramatic part of the whole world...just so, pausing for as long as necessary over a work of art. If it is working on you, let it grow out of proportion; let it become the most important thing in your life. Revisit it as you proceed around the room or the town where you came upon it. Enter it; let it work on you until you are it and it is yours, even if you do not buy.

STAGE THREE: ILLUMINATION

> Secret: Do not think actively about buying prints.

Don't allow yourself to concentrate on buying prints. Only exercise your senses and aesthetic reactions; float. Look at art; absorb and enjoy the prints. You might find yourself dreaming of a particular etching.

Buying a print involves a courtship that cannot be hurried. The stages and the process of being won by a wonderful image can go slowly or quickly; but finally, you realize that you want it. This

Etching by Peggy Bacon, The Girls. *Note the gentle curving lines.*

Two Plants, *a vertical format still life, by Mary Ware.*

is called the *illumination stage.*

The timing of illumination is instantaneous. A decision that "you want it" is best made quickly. This is that high point that can happen after just thirty seconds in an art gallery. Psychologists I have queried about this have noted that many people's perceptions work incredibly fast. With confidence they can glance over hundreds of items and make judgments within seconds. However, most of us need incubation time. This might involve taking a short walk, having a cup of tea, a time of resting.

Secret: Be ready for the "Aha" reaction.

The "eureka...aha" reaction, the "this is it" feeling is a euphoric experience. It triggers confidence, a powerful sense of self to take a piece of art, to say, "This speaks to me. This is me. This is what I want. I have confidence to know I will

delight in this. I have the confidence to say that I deserve this work of art, to feel that I can spend money on aesthetic pleasure—a spiritual feeling, as well as practical."

During this magical moment, the conscious desire for art in your life and the unconscious search for art that grounds, provokes, or inspires you, for an instant becomes a creative unity. It turns around. Instead of parts, the wholeness of the statement is what you appreciate and want in your life. You decide delightedly in that moment to acquire this beautiful thing. Part of that artist's pilgrimage is forever yours.

Owning a particular print that delights you is a constant involvement. It gives a sense of personal pleasure. That is why art buying is addictive. The sense of personal pride in one's self, growing, strengthening, loving, and now com-

Lithograph by Ben Shahn. The face fills the whole sheet of paper.

mitted to beauty is what impels people to keep looking at and buying prints even after their walls are full.

If you don't buy it when you see it, your disappointment will last just as long! A story was told to me by a man who came in to see our Japanese prints. He was furtively looking about. For what, I asked. "Have you ever seen a Japanese print of a boy and a kite? I've been looking for it ever since I returned from Japan where I decided against it, and instead followed the friend's opinion that I should invest in the three Hiroshige prints. I have been looking for that print of the boy and the kite ever since."

ASK GALLERY PEOPLE FOR HELP

The most irresistible call in the human vocabulary is the call for help. This basic fact of human re-

lationships can easily be turned to the buyer's advantage, simply by approaching gallery people as advisers and collaborators. Virtually, every gallery person I can think of will go out of his way to help; no responsible gallery owner will ever take advantage of a client's uncertainty.

Every gallery person knows that even if he should want to take advantage of someone, he could only do so once. A novice art buyer who has been abused will discover it sooner rather than later, will never be back, and will speak ill of the dealer all of his life. Conversely, a satisfied client soon becomes a friend of the art gallery and a walking advertisement for it.

> Secret: As you browse, refine your goals.

Decide why you want to buy prints; your motives and values. This step involves deciding if your goal is art for love, art for decoration, or art for investment. I discuss these notions in greater depth in other chapters, because they are at the heart of buying prints. Buying art for love is the easiest motivation, but we all buy art for many other personal reasons: aggrandizement, status, decoration, instant gratification, wall coverings, anger or appeasement in a power struggle. Define and clarify your goals! They are all okay.

A DECISION MADE

When the woman came down the stairs, I was aware of the brownness of her tightly tied raincoat and her worried face. She had close-cropped hair, tucked behind ears that were the only decorative accent on her narrow head. Even her glasses seemed plain and utilitarian. Her face was closed as she handed a brown paper-wrapped parcel to me, which contained the framed print of a flower.

I recall feeling hungry and tired as she stood in front of my desk, but once she spoke, I pushed away other thoughts and focused on her. "It does not suit my living room. I cannot find a place for it." "Why did you buy it, if I may ask?" I said. "It is so beautiful, so rich," she replied, referring to the small mezzotint of a single orange lily tilted on the edge of a white plate and focused by a

Lithograph by Ben Shahn. A small face on a large sheet of paper.

The hands-on influence of the printmaker is evident in this collagraph, Baseball Ballet, *by Mary Ann Wenniger.*

blue-black velvety background, typical of the layers of ink that make a color mezzotint.

"I loved it when I saw it in your other gallery. It looked like a jewel. I should not have bought it. My job is only part-time. I am looking for a better one."

"You seem to like it so much, that really is the way to buy art, even if you buy it slowly."

"But I can't put it over my couch. . ."

I moved towards drawers full of a nice variety of original prints. "I am sure we can show you many images that will please you and fit nicely; now, what colors are you working with?" It really was not giving up; I felt new energy as I moved into a familiar gear.

The woman told me the colors; they really are not important. As I pulled etchings, lithographs, and silkscreens out, we became friends. She told me that this mezzotint of a lily was the first work of art that she had ever considered purchasing. I confided that I had been toying with theories about how people should buy art with the right side of the brain; how they should be relaxed and just let it happen; how people were right when they chant the familiar, "I will know it when I see it."

The end of my tale is that she got sadder and sadder as we found perfect prints for over her couch. "I just do not like anything as much as that lily," she finally said. I stopped, turned, and we looked across the bins at each other and smiled. Feeling relief, I asked, "All right, what are you going to do?" It does not always end so well but this time it did. She agreed to pay for the mezzotint slowly, and made a plan to bring in payments in installments. And because she will be coming in frequently, there is a good chance I can encourage her to do more creative browsing.

DECISIONS
Common Sense Ways to Choose Prints
6

Alexandra looked up at her roommate, Steve. "I think I'm going to buy it. It really is fun. I've never seen anything like it." The silkscreen she described hung with its red, yellow, and blue shapes on the wall opposite them at the gallery. Steve said, "Well, hurry up. I'm supposed to be at the university in a few minutes. Hey, have you thought about where you will hang it?" To facilitate her decision, Alexandra asked me if we could deliver the serigraph to her apartment on approval. Her intuition was correct; it looked great.

This chapter moves the reader from the secret of making a print purchase, by following your gut reaction and buying for pleasure, to the next secret: Don't wait; buy it when you see it or try it on approval.

> Secret: Buying prints is an easy way to begin deciding on art.

• Prints are relatively inexpensive.
• Prints are accessible throughout the world.
• Prints are understandable as crafts, as well as art.
• Printmakers enjoy explaining their print techniques.
• Prints can be shipped anywhere.
• Prints can be matted and framed so they suit one environment and then re-matted so they can suit another room.
• Prints can be given away or resold at auction. They can be given to hospitals or charity sales when you grow tired of them, and you can do this without guilt because you will have gotten your money's worth by that time.

MAKING UP YOUR MIND

Many people buy as an immediate response to one print that they find without the aid or advice of a gallery person. It always amazes me how quickly the average person's perceptions work to note what is available. Within less than a moment, there seems to be a scanning operation that singles out a few pictures for special attention.

There are so many reasons for people's choices: association with places, events; people remembered; pleasing colors or forms; interesting textures or shapes; and any combination of these working within space on the two-dimensional surface, to delight or at least start a spark of interest in the viewer's eyes.

For other people, it is a slower courtship between taste, needs, pocketbook, or simply between a work of art and themselves. They come back to look many times; they ask questions about the provenance of a print and want to know all about a certain printmaker or how he works, what his artistic significance is.

Many clients take a walk, or a week, to think about what they've seen or experienced in a gallery. They put this discipline on themselves so they can sort out which pieces they truly like so they will be sure that a work will always delight them.

HOW TO FIND
WHAT YOU WANT TO BUY

Recognize what kind of buyer you are. Some people decide on everything quickly; others prefer a gestation period before they decide. Both ways are fine when buying art. My plan is to share secrets that will help you feel comfortable and secure about deciding to buy a print. Recently a customer asked me if most buyers went through the process he found so necessary, which is to return two or three times to look at work he liked before choosing. I replied that it is surprising to me how many people actually make fast buying decisions and that these are usually their happiest, longest lasting decisions.

The first step is to recognize why you are considering this print; analyze what the print does for you.
• Does it give you pleasure?
• Does it touch you, shock you or others, or make you laugh?
• Does it decorate?
• Does it evoke an emotion?
• Does it seem like an investment?

Buying anything is idiosyncratic and extremely private. However, there seem to be some common realizations about buying art that have helped me and others when we consider taking the big step, which is to make a financial commitment to a work of art. Within the art industry, the "lovers and lookers" can be recognized: Those people who love everything, but never buy anything; or research everything, but never buy. One print dealer confessed that if a person repeatedly visits his gallery and asks questions and does not make a commitment, he actually confronts the person about this non-buying stance, tries to find out what the problem is, and defines his limits as a source of free information.

Secret: It takes courage to buy art.

It takes courage to buy art. More than buying any other commodity, art buying is difficult for the novice buyer. A buyer comes out of the closet and asserts that this is a wonderful print. It lays you open to criticism from family or friends. It advertises your values. You have to have confidence to do it. But once you realize that buying art is hard, then it becomes easier. And once you start to buy

art, it can become a powerful addiction. It will enhance your life.

Secret: Buy prints for love.

You will grow more and more involved with a print bought for emotional reasons. The more we understand about why we love it and by whom it was made and why, the more we love it. That's where gallery people can be helpful to you; they could help you to understand the background of an original—where it was made; by whom, who he is or was, both as a person and as an artist; where he stands in relation to other artists; what collections and museums include his work.

If art is bought as a furniture or as an accessory, it will not be noticed after a short while. If you find an image that knocks your socks off, buy it, even if it doesn't match your decor. Redecorate your room to go with your new print. You will not be sorry. You will not regret purchasing it.

There is a geometric progression in the effect of beautiful prints. They work on you daily; you grow to love them more and more. I fell in love with an etching of a small boy sitting sifting sand into a bucket. It looked like my son when he was very young. Because I am an art dealer and not often a buyer, I played games with myself and the picture. I had bought it from Joseph Margolies, an artist in Gloucester, Massachusetts, who died the following winter. I realized as I showed it that there were no backup prints. I could not get another print just like this ever again. It was unique because it was hand-colored by the artist. Every time someone picked it up I panicked. But I would not admit that I wanted it. What if I bought everything I liked, we couldn't stay in business. I loved it, in a different way than just admiring a fine work of art. I found it exquisite and haunting, deeply touching.

Finally, a man asked me to hold it for him. He left his telephone number and said he would be back. When I started to call him, I hung up and thought, "Why I am I torturing myself? I deserve to collect prints that I love too."

This print hangs in our upstairs hall. I pass it on my way to bed. It marks my son's departure and my memory of days sitting by him on our favorite beach, watching him systematically sift sand as carefully as he now sorts the law. My life stops and becomes momentarily happier through seeing that small etching.

PRINTS ARE WORTH IT

"I am still horrified at the idea of spending money on pictures. The kind of life where you can just buy a print because it pleases you or looks pretty is something I am not used to. I feel as if I've spent my life scrambling just to keep up, just coping, and at this point, spending money just for aesthetics rather than 'to get the best deal' seems irrelevant."

This querulous protest came from a friend whose conflicting feelings about deciding on a work of art are shared by other Americans when they confront the same decision. Researching this, I found this supported by a *New York Times* general public poll, which found that about 70% of Americans do not feel comfortable about buying art. I can identify with this insecurity about buying art.

Even if you feel you deserve art, adding to your conflict is the fact that your parents or grandparents probably scrambled during the Depression and consequently left you worried about spending money frivolously.

Let's focus on guidelines to help you buy a print today. The first step is to develop your own taste in art and learn to trust it and indulge it. I want you to come out of the closet as a secret art lover. I will help you begin to buy a print intelligently, sensibly, and for the sheer pleasure of it.

Is the print you like worth purchasing? Answering this question involves two phases: listening to your gut reactions and listening to gallery people's summary of an artist's worth.

Secret: You have good taste.

DEFINING YOUR REACTIONS TO ART

Of course, you have taste. Everyone has taste. We all have aesthetics in our lives. A cat on the window sill, a branch of fall leaves in full color stuck in a jar. These are fragments that bring a restful pause into our busy lives.

If you ask "What kind of taste do I have?" the answer is that your taste is not good or bad. You have your own individual taste; there are choices involved. These choices include colors, shapes, sounds, ambience, and feelings. In other words, you can shape, mold, and design your habitat to your absolute personal taste. You are the one who lives in it, and you are the one you have to please.

While a print in neon colors may not be your mother's cup of tea, it may please you. Just because she doesn't like it doesn't mean that you have bad taste. It means that you are an individual, and you will be more interesting than ever before to those who come into your home if you buy art that reflects your specificity.

Never let yourself be intimidated by someone who thinks they have better taste than you. If you are inexperienced in exercising taste, it comes with practice. It is like bicycling. It gets smooth and easy the more you do it. You can ask a knowledgeable person, a good friend, an interior designer, to guide you, to work with you, to act as a foil for your taste. However, never let anyone else tell you what is aesthetically good or bad. You and only you can make that decision for yourself. If you like it, buy it, even if the artist does not have impressive credentials. There are 350,000 artists in this country. Not many get into the Metropolitan Museum.

Try to voice the dominant impression the print you like makes on you. Is it the feelings it evokes or the lines, or the tensions, colors, shapes, textures you like best? Then listen to your inner responses and be faithful to them. If you truly like a work of art, it will always make you happy. Conversely, no matter how many people recommend it, if you don't care for it, you will never like it. Do not buy it.

Secret: Determine why a print attracts you.

When I think about watching people's choices and decision making, I remember seeing a certain light coming across their faces, almost as if they recognized something. As I've said before, the old saying, "I'll know it when I see it," is true. Plato's theory of beauty being like the reflection of a candle on a cave wall is borne out. Recognition is the core of an aesthetic decision. To say it another way: *The artist, printmaker, translates for the viewer what the viewer has seen or felt, but never has been able to realize fully or describe as concretely as this print does.*

ASK FOR HELP WITH YOUR DECISION

Most people need to have input from another source when making any major decision. This is where a relationship with a print dealer helps. The dealer has been looking at the work longer than you have and should be ready to point out weaknesses and strengths in the work, aesthetically and technically.

An amazing thing about art professionals is that they know something about the technical attributes and the aesthetic qualities of the works they exhibit. It is your right to ask them questions and draw out their professional opinions about the work you like.

I also have found that most buyers feel best if they are helped by a friend, relative, or even a child, as well as an expert who lets them mull over their decision and gives support, or at least acts as a foil for their decisions. Years ago, when I was selling small prints at a hospital benefit given at a country club, a young matron obsessed with buying a frog print for her bathroom, brought dozens of friends all day long over to my table, to analyze if the frog was too green or too "froggy." In this case, insecurities about decorating and a lack of confidence about spending money for something frivolous overcame all the pleasure and fun of buying a print.

THE TRIUMVIRATE SOLUTION

> Secret: Develop a print-buying support system.

I have suggested this approach in other parts of this book. It involves developing a relationship with other art professionals. How can you cultivate the desired relationship with them? Try my "Triumvirate Solution." It will help you work with art gallery people, museum people, decorators, architects, and space designers. Shop for people you can trust, who take this as seriously as you do. Offer to pay them for a consultation. Note: Many museum people will not work readily with the neophyte, unless there is the possibility of a bequest to their collection. Do not be hurt by a rejection from this quarter.

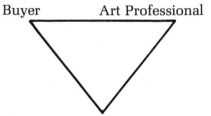

Buyer   Art Professional

Architect / Interior Designer / Decorator

The triumvirate approach involves building a trusting relationship between yourself and the art dealer and other art-informed persons you feel you can trust. The third point in the triumvirate can be a decorator or even another gallery person. To make the triumvirate method work, the buyer must agree to listen to advice. Most important, he must be mindful that establishing print-buying goals and plans takes *time* and *listening, true listening,* on both sides.

THE SEAL OF APPROVAL

So many of us in America seem to need a stamp or seal of approval on our art purchases. Every subject has its appointed place: nudes only for bathrooms, landscapes over the couch, horses and fowl over the dropleaf tables, flowers to match Laura Ashley prints in the bedrooms. Sometimes the mix-and-match complex is so gripping that if one piece is selected for a room, all the other art chosen for that room must match the first purchase.

This type of panicked art buying is based on a deep-seated fear of being found out that we are not as sophisticated in our tastes as someone else; that we are peasants who do not deserve to own art; that art is the rightful property of collectors, museums, and other aristocratic types, not humble folk like us.

Does this not harken to a superficiality in the American character, focusing on outer directedness rather than inner directedness? Outer directedness or other directedness mandates that everything has to be agreeable, okay, acceptable, new, slick, and perfect, and above all, matching.

> Secret: Interior designers recommend that you *not* match artwork to furnishings.

THE HAND OF THE ARTIST

The hand of the maker, the artist, who is or once was a living person, is all-important. Marks of manipulation on a print can be a wonderful way of bringing the viewer into the process of making the print. I like seeing a print with an extra mark or a print with some options in the sequence of work. In fact, every now and again a customer, too, appreciates a smear, the trace of the hand of the artist, on a print that I sell. But that client is the very rare confident, secure art buyer.

When the editor of a prominent newspaper bought a collagraph of mine that revealed a change I had made in the plate, I was surprised. When I asked him why he decided on it he replied that he was delighted to see some indecision revealed in the print. He had had enough of perfectly produced prints. He was pleased to find traces of an artist's effort.

That this is a new direction in the print industry on a widespread level was corroborated by a major print publisher, who encourages his printmakers to work on each print in an edition to make it slightly different from all the others. This makes them more valuable in his opinion and radically different from prints made on an offset press.

BUY A PRINT
WHEN YOU CANNOT *NOT* BUY IT

Don't buy unless you cannot not buy. Don't be lukewarm about a work of art; you have to live with it longer than you do your furniture. It will not wear out; it goes with you on to your retirement home and often, on to your children and their children. Even if the color is perfect and the price is right, if the work is for your home or for over the desk in your office, make sure it pleases you so much that it gives you pain to think of not possessing it.

> Secret: Use the palm of the hand test.

I have talked to psychologists about the following process. Most people are capable of doing a quick fifty second skim of a gallery, ever so quickly selecting their piece. After that quick selective process, everything else might be called obsessing, or getting a stamp of okay. Many people—even a year later—seek that first beloved piece. I would urge you to note and respect your first response.

The first step towards buying: Follow the advice of Thomas Hoving, who wrote in his book, *The King of the Confessors*, how he acquired art for the Metropolitan Museum of Fine Arts in New York City. When he first looked at a piece that interested him for whatever historical, technical, or aesthetic reason, he would pause, take out a ballpoint pen and write "yes" or "no" on the palm of his hand. This recorded his gut reaction to the piece.

After hearing about the piece's provenance, its rarity, and its incredible attributes, Hoving counterbalanced all he had heard against the initial response to it, which was recorded on his hand.

> Secret: Take your time.

Galleries and artists encourage customers to take time to think about the art that particularly interests them. I suspect gallery owners have learned that most people do not spend sizeable amounts of money in half an hour; that allowing them time and space ultimately helps them buy art.

If money is a problem, ask if you can pay slowly for a print so you will not miss something special that you fall in love with or a print that reminds you of a particular moment or conveys an emotion to you and can crystallize it for you forever.

SECRETS OF GOOD PRINT-BUYING DECISIONS

We have asked many print buyers how they determine what to buy. The following criteria are given most frequently.

Aesthetics

The beauty of an image or object draws the viewer into it. Sometimes this experience is so creative and so intense, the viewer almost becomes one with the piece and even sees more in the image than the artist intended. When it all comes together just right—emotion and beauty—the viewer can be moved to tears or other intense feelings and can pinpoint perfect insights into the nature of things. If the person cannot purchase that work of art, it is still theirs. Often, people have asked me to track down prints that caught them this way years before.

Content

Good art always contains thought or visible evidence of an idea. In abstract work, the content is the tensions on the two-dimensional surface. An abstract print has subtle content which, although abstract, rewards the viewer.

In figurative work, the content is narrative, telling a story; or realistic, freezing or interpreting a real or imagined moment in time or place.

Expertise

Most people noted that the quality most admired in a print is genuine skill, a mastery of materials that does not dominate, but instead serves to strengthen a print's aesthetics. Refinement of printmaking technique makes you realize that the artist is professional. However, many pieces are captivating in their awkwardness. A genuine emotion can shine through a naïve or unfinished piece.

Emotion

Another factor that has a major bearing on print buying is its emotional content. Sometimes called a rush, this quality of realness and warmth makes a work arresting.

Credentials

Ask what institution, corporations, or museums have pieces of your artists' work. Ask by whom the prints are collected. The answers to these questions will show if their work is consistently considered admirable and of lasting value. This is not a necessary criterion for up-and-coming printmakers or the provincial artists you meet in resorts or at street shows.

Utilitarian

The best clue that can be given to any buyer is that he is actually going to use his artwork. By that I mean that if he makes a wise choice and buys something he loves, it is going to touch and affect his life. Selecting a print, at any price at all, can be an enriching experience in many unexpected ways.

BUY THE BEST

Art dealers agree on only one buying theory—buy the best! When sorting through a printmaker's work, pick your favorite without looking at prices. If you are confused, this is a good time to ask for advice from a gallery person. Get input about which is the best work from different periods in the printmaker's developing style. Ask about the genesis of the printmaker's imagery so that what is special to you will be even more understood and appreciated.

> Secret: Give yourself the gift of a print.

It is a myth that all original art is very expensive, or overpriced and out of the range of ordinary people. Such myths work financial hardships on many artists and deprive people of the joy of owning and living with original works.

HANDLING BUDGET CONSTRAINTS

I love the person who comes into my gallery and admits, "I don't have much money to spend right now, but I am interested in finding out about contemporary prints." I will drop everything and try to show him our best work and help him in any way.

It saves embarrassment for everyone if the potential buyer says at the outset that he has "x" amount to spend. One way to manage budget print buying is to buy unknown and/or unestablished printmakers, whose work you admire and covet. Most of these artists never will become famous. Unless you are exceptionally prescient or lucky, it is unlikely that any of your print purchases will increase in value.

Love of a print must be your guide, a difficult adjustment in a world where art is often advertised as an investment. Be aware that investment art is created by marketing experts, not better artists.

Secret: Set aside a percentage of your income for art.

Another way to budget is to set aside a percentage of your income for art. The first step in this involves figuring out your values. Do you really want original prints in your home and in your life? Can you spend some time researching what prints are available? Can you decide what type of art you like and how you can expect to spend to acquire it?

Are you sure that you want to spend money on prints? What percentage of your annual income can you afford to spend on art? Do you want reproductions at a low cost of $20 to $100 unframed; works of art on paper, such as watercolors and original prints, priced at the middle range of $100 to $500; or paintings at a higher price of $500 to $10,000?

A handy device some people use is the same as that used by the federal government to budget art, designating 1% for art out of the total cost of every building project. Many couples agree to set aside a certain percentage of their annual income, such as 1 to 5%, for art purchases. I have also found that many people set aside a yearly amount to spend, such as $1000.

ASK IF YOU CAN TAKE THE WORK HOME ON APPROVAL

Galleries allow work to go home on approval. This means that the customer leaves a check or charge slip to be held aside by the gallery while they live with the work of art within their own environment. This helps a person know if she will tire of the work and if it suits her home. The idea is for it to continue to interest her and, in fact, to appeal to her more in the setting of her home, because it is quieter and more intimate than a gallery. If you take a print home on approval, you can figure out exactly how you feel about this print. You can see how it looks in your light and ask if it will wear well in your house.

When a person is intrigued by a few pieces and cannot make a comfortable on the spot decision, I encourage him or her to take several pieces home using the approval arrangement. This eases the problem for us both.

The mechanics most galleries suggest are the following. A charge card slip or check is made out for the full price of the work taken home. This is held in reserve by the gallery before you leave. Be sure that the gallery will not process the charge or deposit the check until a purchase decision is made.

If a gallery owner resists this approach, it might be that he or she wants to close on your purchase quickly, or hopes to get rid of the work that you have shown interest in, and knows that he can succeed best by pressing you to make the decision to buy on the spot, rather than at home.

The point is that taking work home on approval is within your rights as a potential customer. It does not demean the work to want to live with it for a short time. One of my favorite memories of selling my art is of a couple who took home a set of four pieces of my handmade paper. They created a new, quiet look in their bedroom. In fact, it was an oasis for two busy people. I appreciated it when the wife said that she fell completely in love with my pieces when she woke up and her eyes delighted in the random white cloud forms scattered on blue/gray areas.

LETTERS FROM SATISFIED PRINT BUYERS

"My mother was delighted with your print.... In fact my two sisters think it's terrific and would like one like it. I suggested that they come out for a visit and get one! So my choice couldn't have been better. The ones I chose for myself fit exactly where I had anticipated. I can't believe what a difference it has made in the rooms where I am hanging them.

"I can't thank you enough for your help and for our payment agreement. I can now enjoy them an extra month! We can settle on the framing for my mother's print in January. I will let you know when my bonus arrives."

"Well, I saw the pieces in the window as I was passing by today—they were similar to [those of] an artist I had loved for years, but I had never seen anything like them for sale. When I seriously started to consider purchasing one, it helped that I had two friends along (by chance) whose taste and judgment I admire, because they encouraged me.

"Still I had to stare at it awhile, and imagine it at home, seeing it every day, looking at it five or ten years from now. Will it still thrill me and will I feel excited about it? Does this sound like deciding whether or not to propose to someone? Perhaps this is why I'm still unmarried. And I wondered, 'Will I like myself for walking away from it?'

"Every time I walk past my print I'm so glad that I made the commitment. The fine line is between hesitation and commitment. You can always talk yourself out of a print—not necessary, but it really is, if you think about it. If you do it, you do it for yourself."

MORE JOURNAL NOTES

Suzanne R. returned to our gallery to purchase the print *Broome Street Marchers,* which she and her husband had looked at two Saturdays prior. Suzanne's husband told me over the phone the week before that he did not think they would buy it because he was sick. When I replied that they had put a deposit down on it and that it would be put aside for their consideration, he said, "I mean I am really sick." Mystified, I put it aside for them.

When she returned to purchase the print, Suzanne smiled as she told me the reason they had liked it so much. It functioned as a talisman or symbol: "One has to just keep marching along... just like those incredible embossed toy soldiers, straight ahead, no stopping, up, down, up, down." I looked at her. She continued and told me that her husband had died from leukemia the previous Friday. She actually looked serene as she left the gallery with the print in hand. That couple had given me quite a gift. Buying art is a two-way street!

COUPLES
Easy Steps for Making Decisions Together
7

A conservatively dressed couple walked down our stairs and floated, transfixed, toward the English etching of *Burknowle*. They glowed. They looked at it and each other so happily, so privately, that I was loath to approach them. They stood smitten, not speaking a word; they just looked, smiled, and nodded to each other. I finally asked—rather clinically, since I had been researching couples' art-buying habits—if they both liked it, and if so, why? They answered readily, "It's beautiful," and he said, "It's so soft." I agreed, since this print had changed my feelings about the month of January. The pale greenish-blue sky on the etching heightened my appreciation of winter twilights.

The couple then backed off after asking the price, saying that they really did not need any art. They came forward, asking about framing. I suggested that they might need to take a walk to talk alone, which they did. Judy, the wife, said that they had gone almost to the corner, and had to come back to buy it. She was a banker, with no art background, but she solved the aesthetic problem of framing more quickly than our framer did.

This couple did not have a problem buying art. They both loved the print and that was that. But many couples deter each other from buying art, as the following stories reveals.

One couple, Art and Kay, told me that when they attempt to buy art, they use another rather perilous method. Each has absolute veto power over the other's choices. Art likes hard-edged abstract prints. Kay likes soft, hazy landscapes and flowers. When Kay returned the two silkscreens she had taken on approval the day before, while accompanied by her parents, I asked if she really thought that their method of buying worked. She

admitted that they did not own any art as she shook her head.

I remember another couple. She was small and wiry, enthusiastic yet tentative. He was a large man given to monosyllables. I remember them climbing up and down the steep stairs of our gallery four times. The woman coveted for her bathroom the watercolor drawings of the figure which my husband created, with a few lines and watercolor washes in pastel colors, priced then at about $200. Her husband, however, refused to spend any money on art for the bathroom. The two argued while Mace and I stood and agonized, feeling pride in his work and her enthusiasm, but dismay about the power struggle we had to witness.

As long as I have kept a gallery, I have continued to agonize over couples buying prints. They can be the most gratifying people to work with; they hug and kiss and adore each other, the gallery, and us when one or both of them buys a piece. Yet, because of the dynamics involved, the power struggles, and the sensitivity of both partners, couples encounter special problems when shopping for prints together.

BUYING STRATEGIES FOR COUPLES

Secret: Take time before visiting galleries to talk about what buying art means to you both and the purpose of your visits.

Since two people often think they both must be satisfied with an art purchase, special tensions are generated when buying art. Differences of values and goals, as well as family pressures, will hinder a free selection process and frequently spawn frustrating art-shopping experiences.

I think that couples should think out and talk about some alternative approaches to their art-buying strategies even before they browse for art. Some of the tensions involved relate to assertiveness. Many stem from who is responsible for money spent and who is responsible for art buying. This in turn relates to a basic issue for a couple in their art buying: home decorating. Often there is confusion regarding priorities, but whatever the reason, I have been amazed at how dramatically couples support or undermine each other.

How then, can couples buy art together? This is a difficult question to answer. My thesis is that couples should be mindful of the hazards of joint art buying and take time, prior to visiting a gallery, to discuss the various options open to them as two individuals approaching works of art with the intention of purchasing art as a couple.

The point about starting an art collection with prints is that they can be inexpensive, decorative, compelling, funny—whatever you want. You can afford a wall for each person. It is not an all-or-nothing situation. You can also each exercise your own taste.

Different kinds of couples experience different kinds of problems, according to the circumstances surrounding their relationship. Husbands and wives are not the only type of couples who buy art. Problems arise between roommates who want to agree on a work of art, but are aware that one may depart in the near future. If they buy art, should they both agree? Both pay? If so, what happens later on? Or if they are lovers with jobs, sharing living quarters, who buys, who pays?

Married Couples

Even married couples come in many varieties. Every couple is unique; yet they still have to decide on a system of art buying that will allow them to live with art that pleases both of them. During several decades of helping couples to buy prints successfully, I have asked many of them how they go about deciding what to buy; how the prints were chosen and by whom; whether or not they negotiate; and which conscious or unconscious selection methods they use and why.

Unmarried Couples

Unmarried couples have the above problems plus additional problems, such as who pays for art initially and who gets to keep it if they break up. This creates different limitations on their art-buying habits. They often buy for the short term rather than the long because they might change residences or partners in the near future.

I enjoy unmarried couples because more often than not, they encourage each other to buy art. They do not undermine each other as readily as married couples do. They give each other permission to buy art.

Roommates

Roommates want to agree on a work of art, but are aware that one person might depart in the near future. They may have bought a poster or two in college and have it taped on the wall.

Now that same person has a $30,000 a year salary from a software company, an attaché case, and lots of white walls. Should she bother framing the posters or search for art with some permanent value? If so, would buying prints be a logical first step? If roommates buy prints, should they both agree? Both pay for the print? What happens later on?

Lovers

Sweethearts who live together should be careful about buying prints together. Should their liaison be temporary, just so is their print collection. Take turns; buy with caution. Exercise discretion; do not buy prints to decorate or to match temporary furniture or apartments unless you realize that you may need to be ready to discard them in the near future. Face the fact that this might be a short-term relationship. Determine ahead who keeps each print if you break up. Or, if that is too hard, assume responsibility now. Buy what you love and want to own.

PRINT-BUYING STRATEGIES

Here are some strategies and tips, as well as the three steps to easy art buying, gleaned from couples who have bought art successfully. These strategies will cure art-buying deadlocks between couples, as well as other common art-buying blocks individuals often encounter. These will start you on your way to beautiful, print-filled environments, which may lead in turn to an addiction to the many pleasures and gratifications of print buying.

These simple steps will help you focus your art needs and wants. If you take the time to get organized before shopping for prints, you will find it easier. If you master these steps, you will be able to shop confidently and comfortably. Mastering these steps will give you the tools you need to talk to each other effectively about what art means to you prior to going to a gallery, as well as allowing you to talk confidently to gallery people as you search for art.

Three Steps to Easy Print Buying

1. Decide whether you want to buy original prints or reproductions. This first step involves figuring out your values. Do you really want fine art in your home and in your life? Can you spend some time doing research about what original prints are and what reproductions are where they are available? Can you decide what type of print you like and learn how much you can expect to spend to acquire them?

There are other related questions to be answered. Are you sure that you want to spend money on prints or any art? What percentage of your yearly income can you afford to spend on art? As mentioned before, some people decide to set aside 1 to 5% for art purchases. Others set a limit of $1000 for their annual art budget, which will probably buy and frame two original prints or reproductions.

2. Try to isolate why you want to buy art just now. This second step involves deciding if your goal is art for love, art for decoration, or art for investment. I discuss these notions in greater depth in other chapters; they are at the heart of buying art.

3. Learn whether the print you have chosen is worth purchasing. This third step involves three phases: 1) listening to your art source's summary of a printmaker's worth; 2) listening to your own gut reactions; and 3) listening to a capable art professional who will act as your support system.
• Is the printmaker emerging, unknown or recognized, blue chip?
• What collections is he or she in?
• How long has he or she worked?
• Is he or she a dabbler or a professional?

> Secret: Listen to your printkeeper's critique of the printmakers you are interested in.

The goal is to make sure that you really want this print and that it is worth it to you, either as a decorative or pleasurable object or as an investment. Ask for an honest appraisal of the artist's status in the art world. Does he hold a solid position, or does his work represent a passing fad? Will the quality of his work be respected years from now? Ask for documented reasons for your source's judgment.

One good thing about most print keepers is that they know something about the technical attributes and the aesthetic qualities of the works they exhibit. It is your right to ask them questions and draw out their professional opinions about the work you like.

> Secret: Check your gut reaction to the print in question.

It is most important to check your gut reactions and be faithful to them. If you truly like a work of art, it will always make you happy. Conversely, no matter how many people recommend something, if you do not care for it, you probably never will like it. Try to elicit the dominant impression of the prints you like: Is it the feelings, colors, or shapes that you like best?

Try to be truly free about your reaction; I want to salute the spontaneity with which men choose prints. They do not equivocate or hesitate as much as women do. Men seem to be more intuitive than women when it comes to choosing art. If they really like it and the price seems fair, they buy it.

I have noticed an ability in professional men and women to make quick decisions. I applaud this ability to trust the gut reaction to art. They do not have the inhibitions that prevent so many of us from enjoying the purchase of good prints. Women are too often influenced by home decorating strictures. I lament the left-brain, overly rational, studied approach that many women bring to art buying. It seems to stem from reading too many interior decorating magazines, which inhibits the impulsiveness that sweetens many print purchases.

> Secret: Let the print draw you to it.

If a print speaks to you, let it, even if it is not the type one of you thought you wanted or needed. Let yourself fantasize about the print. What in the world was the artist thinking? If the print challenges you, so much the better. It will be of lasting interest to you.

Only buy what you cannot not buy. This is an esoteric buying principle that all art professionals recommend as the core principle of buying any art. It means that the print under consideration would almost break the heart of one or both of you. It means that at least one of you wants to buy it so badly you are willing to store it until you build a wall on which to hang it. This sounds extreme, but it can easily happen if you listen to yourselves. That means buying the wrong size and colors but enjoying the print totally all your life.

> Secret: Apply the triumvirate solution to yourselves as a couple.

Have you developed a relationship with art professionals? How can you cultivate the desired relationship with them? Try the triumvirate solution. It will help you to work with decorators, architects, and space designers, and other artistic people, as well as yourselves.

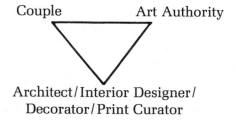

Couple   Art Authority

Architect / Interior Designer /
Decorator / Print Curator

To make the triumvirate method work, the couple must agree to listen to advice and to each other. Most important, they must be mindful that establishing art-buying goals and plans takes *time* and *listening* on both sides.

HINTS FOR COUPLES WORKING WITH ART DEALERS

It is best to make an appointment with the dealer in advance so that he will be free and can contemplate your needs ahead of time. Often dealers are artists themselves, extremely creative and resourceful people who can obtain art from other sources if you do not see what you want in their gallery.

I remember the art needs of my clients when I am traveling. Sometimes I see a fit between a piece and a client at the oddest times: when I am turning the bacon or waking up in the morning.

Give your art dealer information about both of you: the type of art you prefer, your purse limitations, your plans for future purchases, and details of your dreams of having beautiful prints on your walls, their sizes, colors, etc. Most dealers take tremendous satisfaction and excitement in finding art that pleases someone and suits their home and dreams perfectly! If the relationship between gallery and client is warm, you will find yourselves making many purchases. I think as I write this of many couples who have come back to me after a few years and thanked me for guiding them towards a printmaker and tell me how they have gotten to know him and have followed his development.

Define your needs and wants; open up your wishes to your art dealer: interior decorating, matching couches, opening walls, looking for an Art Deco look, creating a Florida look, making an investment, having a moving emotional experience. Then let the dealer make suggestions. Let him share what he is proud of. Listen to him, but listen prudently. The minute the word "investment" is mentioned, start to worry a little bit. I will discuss this later on in this book.

Determine exactly how you will negotiate the decision to buy. This step involves figuring some alternative ways to negotiate art decisions between yourselves as a couple, when confronted with the possibility of buying prints. You need to clarify the steps you will take. Some couples make an agreement with themselves to leave the gallery or their partner for a while before they make decisions. Others know that this would make them give up, because they feel that any art, even prints, is such a luxury, that they make a pact that they will try to give themselves a treat, and vow not to leave the chosen gallery emptyhanded. Many couples agree in advance whose choice it will be in the final moment of saying yes or no.

HOW A FEW COUPLES WORK OUT BUYING ART

> Secret: Do not expect to agree 100% about print purchases.

Two people may have different backgrounds, tastes, and aesthetic expectations. For example, one might like lots of color, while another might want the status of a known artist. Define your values and needs beforehand. Allow time for seeing something other than what you think you are looking for. Allow yourself to look with pleasure at anything that appeals to you in the gallery. Define what you like best, and then summarize why this or that print speaks to you. Be open to new ideas in art and to art that is different from what you have imagined.

Work out a neutral strategy; let each person pick out three pieces from the gallery or galleries you visit. Take work home on approval, edge up to a decision slowly, again listening hard to each other's reasons for liking a work, and juxtapose these preferences with your decorating needs, demands, or aspirations. Live with the prints for a while in your home on an approval basis. Ask your gallery if you can take prints on approval for a few days. Then discuss the prints as you experience them within your home environment. Does one still look beautiful on a dark day? Does it look richer and more interesting at home than in the gallery?

> Secret: Agree to buy only if one of you cannot *not* buy.

Agree not to be lukewarm about your art. Even if it is chosen to go with draperies or wall coverings, agree that it must make one of you feel good. Your art will not wear out. Whoever feels most strongly about a piece and cannot *not* buy it, should go for it and pay for it.

Occasionally take turns; decide who can make the selection. Find a way to make a celebration—an anniversary, a birthday, a name day.

TAKING PRINTS HOME ON APPROVAL

> Secret: Prints will look better at home than in a gallery.

One of the more common nightmares a buyer can have is that he will buy something on impulse and grow to hate it. Art appears quite different and often better when it is seen in your home, rather than in a gallery or an artist's studio. There are not as many distractions at home, and no one is waiting for a decision there. However, expect to experience a touch of a well-documented art buyers' ailment—buyer's remorse. This can be best described as an attack of anxiety coupled with an overdose of responsibility. Breathe deeply and let the attack pass. Relax and enjoy the print, even if it is only for a few days. The best way to ensure against disappointment is to take works of art home on approval and live with them a while before making a commitment to purchase them.

This is especially true with large-scale works. Since no gallery wants customers to end up with expensive prints they cannot stand, good dealers encourage this practice, usually billing the collector for shipping, delivery, and other out-of-pocket expenses, but for nothing else.

Having a print at home allows you to look at it in different ways. We can look very hard at pictures on an easel, but in our daily lives we also see them subliminally: as they hang on a wall, while walking past them, eating or reading near them, while falling asleep or waking, seeing them as the light in a room changes with the passing sun and from daylight to lamplight.

One of the worst things about seeing prints in galleries is that they are always bathed in the same unchanging, artificial light. Artwork changes with different kinds of light; that is one of the things that is so wonderful about living with them. This enables you to grow with the work of art; your experience of it should deepen the longer you own it.

When you bring a print home on approval, try evaluating it by juxtaposing it with a touchstone, with something you know and appreciate as a superb work of art. For example, try hanging a reproduction of your favorite artist's work on your wall, then compare it with whatever you are contemplating acquiring. This kind of juxtaposition will sometimes reveal the new work to you as weak or flawed. But sometimes—and this is the moment of supreme gratification for any buyer—you may find yourself saying, "By God, it holds up."

CASE HISTORIES OF SUCCESSFUL ART-BUYING COUPLES

I watch and share in the pleasure, one of doubled intensity, when a couple buys something they cannot *not* buy. Faces brighten when an affirmative decision on a purchase is reached. I feel as if I have been midwife to their agreement. Years later we hear how prints have enhanced couples' lives. English, Scottish, German, Czech, and French prints suggest their European travels; a small print for every anniversary celebration; and the story of a Christmas print treasure hunt focusing each year on hiding a print and finding it with clues left over the whole house.

One of the pleasures of having been a print dealer for such a long time is watching more and more couples who are buying prints today in far happier, more reasonable, and more considerate ways than ever before. Many couples have taught me the secrets outlined above. They manage to negotiate on dual aesthetic encounters.

Two alternative art-buying approaches used by similar couples are worth studying to explore strat-

egies for those of us who want to grow confident about art buying. I would like to mention that a lack of confidence is sometimes endearing to gallery people who often do not feel altogether confident in dealing with the public. It brings out the best in those who want to help couples buy art. They generously share their knowledge and experience in the field.

Here is a true story from my notebook. I was arranging a print display in our window, near the front steps, when a couple walked in with fabric swatches in hand and made apologetic remarks about a blue room. I poked my head out between easels and said, "Yes, you can find art to match color swatches and still be excited by the art. I will be right there. Just browse." The fact that they had swatches saved us time. They defined their goal, which I will summarize as primarily "decorative" and secondarily "status." Their needs were: 1) an elegant look in blues, beiges, and peaches; 2) low to medium price range ($200 to $400); 3) a work of art on paper; and 4) framed within two weeks.

It took half an hour. There were no surprises. This is the point. They took the time to think. They asked me for advice, but mostly negotiated without me. It went almost too methodically. In fact, when the choices were made and the wife sat down, she suddenly seemed to enjoy what she saw. Her face visibly relaxed as she came back to herself and left her house's appearance behind.

They did not get the high that the next couple did. They came in to look at Oriental prints. I was finishing a letter so I left them alone, which I sensed they might prefer. They spent two hours poring over the Chinese prints, even translating titles and marks on them, selecting a small group for a second look. I pulled out a wonderful print of a beetle silhouetted on a branch against the moon, which I could not believe they had overlooked. The slightest smear of black ink on the beetle apparently made them pass it by. "I think we can correct that smudge if you want it," I said. We discussed the problems of framing, paying, and shipping in that order, and then they left for lunch to think it over.

They must have done some major negotiating because they decided they could afford two prints and where they would place new artwork in their home. They were happy to tell me that one selection was the unique Chinese print with the beetle and another was a Japanese print. They wondered if I could send them prints on approval from time to time.

They so impressed me that I showed them other prints that I thought were especially fine. They left with several instant photos of possible future purchases in hand, having arranged for their selected prints to be shipped. Their good mood was infectious.

Similar commendable steps were taken by both couples:

1. Both came with specific goals.
2. They involved me in their needs so I gave them more than the usual attention, information, and help.
3. They negotiated with each other about what to buy.
4. They bought what they could afford and what each partner liked.

Ken and Cindy

Ken and Cindy's children are grown. They enjoy buying art to the point where they deliberately added a print room to their small house so that they could rotate their art acquisitions according to the seasons. The room would delight any art buyer. Three walls have no windows, the fourth is a glass wall facing their wooded lot—artificially lit in the evening. At one side they put in a Jacuzzi, so they could relax after work and really enjoy their art.

When asked how they choose between two pieces that they like, Ken cheerfully said, "That's easy. In that case, we buy both and we are never sorry.

"Our technique in a gallery is to first ask the owner many questions while trying to put him at ease so that he feels good about giving us time and information. Usually," Ken volunteered, "Gallery personnel feel inadequate about their own expertise and take a bit of jollying not to feel threatened

by questions that might stop sales. A light mood and genuine interest in a gallery's struggles and successes, as well as in their artists, has resulted in some wonderful friendships and purchases for us.

"Second, we feel that it is appropriate to draw back from the client–gallery relationship and *reconnoiter* between ourselves. There are ways to do this, such as the direct approach, asking the gallery people to leave us alone so we can talk; and the more subtle method of drifting away for a meal or walk so we can share our aesthetic responses without the pressure of an audience."

Jeff and Kathy

A game is played by this couple using three criteria. They challenge each other first to rank their final choices silently, starting with the ones they like best and least. Their first and most important criterion is their "gut reaction." Through responding to the impact of their gut reaction, they narrow down their "likes." Eighty-five percent of the time they agree! If they do not, they challenge each other.

A sample dialogue: Jeff: "I like it." Kathy: "I think it's garbage." Jeff: "Why don't you like it?" Kathy explains: "I'm just not sure about it." Jeff adds: "Where could we put it?" This is their second criterion—the place to be used for the art. Jeff and Kathy's house has a free, artistic feeling, they choose art eclectically to reflect their spontaneity and their serendipitous approach to art. "But can we pay for it?" The third criterion is aired. At this point they ask the gallery person to leave them alone to make a decision based on their three criteria.

Ellen and Al

Ellen, a lawyer, who is living with Al, an economist, replied in response to my probing that they agree that whoever pays, chooses. She testified to saying, "What, you think that's art?" to some pieces he had brought home. Since each of them pays his or her own bills, if either wants something, he or she buys it and hangs it in his or her own space.

Cary and Jerry

Cary and Jerry consistently say "maybe" to me and to each other. About half the time, after thinking it over, they return to purchase something that one or the other liked. Sometimes they pay slowly because he is a writer whose income fluctuates. They always seem to give themselves a great lift when they do buy art.

The last time they came in, Cary and Jerry were out of tune. She was psyched up with the purchase of finding a print that her mother saw in our gallery window during the summer. She really has a good eye and enjoys evaluating our prints. He seemed depressed and rattled as he looked at a few prints slowly. Cary ended up focusing on a piece that was expensive, a point that did not impress him favorably at all; in fact, it created a black cloud for him. His response was, "Do we like it enough to buy it, and would it fit somewhere? Let's think about it over lunch." They came back in harmony, and she bought the piece that she had liked so much.

I like the "maybe" style. It suggests maturity and cohesiveness in the couple and implies the possibility of developing a long-term buyer/art dealer relationship. I do admit that this style might not be as rapidly gratifying for the art seller. You might find that some gallery people try to talk you out of this approach.

Jean and Jeff

Jean and Jeff have arrived at art-buying decisions by making compensations. He likes realistic art, while she usually prefers abstract work, but she will go along with Jeff's choice as long as she can choose the framing. Their art has to feel good to both of them.

Jeff writes:

"The secret of successful art shopping for us is waiting to make decisions until both hearts are going the same way. That's why we always speak in French when we shop for aesthetics. Art has too much emotion to be confined to one language. We like to debate in what to us is a foreign and beautiful language. When we both feel one way, then we can speak concretely—in English."

FRAMING
Supporting and Enhancing Your Prints
8

Audrey had been planning to look for prints for her new suburban home, but her chiropractic practice often keeps her in the city until 7:30 at night. When she met her husband, Tom, a busy lawyer, for a run through galleries, it was frustrating to both of them. Since I am one of her chiropractic patients, she was a captive audience to my excitement about showing Joe Price's still life silkscreens. When she finally made an appointment to meet me at the gallery on her free day, she remarked that if she saw something that she loved, she would just buy it. When she came by the gallery a few days later she swore that she had dreamed of Price's pomegranate print. She bought it within five minutes. But what about framing? Since she had been listening to many of the secrets in the book as she straightened out the kinks in my back, and had even persuaded me to include the Couples chapter, she had absorbed some of the principles and secrets without our knowing it.

We looked at choices of frames: cherry to match her kitchen, gold to go with her dining room, and a muted silvery wood that complemented the background behind the pomegranate. Audrey laughed and recited the most basic framing secret: *frame to the piece.* She picked a gray inner mat, with a white mat over it, and used the silvery gray molding as a frame. I'm sure that this framed piece will look rich and beautiful wherever she hangs it. The frame will not dominate the artwork; in fact, the frame will hardly be noticeable because it suits the print perfectly.

THE PURPOSE OF A FRAME

Secret: A frame is a jewel box.

A framed print is a beautiful treasure chest wherein the art is carefully placed with room to move according to its reactions to its environment, yet is protected from and within its environment, so neither framing materials nor contaminants will affect it.

One of our favorite miniatures, a mezzotint Christmas greeting by Joop Vegter, framed using a triple mat in a manner that enhances the jewel-like quality of this tiny print.

The closed, airtight environment is produced by wood or metal frames used on the sides of the mat package. This safe containment is further enhanced by the glass in the front and the backing on the reverse side of the frame package.

Do not fall into the trap common to young art buyers: Do not put a work of art between two pieces of glass or Plexiglas and fasten them with inexpensive clip sets available at art supplies stores. Besides allowing dust to seep in the frame package between the clips and cause rot and disintegration of the artwork, it also causes the devastation of cockling, or rippling of the paper.

Art on paper needs air space. Paper responds to the atmospheric conditions surrounding it. No frame can seal out atmosphere completely; you have to expect that paper will buckle, warp, and throw up waves. When these changes are excessive, you need to suspect and investigate the framing. For example, in our two seaside galleries, prints often look warped after a rainy week. Amazingly, they settle down again after a few clear, dry days. Only when glued or taped with masking tape rather than hinged with two or three small hinged tabs are they unable to expand or shrink. All paper repair work should be entrusted not to a framer but to a paper conservator, readily available through a museum.

> Secret: Frame to suit your art.

When considering frames, aesthetics is the prime consideration. Your framing goal should be to enhance your carefully selected, beloved original print, not necessarily to match the furniture.

It is difficult to describe exactly how to determine which molding and mat will best enhance your artwork. Work with a reliable framer and take time to review your options before making a decision.

FRAMING PARTICULARS FOR PAPER-BORNE ART

There are three prime considerations for framing: using correct framing materials that will conserve your art, keeping costs moderate, and picking aesthetically pleasing frame parts. First, we will consider the aesthetic choices available to you.

> Secret: Preserving the integrity of your art is what really matters.

There are many framing alternatives. For works of art on paper, I recommend using restraint when considering the mat and frame. Select a mat, made of acid-free materials, that matches the print paper, which varies from a cool white to a warm pinkish off-white or a gray to tan. If you use a colored mat, choose a subtle color to complement the image.

Don't be tempted to add elements that distract from the statement of the art itself. A framer I know sprayed black paint on the reverse side of the glass. This acted as a mat for art and print. A novel device, but not suited to the delicacy of the small etching of a medieval church. This was an inappropriate recommendation made by the framer.

> Secret: Don't settle for passive framing.

Selecting mats and frames that please you is part of the aesthetic experience of choosing art. Use the same please-the-gut test you used in selecting the art. If it feels wrong, don't let any framer persuade you otherwise.

I recall how much the first mat and frame I selected thirty years ago bothered me. The framer had insisted upon a cocoa-brown inner mat. After disliking it for a whole year, I finally replaced it with a white one. Don't settle for "passive framing" as I did. Think about how *you* want to present your art. Try different matting alternatives. Arrange them, think, walk away, come back and tell the framer what mat and frame you want.

> Secret: Crystallize your frame preferences.

It is important to develop your own framing taste. Many questions are raised about framing: Should the frame suit the historical period of the work of art? Should the frame match the furnishing in a room (brass lamps, steel coffee tables)?

Should you de-emphasize the frames so the viewer will look only at the work of art? To illustrate the latter, I should point out that the Museum of Modern Art recently replaced the antique frames on its works with simple gold moldings, hoping that more attentions would be drawn to the pictures themselves. Many museums, including the Philadelphia Museum of Art, enjoin that emphasizing historical correctness might lead to over-framing.

Other museums say that big, old frames give a dimensional quality to paintings, gearing the eye to a painter's level of intensity, setting the painting off from the wall, and drawing people in to see the picture better. Frames work to complement the look of the particular work of art; the room it will be hung in; and the personal taste of the owner.

Your goal should be to develop a unique personal approach to framing. I suggest that you try to create a variety of visual experiences with your prints and drawings; a function, in part, of the way they are framed.

Framing involves the following components: molding, splines, fillets, mats, hinges, and glass.

Molding

Molding is another word for the frame itself. There are many moldings to choose from: woods turned in flat or rounded shapes; articulated in oak, ash, maple, walnut, or mahogany. Wood moldings are treated with many surface finishes, as you choose, stained or lightened, polished or not. Today, a popular style is to rub paint thinly on the surface, reflecting a color in the artwork. You will find moldings made of applied gold and silver on wood, simple and carved; real metal or imitation in metallics and colors; lacquer applied in all colors and widths; geometric shapes made from knot free, plain woods; woods covered with paint, Formica®, velvet, gold, and silver; as well as decorative frames made with subtle stripes and designs.

Early frames were made of wooden and gilt frame molding, designed either to complement furniture or to enhance a painter's work. Louis XIV moldings suited the furnishings of that period. Victorian frames were designed to complement the furnishings popular in Queen Victoria's time.

Employee selects raw wood to put into the computerized mold sanding machine. The wood has been milled under the company's strict supervision, eliminating woods with imperfections. Photo courtesy of Nurre Caxton.

The Whistlerian molding was designed to enhance the work of American artist James McNeill Whistler. Each style of molding had its own ornamentation.

There are two factors that led to standardized frames being manufactured in America. First, the early Shakers mass-produced wooden moldings, and during the early 1800s the inexpensive process of mass-producing chromolithographs, such as Currier & Ives prints, brought simple factory-produced frames into middle class American homes.

Secret: Select strong, sturdy moldings.

Beware of skimpy moldings. I tend to choose frames that are as light and thin as possible. Many of the frames in my house have split because the weight of the glass has pushed their corners apart over time. As I worked on this chapter, I noticed that the frames in the homes of my friends and

Setting the computerized sanding machine before feeding the wood molding into it. Photo courtesy of Nurre Caxton.

Mold staining is done completely by hand. Color washes of watercolors are also rubbed over hardwoods such as maple to satisfy contemporary tastes. Photo courtesy of Nurre Caxton.

acquaintances also have these split corners. A framer whom I interviewed had a frame that was splitting on the wall above the matting table in his own shop. Take a quick survey of your pictures right now. I venture that if you are older than forty, some of your frames have split corners. Be sure to use frame molding that is sturdy enough to support the weight of the glass and other materials. You should also consider the following: Is the size of the frame appropriate to the size and weight of the picture? How well is the frame made? Note the quality as well as the type, color, and shape.

The finishing and sealing spray machine completes the twelve-step process of manufacturing wood molding for framing. Photo courtesy of Nurre Caxton.

Consider, too, whether a frame will endure mechanically as well as aesthetically. For example, a large piece will not be carried as sturdily in a plastic laminate-type frame, which has a soft wood core, as it will in a metal or hardwood frame. Laminate frames are appropriate for decorative pictures but not for heirlooms.

Gold leaf moldings are usually made of imitation metal skins overlaid on wood. Ask if the gold leaf molding you see is real. Be aware that imitation gold leaf will vary in color. For years I sold imitation gold leaf without full disclosure to our customers. Why didn't I know what I was selling? Because I didn't ask. Brass-covered gold frames have an orange or brassy appearance, and the seams of the frame are visible. Real gold leaf is attached to the molding by a process that requires great skill and time. You can tell real gold leaf by noting overlapped 1-inch segments. In a real gold leaf frame, the corners are filled and smoothed with gold leaf, creating a welded look. Genuine gold frames are at least three times as expensive. They have the warm rich look of a gold coin.

The consensus today is that metal frames are best suited to posters. There has been a resurgence of interest in wooden frames, which conservators applaud because wood expands and contracts with the weather, coinciding with the movement of the paper, whereas metal stays rigid. Conservators support the use of wooden inserts, called *splines*, to strengthen corners. If a frame is large,

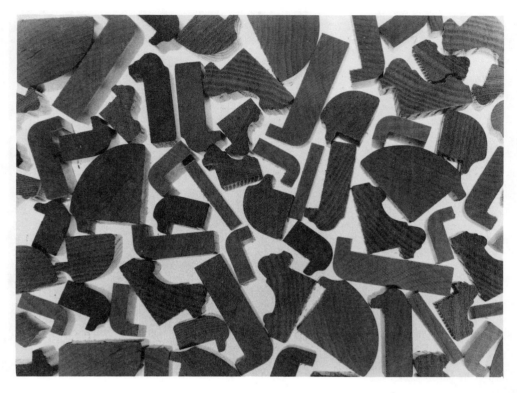

The meticulous process of creating wood moldings begins with the selection of top grade raw woods such as ash, cherry, maple, oak, and walnut, gathered from suppliers around the world. Photo courtesy of Nurre Caxton.

building a wooden strainer, which is inserted at the back of the frame to carry the weight, is also a recommended practice, well worth the additional cost.

Splines

Splines are wooden inserts used in frame corners in place of nails. These are the best solution to the problem of "gaposis." While not all frames need their corners reinforced with splines, they should at least have the raw structural strength to hold the weight and stress of the framed picture. This can also be accomplished by adding stretchers (extra wooden braces behind the framed piece) to reinforce the frame.

Mats

The supporting board and a covering mat with a window to display the art should be cut with a beveled (slanted) edge. There are two ways to posi-

tion work in a mat: under the edge of the mat, or floating within the mat window opening so that the edge of the paper is visible. It is important that the mat and back board be acid-free. Most mats are at least 2½ inches wide on each side. For larger works, wider or much narrower mats can be aesthetically pleasing. Mats create air space to prevent condensation from harming the art.

Use acid-free matting materials. Insist that all the materials touching your work of art be of the highest quality, inert, and acid-free. The mat board with its window and the mat backing board should be cut from non-acidic, 100% rag board. If wood-pulp board is used in any part of a frame, make sure that the framer inserts an acid-free buffering paper between your art and the board.

Play with colors of mats. You have many choices, however, for mats. Color mats are not imperative, but carefully chosen they can enhance a work of art on paper. In rag mats there are at least half a dozen shades of white, from cool to warm. Mats can also be covered with natural or neutral linen or silk to lend an air of preciousness. I prefer to use only one mat on my work or my

A wooden strainer or stretcher can be added to reinforce the frame. It is used more commonly with larger framed pieces to relieve stress on the frame.

Shown at the corner of this frame sample are wooden splines used to reinforce the corner without using nails.

collection, preferably an exact match of the color of the paper on which the art is created.

The window of a mat should be fitted to the *optical center* of an image, not to the mathematical center of the frame because the weight of an image might be off center.

Matting can also be used creatively to enhance your paper-borne art. In the frame room attached to our gallery, we have created a variety of dramatic mat treatments that set off the artwork, such as three mats, each silk covered, stepped back by ⅛ inch, surrounding an old master drawing to be shown in a museum.

Other mat enhancements are French lines (a thin line inked about ½ inch away around the mat

Miniature etching by John Taylor Arms. The piece was "floated" on a back board and a gold fillet was used around the mat window to hold the glass off the artwork and provide more "finish" to the mat.

mat window) and English lines (similar to French lines but with an added color border ¼ to ½ inch wide). Another design involved a V-shaped groove cut into the mat around the window.

Fillets

An impressive mat treatment is the use of a fillet. There are two types of fillets. One is a thin strip of wood or plastic measuring ⅛ inch or more in depth, and inserted by the framer around the edge of the frame to keep the artwork from touching the glass. In this regard it replaces the function of the mat and is used when a mat is not appropriate or feasible, e.g., when a print is "floated" on the backboard so that the entire sheet of paper is visible.

The other type of fillet is a strip of thin molding, often finished in gold or silver, which is added to the border of a mat window. The frame within a frame approach creates a quality look for the total treatment.

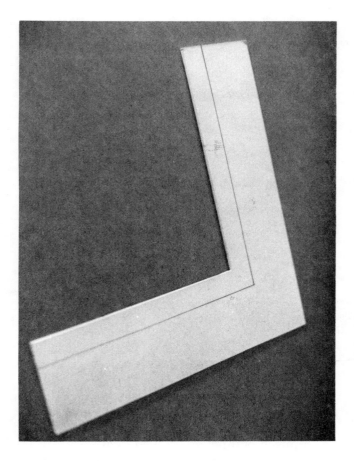

A French line inked around a mat window can enhance a mat.

An English line, which is similar to a French line but with an added ¼ inch wide color border around the mat window.

Fitting

The framer should *never* cut the margin of a print to fit a frame or mat; if the paper is to be made smaller, leave that to the owner to do or leave the extra border folded under. The reason for this is that the condition of a print's margins will be under consideration if a print is advertised or auctioned or evaluated by a museum or collector.

Glass

Glass functions to highlight the work beneath it. The sheen of glass unifies and enhances your paper-borne artwork. Check that your glass is first quality. Be sure that your glass does not rest on or touch the artwork because paper-borne art needs space to breathe and move. It takes on some moisture, even if the frame is sealed; thus, it must have room to move ever so slightly, to curl and uncurl. The glass resting on a mat or on the frame inserts (fillets) creates the dead air space in which the artwork can be free. If glass rests on the paper-borne art, the art will become more and more distorted as it moves.

Types of glazing include picture glass, UV glass, and Plexiglas. Plexiglas screens out some of the glare and ultraviolet light. Be sure that the glass used by your framer is first quality. Plexiglas should be used within a large frame; glass larger than 30″ × 40″ is impractical to use because of its weight, which tends to split the frame. UV glass is

Hinges

The back and front of the mat should be held together by a folded piece of linen tape. This tape is commercially manufactured and sold by framing supply companies. The reverse side of the linen tape has pH neutral glue that needs to be wet to stick. Do not let your framer use masking tape, Scotch® tape, or surgical tape.

Framers attach artwork to the back of the mat window with hinges. They create a flap made of Japanese rice paper, often *kozo* paper, which comes in many different weights and is made with long fibers that will bear the weight of heavy artwork. The hinge is folded and attached to the art and board with wallpaper paste (methyl cellulose) or wheat paste. Talk to your framer about this method of hinging; it lasts longer than the linen tape, which dries out after a few years, and leaves less of a mark on the back of the artwork.

Artwork is attached to the back of the mat board with Japanese rice paper hinges as shown. For heavier work, linen tape can also be used.

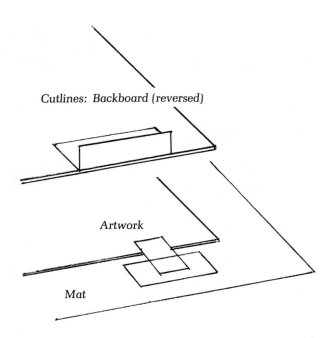

Cutlines: Backboard (reversed)

Artwork

Mat

Artwork is hinged to the back of the mat. Then backboard is hinged to the mat to protect the artwork.

specially designed to screen out ultraviolet light if you have to hang your print where it gets sunlight.

FRAMING AS CONSERVATION

Secret: Framing functions both curatorially and aesthetically.

Works of art on paper are soon contaminated in an unbalanced physical environment. Safe containment is especially important. Frames have a caretaking function as well as serving as enhancement for the artwork.

The earliest drawings and prints were kept in files or put into drawers, books, and boxes. Those are still options; many people put their paper-borne artwork into boxes specially built to preserve works of art on paper. These are sometimes called solander boxes, and are readily available in various sizes.

Paper-borne artwork has been casually hung on walls, without cover or frame, much as students hang posters. Most people now frame their prints attractively, to preserve it and let it enhance their homes and offices.

A frame creates the distinction between picture and wall space. It also aids the viewer in the transition between reality and the imagery of a painting, in the best case serving as an aesthetic but not distracting link. At the same time, a frame

exists to present a picture in the most harmonious manner possible.

Frame moldings are considered works of art today, designed and crafted to be aesthetically beautiful objects in themselves. They also have work to do, enhancing, protecting, preserving, and housing artwork. A frame with glass and mat shields the front of a work of art from dust, fingerprints, animals, and atmospheric conditions. In addition, glass mounted over paper-borne art is an enhancing finish to the work.

I realized that we all need to check our frames and mats periodically to ascertain the safekeeping of our carefully chosen artwork when I glanced over the desk of one of America's most prestigious conservators. There was a badly housed print. The mat had buckled, the print had come unattached at one edge so it was crooked, and the mat had a telltale yellow bevel edge that gave it away as an old-fashioned wood pulp mat, made before our new framing consciousness was raised to insist on rag mats.

A new awareness came to me that my audience for the secrets of framing would not just be the

An example of poor framing. No mat or spacer was used to separate the glass from the artwork. Consequently the paper could not expand or contract with atmospheric changes, and the tightness of the frame and glass caused the paper to cockle. Wood engraving by Fritz Eichenberg, Seven Deadly Sins.

young, with their new works of art, but everyone —old and young. Anyone who has a photograph or print in their lives needs to know why a frame is important as a preservation aid and how a mat and glass protect art. My job is to increase your knowledge and understanding of the fundamentals of framing so you can take a new look at the art on your walls and know when it needs help. I also want you to know what to ask for from a framer.

I remember one year, while preparing for our Thanksgiving gathering, I dusted and cleaned the art on our walls and rearranged the prints in our family room. I felt a wave of pleasant memories about each print, watercolor, and painting as I wandered backwards, revisiting artists and friends connected with my art.

But as I rehung the works, some bad framing confronted me! *Seven Deadly Sins*, a wood engraving printed on the most delicate tissue by Fritz Eichenberg, had *cockled*; that is, the print no longer lay flat within the frame, and the tissue on which the print was made had gathered and rearranged itself into concentric waves extending out from the middle of the picture to the frame.

Years ago, in my ignorance of the rudiments of curatorially correct framing and matting tech-

niques, my caution about spending money on art-related luxuries, and my delight with the aesthetics ics of the paper and the image, I had the framer omit the crucial step of placing the print under a mat or putting a spacer in the sides of the frame to hold the glass *away* from the paper surface, to build an air space between paper and glass.

Instead, I had him place a narrow black frame at the edge of the paper. Consequently, the tightness of the frame extended up and over the paper, and the weight of the glass eventually compressed the delicate Japanese tissue, which had expanded and contracted as it interacted with the prevailing humidity of the changing weather here in New England.

> Secret: Curatorially safe containment is your first goal.

Frames must be curatorially acceptable housing containers for your paper-borne works of art. There are basic facts that you, the buyer, need to know about containing your art purchases in order to protect them, whether they are prints, drawings, watercolors, photographs, or any two-dimensional paper objects. After selecting a work of art, you need to make sure that it is properly contained as well as beautifully presented. Creating a safely buffered environment with necessary air spaces, and choosing appropriate framing material and acid-free mats are your goals.

A two-dimensional work of art, whether painting or paper-borne art, needs the following:
• Acid-free backing to protect it from dust, air, insects, and deterioration.
• A frame that is strong enough to hold the screw eyes for the picture wire and carry the weight of the glass.
• Glass or Plexiglas to protect the front of paper pieces.
• An acid-free, 100% rag mat, which holds the glass off the art and provides a dead air space in which the paper can move freely. This mat needs a window or hole cut in it to reveal the image. How far the edge of this window is from the image is usually decided by you and your framer, but I find ½ inch works well. The same measurement,

called a *reveal,* is used on all four sides of the image.
• The artist's signature revealed when the mat window is cut.
• Behind the paper piece, a supporting mat board cut to the inside dimension of the frame.
• The work of paper art must be mounted on an acid-free backing board with a hinge made of linen tape. Do not let your framer hinge your art to the mat with the window. The mat is attached to the backing board by means of another hinge.
• The two mat boards attached to each other in a mat package by a folded hinge of gummed linen tape, attaching edges of both mat boards. Check to see if your framer uses masking tape or surgical tape. Both are curatorially incorrect and can be damaging.
• Buffer your paper-borne artwork. Certain parts of the frame package should not touch each other because the acidic content of wood will hurt your paper, and you need to allow for the natural expansion and contraction of a work of art. Your art should not touch your frame. The front and sides of a paper piece are buffered by a mat, glass, and backing board of mat board or Fome Core®.

Metal frames should not be used in bathrooms because moisture can seep around the edges of the backing. Wood frame packages with their dust covers and paper backings are almost moisture proof and buffer your art better.

Buffering a work of art also means that you consciously provide for an air space behind your art when it is hung. Add felt tabs (bumpers) to the four rear corners of the frame. This will hold it away from the changing humidity of the outside walls of your house.

FINDING THE RIGHT FRAMER

> Secret: Search for framers who care about presentation.

When people say to me, "You are the artist—you frame it," I wince. Maybe I should have an idea about the presentation of my art, but as an artist,

my creative effort to solve the problem of putting an image on paper usually dries up the initial creative surge.

But as an art dealer, I look hard at an artist's work and make plans with him or her as to how we could best present it. When the handsome handmade paper pieces by one of our artists didn't sell, I told him how bad they looked squeezed in their metal frames with no mats or air space around them. He later floated them on rag board, with plenty of space surrounding them; he used rag mat and a recessed, lightly colored wood frame with a fillet inset inside it to hold the glass off the textured paper. It made a tremendous difference. His cast papers looked wonderful and started to sell immediately.

> Secret: Be assertive about personalized framing.

When considering taking a print to your framer, do not be humble. Be assertive; remember, it is your carefully selected treasure that you are focusing on. Take your time—framing skills are important for the preservation and presentation of your carefully selected prints.

There are some principles to practice when you frame your artwork:
• Search for a framer who cares about costs, conservation, and preservation.
• Take time to work out a personally satisfying aesthetic solution with the gallery person or framer. It is as gratifying to select the right frame components as it is to select your art.
• Framers should provide you with a cost estimate. Alternative frame and mat combinations vary considerably in cost. You should review the alternatives before making your final selection. However, keep in mind that the cost difference between a wood pulp mat and an acid-free mat might be only a few dollars and well worth it in terms of ultimate preservation. You should not, however, feel that because the framer is the most expensive around, he will do the job correctly. Take time to check each piece before you leave the shop.
• Framers learn aesthetic solutions for framing and matting from clients. There are no pat, ready-made answers to framing your art. Look for, in

fact insist upon, a patient, cooperative attitude from your framer.

• Be sure to use good quality glass and curatorially correct materials.

• Find out exactly how the materials are positioned in your frame.

• If art is to be hung on an outside wall, use felt buffering pads on the reverse of the frame.

• Research available moldings, decide what type of mat to use, how wide it should be, how many mats you need, what color or colors, and whether mats should be with or without lines or fillets. Examine types of glass, backing materials, and buffering techniques. You may need to teach your framer, as you teach your hairdresser, to adapt to or help you invent your own personal style.

• Avoid cheap, unsound framing or acidic framing materials. Avoid needlessly expensive framing solutions.

Secret: Frame to suit yourself.

Now that you understand what goes into a frame, you can create variations to suit your taste. The point is that there is not one correct solution. Be creative with framing. This permits you to get away from the stereotypical solutions.

Take pleasure out of designing a perfect frame for each artwork you buy. One of my convictions, as a former art teacher and a present day gallery keeper, is that everyone enjoys being creative. Some customers shy away from this; others search for ways to activate this creativity. Framing is a perfect creative outlet. Take time to explore framing alternatives and possibilities; juxtapose mats and moldings around your artwork. Play until you think the arrangement is appropriate.

I like to think that creating a frame creates a link between you and the artist. You can be as inspired and free when you frame the work as the artist was when he created it.

Recently a woman asked me to tell her how to frame two works of art on paper. I gave her a few suggestions and then showed her mats and frames while I answered the telephone. Her choices were creative and fantastic. I wouldn't have thought of arranging the blue and white mats with a thin but expensive gold leaf frame for the inexpensive lithograph she had purchased. She made a wonderful creative choice that resulted in a quality look.

I visited my clients Ken and Cindy at their Arizona home. Ken and his wife worked with their framer collaborating to present and enhance their prints perfectly. I enjoyed seeing the art I had sold them over the years hanging on their walls. As I walked around, I saw that each frame was designed specifically for its work of art. The frames didn't stand out; they disappeared into and merged with the art because they were so well suited to it. This reinforced my appreciation of them as impressive art buyers. Ken spends as much time designing frames and mat arrangements as he spends selecting his art.

Secret: Use the triumvirate approach with framing.

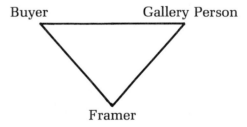

A good approach to framing is to get more than one opinion on a particular mat color and frame combination to suit a print. After you and the framer have chosen one or two possible combinations, bring in the gallery person as a final check. If he or she also agrees with your choice, then you are better assured that you have made the right one.

WHERE TO HAVE YOUR PRINTS FRAMED

When I decided to learn the facts of framing, I interviewed large and small frame shops, do-it-yourself setups, and very expensive framers. You should do the same. Search out a good framer just as you would screen for an informed and reasonable doctor.

Do-It-Yourself Frame Shop

Advantage: The fun of learning a new skill and 10% (or more) savings on framing.

Disadvantage: Your time, which might be more valuable; your inexperience in choosing, cutting, and assembling materials, which might lead to bad consequences such as the frame coming apart after a time.

Small Frame Shop

Advantage: They will take time to help you design a good-looking frame package, and they will try hard to please you, generally being fully responsible for quality framing and interested in quality presentation and preservation of your art.

Disadvantage: They may take too long or use unsound materials. For example, I recently went to a framer in a nearby village to pick up some linen tape for hanging a framed print for a show. He said he never bothered with linen tape and suggested that I go to the drugstore for surgical tape, which he always used since it was inexpensive and readily available. This was wrong on two counts: Surgical tape is not acid-free, so it could damage a work of art on paper, and it would not support a work within a frame longer than a few years, due to the sticky, dissolvable adhesive used.

Art Gallery with Framing Capacity

Many galleries have in-house frame shops attached. Other galleries subcontract their framing to a wholesale frame shop. Ask how your gallery works.

Advantage: The gallery owner makes sure that every work of art he is responsible for is well framed and looks great.

Disadvantage: When galleries subcontract their framing, the artwork might end up with a large, impersonal framer and mistakes can be made. Find out whether the work is done in-house or, if subcontracted, to whom it is given, and then review the gallery's framing standards and procedures. Also be sure to unwrap and check your frame before paying for it.

Gallery people are more interested in how your art looks framed and how happy you are with it because they want your continued business. On the other hand, gallery owners have more pressing work to do: finding art, selling art, and paying artists. When framing your work, they might not give you the framing supervision you need. Review all of this with your favorite gallery.

Large Production Framing Stores

Advantage: They are a good bet for quality framing.

Disadvantage: They might take your orders too fast and not give you time to work out solutions as I have urged you to do.

Custom Framing Shops

Advantage: Custom framing should not be intimidating. It is a joint venture in which you and the framer will design, piece by piece, the mat, glass, and molding frame package you need and want for your art.

Disadvantage: Custom framing is often intimidating and expensive, and you may run into the particular frame prejudices of the custom framer.

COMMON FRAMING MISTAKES

• Prints glued to acidic corrugated board, a common practice until a few years ago. Mat board and corrugated board are made of acidic wood pulp, which will destroy paper artwork.
• Light woods stained dark to approximate mahogany or walnut. Be sure the framer uses the wood you choose or reveals exactly what wood he is using to achieve a certain effect; for example, an ash wood can be stained to create mahogany but will not look like mahogany because of the strong grain.
• Using thick window glass instead of thin framing glass.
• Not using wooden strainers on big frames to keep corners from splitting.
• Use of acidic mat board that burns paper-borne art. Look for yellowed paper under the mat. This is your signal that an acid-free mat is needed.
• Hinges of common masking tape, used to attach artwork to backing board, which will decompose your print.

• Fake gold-leaf frames sold as the expensive real thing. Ask your framer the price before paying for it.

CHECKING FOR QUALITY

Framers must give glorious Christmas gifts, as they surely know how to wrap packages; your framing job will be presented to you carefully wrapped in brown paper. Please don't let this inhibit you. Before you pay the framing bill, ask the person at the desk to open the brown paper so you and he can examine the work done. Be sure that no glass chips, small hairs, or lint float within.

If there is any hesitation about the placement of the art, the color or shape of the mat, or the craftsmanship of the frame, speak up! Leave it behind to be made right. If you get home and find the glass broken, this is not the framer's responsibility. *You* will have to pay to replace the glass.

BASIC FRAMING FALLACIES

"In an inexpensive shop, I will save money."

Fallacy: The danger is that they might use acidic matting or backing, poor quality framing materials, incorrect and potentially destructive hinging. The piece may buckle in the mat or have hidden mechanical problems, which may endanger the art.

"Leave it to me—I'll take care of everything."

Fallacy: The dangers of over-framing, tasteless framing, and/or incorrect framing cannot be over-emphasized. For example, three mats might be used where only one would serve the purpose. Often, unnecessarily expensive framing materials are used, without letting you know the more inexpensive but curatorially sound alternatives now on the market.

"He's the artist; he knows best."

Fallacy: The truth is, artists often use materials at hand, or inexpensive and incorrect framing materials—even dull and tasteless materials—just to get the job done. By the time the piece is framed, the artist has usually "burned out," lost interest creatively or moved on to a new project.

FINAL AESTHETIC CONSIDERATIONS

Each work of art needs to be housed in materials that suit and enhance it, just as each of your children needs clothes that fit his or her temperament and coloring. I saw this when I visited the home of clients, a couple who work with their local small-town framer designing the perfect frames for their art as they buy it. As we walked around their house, I was struck by the subtle variety of frames and mat arrangements. There were prints with gray mats; cream-colored French mats with thick lines; black mats with black fillets (more later on this technique), which provided a stepped look; and more, each perfectly designed for the piece. I cannot remember the frames; they virtually disappeared because each was perfectly suited to the art and mat. In each room, each frame was different from the others in the room, but they all worked together.

HOW ONE FRAMER WORKS

Here is a story of a custom framer I know. Paul combines a collector's eye with a craftsman's expertise. He is an active buyer of art. He has twenty years of framing experience, and his background as a child psychologist enabled him to help customers make practical and aesthetically appropriate framing decisions. His story was that as a teenager he bought and framed copies of prints and paintings from museums. He even framed reproductions from old books found in secondhand bookstores. His career as a collector of original prints began when his grandfather gave him two etchings of ships, as a reminder of his youth spent on boats in Portugal. Now in his early fifties, Paul owns an impressive art collection.

Paul does not sacrifice his commitment to preserving the artwork; he offers options in a straightforward manner. For this custom framer, each work of art offers both creative framing possibilities and curatorially correct preservation alternatives. He suggests that you actively work with him or his assistants as you make decisions regarding framing presentations and mat arrangements.

Being an active buyer makes Paul an ideal framing consultant for art buyers. He takes their art purchases more seriously than they do. "Balancing the practical and the aesthetic creates an interesting tension in framing," he told me.

"What do you do if a customer wants a mat or frame that complements the furniture of a room but isn't the best solution for the work of art?" I asked.

"You mean, someone who wants to put a purple mat or frame on a black and white wood engraving so the piece will match the rug?" He leaned on the heavy oak counter between us and sighed. "If a person insists on something like that, I might do it, but I tell them that I won't put the name of my shop on it.

"However, there are neutral matters such as selecting particular woods for a study or a particular metal for a high-tech office. With the latter, once they see how easy wood is to live with and how it softens a sterile environment, they often choose it."

HANGING
Ways to Display Prints
9

Angela was in stockinged feet, hammer in her hand, and shaking her head. "I'm so disappointed. Our very first work of art looks so odd now that it is hanging up. I wonder what is wrong," she muttered to her roommate Julia. They stood in their new apartment facing their recently painted wall and speculated: "Why is it so high...so anyone sitting below won't bump it...well, he would have to be a giant." Their dialogue is typical of first-time picture hangers. We hope that some of the tips in this chapter will help you realize that it just will not please you if, like Angela, you cautiously hang pictures too high or so that they appear too small on a large wall. We hope that some of the secrets we have learned about displaying and handling prints will help.

USUAL METHODS FOR HANGING PRINTS

1. Suspend wire from the molding separating the top of a wall and the ceiling. Hang an "S" hook from the center of this and attach the frame wire to it. This method saves the wall from holes.
2. Buy picture hooks from a hardware store and install on the wall, 54 inches to the bottom of the frames (or 40 inches from the floor over a sofa or for complicated arrangements). Put Scotch® tape on the wall before inserting a nail, in order to preserve your paint or wallpaper.
3. For heavy, large prints do not take a chance on having them fall off the wall. Instead, insert hollow wall anchors, which can be bought at any hardware store, in the wall.

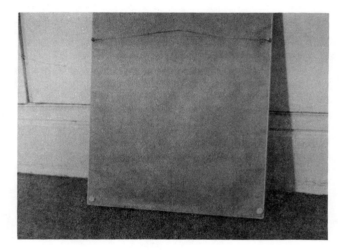

Use buffer tabs at the bottom corners of the rear of the frame to keep it off the wall and allow air to circulate.

Our Favorite Way to Hang Prints

One easy method we recommend is to first place the framed print on the wall at the recommended height—the center of the image at eye level. Then mark the upper left corner of the frame on the wall with a pencil. Measure the distance from the corner of the frame to the center and transfer that measurement to the wall. Measure the slack of the picture wire from the center of the top of the frame and transfer that to the wall. That mark will be where you will place your picture hanger or nail.

If you have more than one print to hang, measure this one from the bottom of the frame to the floor and mark it on the wall. This will locate the height of the bottom of the frame for your next picture.

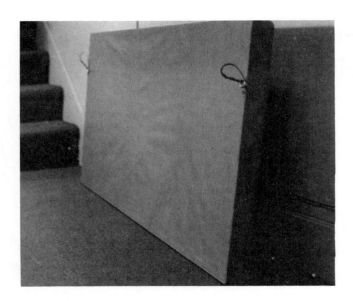

On a large frame use two hangers, one on each side at the back of the frame, so that the strain on the frame is equalized and will not cause bowing or splitting.

> Secret: Hang prints with their centers at eye level.

Placing a piece of art on a wall is like creating a window. It becomes a focal point and center of interest to which your eye travels.

When hanging prints, it is most comfortable to the viewer if the center of the print is hung at your eye level. The general rule here is to keep the center of your print somewhere around 60 inches from the floor. If you are short, obviously you want the center line to be on the lower side.

> Secret: The center line holds a grouping or a show of prints together.

If you want to hang many prints you can make groupings that will still look orderly, if you keep a uniform center line. For example, when hanging four pictures of varying sizes together, keep an invisible line going through the center of them. This creates an irregular but balanced grouping.

Avoid hanging one too-small picture on a large wall by grouping a large print with two or more small prints.

Japanese asymmetrical gestural prints can be grouped in inexact modules of 2, 3½, and 4 inch spacings so that the total effect is slightly uneven. Also note that the images flow from left to right, with the prints on the right flowing to the left.

> Secret: Keep the tops or bottoms of frames in a straight line.

You can also elect to hold the bottom or top line of the low frames at the same level. This can be done by eye. Do not worry if this is not exact. When hanging a line of prints, I like using as a guide 53 or 54 inches from the floor to the bottom of the frames.

Design groupings of pictures so that the frames are an interesting arrangement of shapes. Consider your wall arrangement as patterns with directional lines and various shapes in the images working together to make a dynamic assemblage. To do this, it is important to consider the shape of the total space around the frame arrangement. This is a negative space, which should be considered and finally read as an interesting shape when your pictures and furniture are arranged.

> Secret: Groupings should be hung in increments of the space between frames.

Wall spaces between the sides of frames in groupings of pictures of different sizes are usually arranged in 1 ½"–2" systematic increments of space such as 3-6-9 inches or 4-8-12 inches. This arranging of shapes and spaces usually happens unconsciously when you have hung many arrangements. To start with the method above, we recommend that you play with a grouping. Place your pictures on the floor; try arrangements of their shapes and the distances between them until they please you. Do not be afraid to ask your favorite gallery person to help you with this while you are still in the gallery. Many galleries will recommend picture installers who work at an hourly rate.

> Secret: Consider the forms and gestures, colors and chronological order of the prints when hanging.

Another important factor when arranging groupings is the subject matter of the prints. Serene

Two pin picture hook, purchased from a hardware store, nailed to wall at eye level. Note tape on wall to prevent plaster from breaking at the nailing point.

English etchings of landscapes with well-defined, level horizon lines demand subtly different arrangements than Japanese gestural prints, which look best in asymmetrical arrangements. Hence, the spaces between prints can be articulated in exact or inexact modules. In the case of the English prints, they might be hung with 4 inches between small prints and 8 inches between the smaller prints and a larger print. In arranging the Japanese prints, the spaces between prints might vary between 1½ inches and 2 inches, or 3⅓ and 4 inches, so the total effect is slightly uneven.

Also consider the shadows cast to the sides of the frames by your lights. They create another element. To eliminate the division between wall and shadow, hang the next picture within the shadow.

If, for example, there is a shape—the bow of a boat or the turn of a head—that faces right, place the image on the left hand side of an arrangement. Then arrange the next picture to flow gesturally from the left hand pictures. End up with the print on the far right of the arrangement with an element that flows to the left directionally. In a historical or architectural arrangement, you can arrange prints in chronological order as well as by size or shape.

Colors also should flow from one image to another. Be careful not to drown pictures next to each other because one is too bright or too busy to be next to a quiet image. But you should also avoid the pitfall of matching colors in your print arrangements. This looks supremely contrived, more like wallpapering than an art grouping.

> Secret: Place a pocket-size level on top of each frame as you hang it, to make sure it is straight.

If you have trouble judging whether a picture is level, buy a small pocket-size carpenter's level at the hardware store and rest it on the top rim of the frame. It is easy then to straighten the frame.

BEWARE OF THE "POSTAGE STAMP LOOK"

Proportion is everything. The size of prints to be displayed, in relation to the wall area, is important to achieving a good balance. A small print on a large empty wall does not look right. The solution is to hang a larger print, or to make a grouping of smaller prints. In fact, it can look better to have a large wall filled with many small prints, rather than one medium-sized, lonely print.

HANGING AND YOUR ENVIRONMENT

> Secret: Avoid damp outside walls, and walls over fireplaces and radiators.

Certain walls are worse than others for hanging prints. Outside walls and bathrooms tend to be more damp than others. If you have to use them, increase ventilation and air circulation by attaching rubber or cork bumpers to the lower back corners of the picture frame. The bumpers will keep the frame away from the wall, enough to allow the free passage of air and avoid the build-up of humidity inside the frame.

Be aware that the favorite spot over the fire-place for a picture can also be the worst location because of the build-up of smoke and fumes, which eventually can work their way inside the frame. If you must hang a print above a fireplace, be sure it is well framed and sealed and be prepared to clean it regularly.

Radiators also create an updraft of hot air carrying dust and dirt with it. It is more prudent to hang your print to one side of a radiator.

> Secret: Avoid sunlit or fluorescent lit walls.

All light will eventually fade prints. Ultraviolet rays found in daylight and fluorescent tube light-ing are the most damaging to prints and over time will discolor ink and fade or darken prints.

The best walls to hang prints are lit by indirect daylight or incandescent light bulbs. If you need to highlight a framed print, do not use a bulb stronger than 150 watts and place it at least 4 feet away. A safe rule is to use lighting no stronger than you need to read by.

If you have valuable prints on an office wall, which is lit by banks of fluorescent ceiling lights, you can still reduce the ultraviolet ray impact by using Plexiglas filter sleeves over the fluorescent tubes.

HANDLING PRINTS

> Secret: Prints must be handled with two hands.

The fragility of works of art on paper requires special attention. When examining prints in a gallery, the print paper should be lifted with *two* hands; one on each side. Do not flip prints over like pages in a book. Lifting a medium-sized silk-screen print with one hand, for instance, will put a strain on the surface inking and may cause the ink or paint to crease, crack, or dimple.

To avoid fingerprints on print borders take a small piece of folded paper and slip it over the print's edge, so that your thumbs and fingers can grasp the sheet without leaving a mark. Another alternative is to wear white cotton gloves. This is a common practice in many print galleries.

STORING PRINTS

> Secret: Store prints in a dry, cool environment.

Unless framed prints can be safely stored in a cool, dry environment and away from light, they will eventually fade. Framed prints should be stored vertically on shelves in a closet. Unframed prints pose another problems. The simplest method for storing unframed prints is to use folders or en-velopes made from acid-free materials. These can be placed in dustproof drawers or solander boxes. A solander box is a flat box with a hinged lid, lined with acid-free paper. These can be ordered from a good art supply store.

If you have a large collection of unframed prints, you should invest in an architectural file or set of map drawers. These are wood or metal shallow drawers that can take sheets of paper up to 30″ × 40″.

Never store prints in damp closets or base-ments, nor in hot attics. Extremes in humidity and heat are damaging to paper and allow mold to grow or the paper to become brittle and deteriorate.

TRANSPORTING PRINTS

Transporting prints to be framed should be done flat, with the print or prints covered with tissue and sandwiched between two boards. Avoid roll-ing prints into a tube because it is easy to crease them, and it takes the framer time to flatten them before he can make accurate measurements and cut the right size mat.

Driving framed prints home from the framer should be done with great care, to avoid sudden jars that could dislodge the print from its hinges. Hold the framed work with two hands, vertically, and avoid carrying it by the wire on the back, which could put excessive strain on the frame. Twisting or placing uneven strain on a frame could crack the glass. When placing a framed work in a car, either place it flat on the floor, or if that is not possible, place it in a vertical position, as if it were hanging on a wall, then pad it well with a blanket or clothing.

SHIPPING PRINTS

> Secret: When packing prints for shipment, build a buffer zone into the package.

Shipping prints, whether framed or unframed, can be hazardous. The preferred method is to package unframed prints flat, interleaved with tissue and sandwiched between a double thickness of corrugated board, with all four sides taped with plastic tape. A 2-inch margin should be left between the edge of the largest print and the edge of the package. To prevent the prints from slipping in the package during transit, they should be wrapped in brown paper. The package should then be taped to the corrugated board.

Sometimes it is necessary to ship prints rolled in a tube because of their large size. Make sure you leave a padded buffer of tissue between the end of the roll of prints and the end of the tube. The tube should be sturdy to withstand abuse. Mailing tubes for prints can be purchased at art supply stores.

HOW ONE COUPLE PRESERVES THEIR PRINTS

"Few people *decide* to become collectors. A person becomes a collector over a period of time, as an interest develops, nurtured by the excitement of the hunt, the satisfaction of the find.

"We started buying prints innocently—because we responded to a certain image and wanted it for our home. Soon these early purchases took on a life of their own, spurring us to investigate their production techniques and the nature of the imagery. As we bought, we framed, using the proper archival methods. As we searched, we became aware of more and more sources, and these sources began suggesting and offering new materials. We were now becoming collectors, and acquisitions began to outpace our ability to frame and hang them. It was not just that we were running out of wall space, there is always room for more; there was a limit to our personal resources. We had to decide whether it was more important to us to collect or frame. Of course, once you have started, you continue collecting.

"Prints started piling up under the bed, behind the sofa. None of this is as deliberate as it sounds, it just happens. As a collection develops, your personal tastes, a sense of the time and place of the imagery, a "shape," an understanding of technique begin to emerge. What also emerges is a sense of responsibility for what you are putting together, a realization that the collection has become larger than the sum of its parts. Here comes the hard part: how to channel our finite resources —do we continue to expand, or do we begin to conserve and store properly? Not an easy choice, but piles and other *ad hoc* storage are no longer acceptable.

"Here's our advice to fellow collectors: 'Grow' your storage and conservation efforts with your collection. Once you have acknowledged your responsibility that after all, your collection will probably outlast you, try to keep ahead of the acquisitions and work out your print storage problems. It is easier in the long run. The way you store and hang your collection gives you access for easy study and enjoyment of them, and preserves the prints for the next generation to enjoy."

Bob Stana, Tom Judy

The yellow block, printed first.

The red block, printed over the yellow.

The blue block.

The final print, created using three separately inked, end-grain wood blocks, Katatjuta Two Gums, by Edwina Ellis. Photos courtesy of Edwina Ellis.

Rocking the plate.

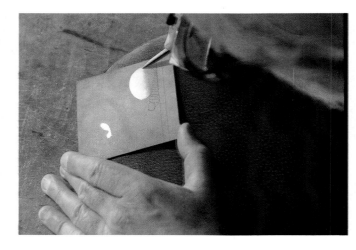

Using a burnishing tool.

Inking the plate with a dabber.

The finished copper plate and finished print by Joop Vegter.
Photos by Sylvia Vegter.

Cutting the stencil.

Ready to print.

Printing.

The final print, Ned's Point Bench, by Lorna Massie.
Photos by Kim Massie.

CUT-PLATE ETCHING

Applying black ink using window stencils.

Multiple plates assembled on press bed ready for printing.

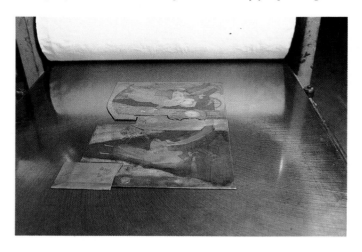

The finished print being pulled.

The finished print, Two Ways To Get More, by David Driesbach. Photos by George Tarbay.

Two Ways to Get More   1/35   David F. Driesbach '90

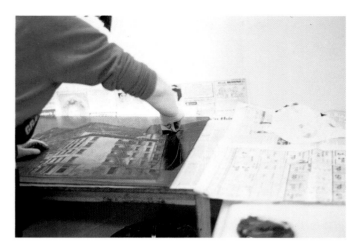

The artist applies a mixed blue-black, viscose etching ink to the entire plate.

Prepared drawing prior to making plate.

Using a small roller to ink high spots on the plate.

The finished print, Shadow Fall/Lampglow (Elegy for Bill), by Grace Bentley–Scheck. Photos courtesy of Grace Bentley–Scheck.

OFFSET LITHOGRAPH

Using printed mylar to register the image.

Paul Stillpass sponges the offset plate in preparation for printing.

Print emerging from the press.

The finished print by John Newman, a multi-colored and mixed media offset lithograph. Printed by master printers Lee Funderburg and Paul Stillpass at Tyler Graphics. Photos courtesy of Tyler Graphics.

Kenneth Tyler etching the limestone lithographic stone.

Inking the stone.

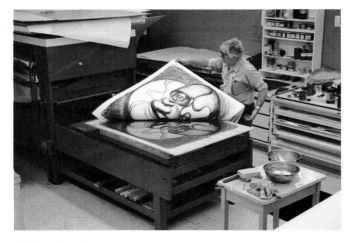

Pulling the print.

The finished print, Twist in Turn, by John Newman. Photos by Marabeth Cohen, courtesy of Tyler Graphics.

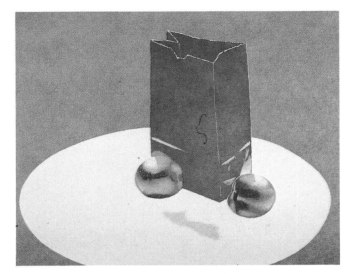

Sixty different screen printings were used, in progressive applications and combinations of only seven colors.

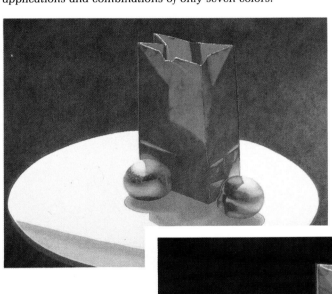

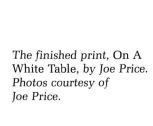

The finished print, On A White Table, by Joe Price. Photos courtesy of Joe Price.

CARE

Conservation and Restoration of Prints

10

It was early on a Sunday morning when our telephone rang and an earnest voice said that he had an urgent question to ask me. Grabbing my towel and trying to dry myself off and be polite, I realized that it was Jerry K., who had bought several large prints the afternoon before, and said, "Okay, shoot." His statement was the most unusual of our twenty year career as gallery keepers. He had put his prints in a folder leaning against the kitchen wall. The folder fell open and his dog urinated on the prints. "What should I do?" he asked. I shuddered and gave him the name of a local conservator who would help him to rectify this calamity by methods and means unknown to the lay person, including gallery people like me, and charge him for this highly technical service.

This chapter discusses the substance—paper—its history, and how it is made because paper is the support of any print. Inks and paints used in the printmaking media are not as likely to be subject to preservation problems except when exposed to extremes of light and even then, etching inks do not fade.

Our intent is to emphasize what a print owner should do to preserve print papers and to offer proper alternatives if there is a problem such as mold, foxing, abrasions, tears, buckling, or cockling in print paper. We also discuss the availability of conservators who can help print owners preserve and restore their prints so they will have permanence and will retain their value, but the secret is that their work is akin to that of a doctor. After years of training, their skills are time consuming and highly technical.

This chapter shares some tips learned from years of handling hurt prints, which will enable a print owner to make emergency cosmetic repairs. Suggestions for simple cosmetic restorations are given, such as in-filling small holes, closing tears, removing creases, lessening water stains and dirt from prints, humidifying prints to relax distortions in supporting papers and drying under weights.

The conservation of prints is based on educated preservation of paper. Paper is such an everyday object in such common use, that we do not stop to think about its composition, much less its durability. However, paper durability is extremely important to you as a responsible print buyer.

THE HISTORY OF PAPER

Early bases for pictures and writing were parchment, papyrus, rice paper, and papers made from linen and cotton plants.

Papyrus was a writing substratum created during ancient times by laminating fibers from an inner layer of bark from the papyrus plant.

Parchment, a writing material predating paper, was invented in Asia Minor to rival papyrus, the writing base from Egypt. Parchment is made from the lining, not the wool side, of sheepskin that has been scraped, washed, stretched, and rubbed with pumice until smooth.

Rice paper is a misnomer for long fibered, fine weight, handmade papers, properly called *tissue*. These tissue papers were first used for Chinese paintings and, like papyrus, were made as a laminate. Early tissues were formed from sheets cut from the inner bark of a tree that grows in Formosa.

What we call rice paper today is actually made from three Japanese trees: mulberry (*kozo*), *matsumata,* and *gampi.* The inner bark of their branches is steamed, peeled, and cooked until the fibers turn to mush. The soft mass is beaten until the fibers start to resemble bread dough. These long cellulose fibers float as slurry on water in a vat. Since they are cellulose, the fibers are attracted to each other and hence cling, bonding, and forming thin but strong sheets of paper when a screen is pulled up through the water and moved backwards and forwards for a few minutes. I have made *kozo* and *gampi* papers from dried barks sent from Japan. They form amazingly transparent yet strong papers.

Paper is made from disintegrated vegetable fibers floating in water and trapped on a screen. According to legend, paper was first created in China by T'sai Lun sometime before 105 A.D. He saved scraps of cloth, then used them for a writing surface, and beat them until they were reduced to fibers. He mixed the fibrous mass with water and poured the "slurry" onto a cloth or bamboo screen. The water drained away through the porous screen, leaving a homogeneous sheet of felt-like paper. Believe it or not, this process of hand-papermaking remains essentially unchanged to this day.

The secret of papermaking eventually traveled to India, the Middle East, Egypt, and Morocco. In Europe, by the 13th and 14th centuries, papermaking fibers were made from cotton and linen plants. Paper was better for printing than parchment and cheaper to produce.

Printing paper requires less sizing and blotting paper almost none. Paper was sized with gelatin made from hooves, hides, and horns. This "sizing" prevents ink from feathering or bleeding out into the sheet. Multiple uses of paper such as writing, painting, and printing require different amounts of sizing. Painting paper requires some sizing. Because of the nature of the various inks used, writing paper requires a hard finish supplied by using lots of size on its surface.

Dr. Jacob Schaffer, 18th century botanist in Bavaria, Germany, pioneered the use of other vegetable fibers such as wasp nests and potatoes for papermaking because the supply of linen and cotton rags was limited and there was increasing need for cheaper paper, due to the invention of the printing press.

> Secret: The type of paper used affects a print's permanence.

Early in the 1800s, American paper companies were so desperate for raw rag materials that one manufacturer, Stanwood Tower in Gardiner, Maine, ingeniously imported the wrappings of Egyptian mummies for this purpose until his employees developed cholera from the ancient rags. Most original prints are printed on 100% rag papers today. Limited edition prints and reproductions are usually printed on wood pulp papers or on combination rag and wood papers.

The development of a wood grinding machine during the 19th century and the founding of the first ground wood pulp mill near Stockbridge, Massachusetts in 1866 gave to the world inexpensive wood pulp paper. This step was significant because artists used wood pulp paper as well as rag papers for drawing and printmaking. Many prints by famous artist printmakers such as Picasso, Thomas Hart Benton, Winslow Homer were printed on wood pulp papers and other poor quality papers which makes them brittle and hard to preserve.

Using wood as a raw material made possible, in the late 1800s, the phenomenal growth of the paper industry not only for newspapers and the like, but for manufacturing objects as diverse as men's disposable shirt collars and embossed coffins. Most important for the future development of hand printmaking, the use of wood pulps for books and newspaper making conserved the supply of rags for use in making fine paper.

Most wood pulp papers contain lignin, an acidic substance that, while it binds the cellulose wood molecules together, also gradually eats the molecules and breaks the wood pulp paper down. However, not all wood pulp papers are bad, from a conservation standpoint. Today, the paper industry has developed techniques to refine wood pulp and turn it into alpha cellulose, suitable for archival papers.

PAPERS FOR PRINTMAKING

According to our source, David Hunter's *Paper-making: The Technique of an Ancient Craft,* rag printmaking papers are made by machines that closely simulate the making of paper by hand. For these fine papers, where strength, durability, and longevity as well as aesthetics are prime considerations, only pure rag pulp is used and often only white rags are employed. The cleaner and whiter the rag and the less severe the boiling and bleaching process, the better the paper will be from a conservation standpoint.

Commercial papers are made by machines. Paper machines transform wet, totally macerated, chemically treated vegetable fibers into a thin web of dry paper. The fibers are flowed onto an endless wire screen which moves continually over rollers. The water is removed by suction and a moist web of matted fibers is transferred to a moving woolen blanket or felt, where it is pressed and then carried to cylinders for drying.

Rag papers used for original prints are macerated without chemical additives in special machines called *beaters* equipped with short blades that rotate and break up the rag stock, leaving fibers that are long, strong, and enduring. It is the fact that rag papers are made without bleaches in combination with the slightly different beating step (using short blades) that makes these papers long fibered and enduring. They are formed either by hand or by special paper machines that carefully simulate the look of handmade papers.

> Secret: Deckled edges and watermarks are clues that print paper might be made of 100% rag.

Deckles

To recapitulate how sheets of handmade paper are formed: a mold or screen of limited proportions with a removable edge called a *deckle* is dipped by a vatman or papermaker into a vat containing beaten fibers suspended in water. After removing the deckle, a worker called a *coucher* (or the papermaker as coucher) transfers the moist sheet of paper from the mold to a felt page where it is pressed and dried. After a sheet of paper is formed in the mold with its thin deposit of pulp, the frame (deckle) is removed. This pulls up the paper on the edges of the piece and creates the uneven *deckled* edge which today is one of the earmarks of handmade papers.

Years ago, the finest handmade papers had their deckled edges trimmed off because deckles were considered an imperfection. Deckled edges have only come in to vogue in the 20th century. Deckled edges can be a clue that the paper is of good quality. However, be aware that wood pulp papers are also made with machine-produced deckled edges. Hence, deckled edges might not definitely indicate that your print is on rag paper. The way to ascertain paper content is to ask what paper the print is on and to develop your connoisseurship so you can recognize papers and distinguish between 100% rag papers and wood pulp papers.

Special machines are used to imitate the look of handmade papers. These cylinder type mold machines form papers that have four deckled edges like real handmade papers, but machine-made deckles are much more even in appearance than the edges of a genuine handmade sheet of paper. It is these deckles that you can look for either on two sides or four sides of printmaking papers. They give an uncertain value to the quality of paper used for a print because pulp papers do not have a rough edge; they have cut edges.

As a printmaker, I print on four types of machine made 100% rag papers: BFK Rives, Arches, Italia, and German etching. They all have deckled edges and watermarks. Some of these printing papers have smooth surfaces and others have rough textures.

Watermarks

Since all 100% rag papers have watermarks that you can see if you hold a piece of paper up to light, it has been assumed by many that finding a watermark is a sure way to know that your print is on rag paper. However, since some papers with wood content also have watermarks, this is dubious. Watermarks identify the maker of the paper. The company or papermaker devises his symbol which is woven onto the copper wire screen or papermaking machine called the *dandy roll*. The watermark wires prevent paper fibers from settling and thus leave a readable impression when the watermark stamp is removed. This type of mark also can be found in money and identification cards. Many printmakers print over the watermark in order to dramatize it.

SIZING

Secret: Sizings used by paper manufacturers affect a paper's conservation qualities.

Giving paper a smooth surface suitable for printmaking uses involves sizing the paper—putting a water resistant substance on or in the sheet of paper. In China papers are finished and sized by rubbing the surface with a stone. Papers are sized with gelatin made from animal hides, hooves, and horns.

Without sizing, paper would be like blotting paper and absorb any printing ink, whether it was used for calligraphy or printmaking. Papers made from hard rags require a thin size at a high temperature, and those made from old soft rags require a thick size at a low temperature.

Sizing is either applied as a glaze after paper is made or mixed internally within the pulp. In glazing with size, an old practice was to put the size in a tank kept hot, and to dip a pile of papers thoroughly in the size, stack them, and then compress them. Today, a mechanical sizing machine is used before the paper is dried and finished, suitable to the paper's intended use. Watercolor and drawing papers are often given a high degree of finish, although some printing papers are purposely left with a rougher surface that appeals to today's printmakers.

The hazard of sizing is that it attracts mold, a fuzzy growth that appears on deteriorated papers. Mold feeds on sizing and paper fibers and thereby weakens the sheets. It is either impurities in sizing

or the type of size used in or on papers that causes mold to grow. Mold takes a variety of forms from small black spots to feathery white strands to an inconspicuous haze. Various types of impurities in sizing are present in old papers, as well as vegetable gum binders which are very subject to mold growth.

When mold growth is seen or suspected on a print, the print should be unframed immediately in order to release any humidity that may be trapped inside the frame. This will stop or prevent further mold growth. After the relative humidity is lowered and your print dries out, you may be able to brush the mold off the surface of your print. Consult a conservator when mold occurs within the structure of the paper or when it interferes with a fragile medium or when it leaves stains after having been brushed off. Only a conservator can restore your prints after mold deterioration.

INTERNAL SOURCES OF PAPER DETERIORATION

Secret: Be aware of possible internal sources of paper deterioration when considering the purchase of an older print.

Poor quality pulp, bleach residues, and unstable sizings are three internal sources of paper deterioration. Although these internal factors are almost beyond a buyer's control, knowing about them can help you ask questions about print papers, particularly when buying older prints. If you suspect that any of these factors might be contributing to a print's deterioration, ask for advice from a paper conservator regarding the condition of a possible print purchase and/or the preservation options available.

Poor quality pulp is acidic in nature. Paper pulp is made of cellulose which has an almost neutral pH when kept in a neutral situation. When exposed to acid, the cellulose separates. Acid can enter paper in many ways. It is present in untreated pulp containing unrefined wood fibers.

To remove these burn marks, made from the wood pulp core of an old mat, needs the expert help of a conservator. This print by John Marin then should be matted in a 100% rag mat.

> Secret: Most reproductions and limited edition prints are printed on commercial papers made in part from wood pulp and coated with various sizings.

Ask about the content of the paper on which an original print or a limited edition print is made. Companies that print reproductions should be up front about the quality of papers they use. One company that makes offset prints which are copies of paintings, Rockport Reproductions, reports that their printing papers are machine made with some wood pulp content and that their papers will last for as long as the householder who buys it, for an average of thirty to fifty years.

Chemicals left from the chlorine bleach used when processing the low grade rags and non-rag fibers used for paper pulps may be hazardous to your print's longevity. Most wood pulp papers are bleached. Any chloride left in a pulp can turn to hydrochloric acid and attack the cellulose bonds in the paper. According to Andrew, Nelson and Whitehead, a major supplier of printing papers to the world, the rag papers used today by printmakers are made from clean, white but unbleached, cotton rags.

DOCUMENTATION

Ask for information about the paper when you are considering buying an original print. This documentation, supplied formally or informally by the printmaker to a print dealer, will list the type of printing paper the printmaker has used as a substrate or printing surface.

Often the master printer who prints an artist's prints, or the printmaker himself or herself, will supply a typed document that lists the type of paper used, along with other data such as number of color plates and screens used. Or a printmaker will send print documentation along with his curriculum vitae (résumé) and statement of purpose.

If this is not readily available, ask your print dealer to obtain it for you if you have the slightest qualm about the feel of the paper that your chosen print is printed on.

As noted in Chapter 3, part of becoming a print connoisseur is familiarizing yourself with the look and feel of the papers used by printmakers. The print on the cover of this book is printed on the handmade Japanese paper known as *gampi*. Its sheen, smoothness, and luster lend a tactile beauty to Hara's work that cannot be verbally described. Hara's papers are unique and of excellent quality; they enhance his work. They are part of the print buyer's confrontation with Hara's silkscreen prints during the browsing experience in our print gallery.

EXTERNAL SOURCES OF PRINT DETERIORATION

> Secret: You can control the seven external sources of print deterioration in order to preserve your prints.

The seven external sources of print deterioration are:
• contact with acidic materials
• ultraviolet light
• air pollution
• high and fluctuating temperatures
• high and changing levels of relative humidity
• insects and rodents
• careless handling
• natural disasters

Humidity

Excessive humidity stimulates the growth of mold. Mold needs a relative humidity level of above 65% to grow. Its appearance can be detected by a soft bloom that appears on the glass or paper surface inside the frame. Mold also takes the form of dull, rusty patches on the paper, known as "foxing."

> Secret: Avoid foxing and mold on prints by controlling the relative humidity level in your home and not hanging prints on damp outside walls.

Air conditioning or dehumidifying machines are good solutions in moist climates and damp building areas, but only if they are maintained. Airtight containers with silica gel, a dehumidifying agent, work well for long-term print storage. It is far more important to avoid frequent fluctuations in relative humidity and temperature than to try to maintain an exact percentage.

In your home, do not store prints in basements or cellars, and be careful with prints in vacation homes, which are closed for an extended time. They may become excessively humid or musty. The prints should be opened and exposed to the air periodically.

As soon as you notice the appearance of mold or foxing, open the frame and take out the print to allow circulation of air and release humidity trapped inside the frame. Simply lowering the relative humidity level will stop its growth. Put the print into a drier environment.

Light

Organic substances in general are degraded by radiant energy. This can result in fading, darkening, or no color change at all. Light weakens print paper and fades many pigments resting on the paper's surface. It is the type, intensity, and duration of light exposure that you must monitor. Less light means less fading, but the reality is that fading does not totally stop when light drops below a certain level. Placing a print in darkness merely slows down the process, until the print is brought out again for viewing.

The question is: How much light should be used for viewing prints? The answer is one of degree. The eye tends to lose its ability to distinguish colors at very low light levels, such as moonlight. It can then only distinguish tonal, or black and white, values. Therefore, when viewing prints, there must be sufficient light to distinguish color values, but without excess light. The optimum amount is about five foot candles, which corresponds to the output of one 150 watt reading lamp.

> Secret: Use the same amount of light for viewing works of art on paper as is required for casual reading.

Hang your prints on walls receiving minimum amounts of natural light. It is deleterious to prints, causing fading of colors and papers and eventual paper deterioration, when sunlight or reflected light hits a wall on which prints are hung. It is best to show your prints by the light of reading lights. Never use those special lights to the tops of frames containing prints. Nor should you use those small spotlights placed on the floor to illuminate artwork. Spotlights from the ceiling should only be used with full awareness that prints gradually can fade over time in this situation.

How do you measure the amount of light? This can be done with one of the older photographic light meters which are calibrated in foot candles. Take a sheet of white unglazed paper, such as blotting paper, at least one square foot in size, and place it where the art is going to hang, then read the foot candles of reflected light by using the light meter. You now can determine the proper amount of light by adjusting the light source and its distance from the art.

> Secret: Rotate your artwork to reduce excessive exposure to light.

How do you guard against unnecessary light exposure? Museums do it by rotating selections of their holdings, so that the art is never left on view for more than a limited time—a few months per year. You can do the same for your print collection by changing the works' positions on the wall in your home, perhaps once every year. You will not only reduce the rate of deterioration, but you will also enjoy viewing them from a new perspective.

> Secret: Avoid hanging prints in natural unfiltered light.

All daylight contains unsafe levels of ultraviolet light, the most damaging part of the spectrum. Do not hang prints on a wall directly opposite windows, since the light there will be greater than anywhere else in the room. Next to sunlight, fluorescent light is the most damaging light source, since it also contains ultraviolet light. Fluorescent lights should always be covered with plastic sleeves or shades that filter out the ultraviolet rays. You can also frame your prints with ultraviolet-filtering acrylic plastic in place of glass.

Heat

High temperatures speed up the deterioration of paper. Do not hang pictures over a radiator or heating register. The traditional spot above the fireplace is doubly poor for works of art on paper. First because of heat, second because of dust, smoke, or gummy residues from the fire attaching themselves to the glass and frame. Do not clip lights to your frames—they are very hot and their light is too intense for your prints.

Air Pollution

Urban dwellers and their collections are subject to high concentrations of pollutants, such as sulfur dioxide, and many other pollutants in the atmosphere. Sulfur dioxide is a gas produced by the combustion of oil or coal. It was particularly prevalent in homes at the turn of the century when gas jets were used for domestic lighting, and many libraries and prints from that period were severely damaged from the fumes. Sulfur dioxide attacks paper, causing discoloration, embrittlement, and eventual disintegration. Older framed pictures that have been partially exposed to the air by inadequate backing show marks or stains due to sulfur dioxide seeping in through openings in the back.

Certain pigments used by artists, such as ultramarine blue and white lead-based paints, react with sulfur dioxide and can be destroyed or turn black from chemical reaction to the gas. The only sure remedy is to relocate artworks to the cleaner air of the suburbs, or install air conditioning. The practice of sealing the backs of frames by using tapes to close the space between back and molding prevents pollutants from seeping into prints.

Insects

The insects that can damage your prints include silverfish, book lice, cockroaches, wood worms, and termites. Silverfish are silvery-gray insects about a quarter of an inch long with three tail-like appendages. They prefer warm, damp, dark places. They are a serious threat to books, but also to any art on paper. They will eat through pictures to get at the flour paste used in hinging and the glue sizing of the paper, or just eat the cellulose. All paper contains cellulose, not just wood pulp papers. Silverfish would probably prefer 100% rag if given a choice.

Cockroaches prefer dark, warm, damp places and usually come out at night. They cause damage to paper, fabrics, and any painting media containing glues or sugar.

Termites and wood worms are thought of as a danger to wood alone, such as home foundation beams, but they will devour anything made of cellulose, including paper. Watch out for their winding, branching tunnels on basement or first floor walls that are close to the ground.

Secret: Infestation by insects is best prevented by regular cleaning and inspecting of dark or damp spaces.

To control insect infestation, use powdered or aerosol insecticides if necessary. Be careful because some insecticides are quite harmful to prints. Pyrethrum is an organic insecticide recommended by professional pest control firms because of its low toxicity to humans. Generally, if the problem of insects cannot be handled through good housekeeping, then professional exterminators should be consulted. Each state requires exterminators to be registered and certified.

Acidic Materials

Secret: When framing prints, insist on museum quality acid-free materials.

Great strides have been made in the last few years to improve the quality of framing materials. You can use papers treated with alkaline chem-

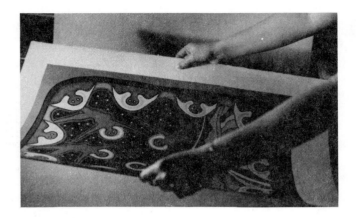

Angela Smalley, gallery assistant, demonstrates how to move a work of art on paper, in this case a silkscreen by Australian printmaker Sally Morgan. The paper's edges are suspended between the palms of her hands.

icals which will neutralize the damaging effects of the atmosphere. "Buffered" papers should be used to protect the backs of prints from long-term damage by acidic wood frames such as oak. Check your framed prints periodically to see if your mats have yellowed edges on their windows—a clue that the wood pulp mat will burn your prints if not replaced with rag mats.

Handling

Always use clean hands when handling prints. The natural oils on one's skin, including the hands, will discolor paper if handled often enough. Therefore, if you are going to sort or handle a number of prints it is prudent to wear cotton gloves.

Lift prints using both hands. Do this by placing your hands on each side of the print to avoid creasing the paper, which will decrease its value.

Valuable prints should be matted rather than left loose. Always open matted prints by the outer edge, not by inserting a finger through the window opening. Unmatted prints, if stored in stacks, should be separated by sheets of acid-free tissue.

Never use pressure-sensitive tapes, Scotch® tape, or masking tape on prints. The adhesive eventually is absorbed by the paper fibers and will leave a stain. The only safe adhesive is wheat or rice paste. An acid-free commercial substitute such as methyl cellulose, often sold for use as wallpaper paste, is readily available.

Transporting prints requires special care. The container or folder should be larger than the work by a few inches, especially if it is to be sent by mail or United Parcel Service. If possible, transport prints flat in a sandwich between two boards, with the corners reinforced with shipping tape. Shipping tubes can also be used, provided they are at least ³⁄₁₆ inch thick board or more. The ends of the folder or tube should be padded with tissue, so that the prints will not shift in transit and damage the ends of the paper. Tubes can be purchased from paper supply firms and sometimes in art supply stores.

CONSERVATION OF DAMAGED WORK

The first level in preservation is a cosmetic one—*restoration.* This step might involve procedures such as dry cleaning; removing water stains; taking out wrinkles, creases, and buckles; sun bleaching to lift stains; humidifying prints to relax them; and drying humidified prints under weights to flatten them. These remedies can be undertaken by the layperson.

Be aware that there are risks involved in any of these restoration practices. By humidifying a print and putting weights on the paper to take out a crease, you might unwittingly alter the texture of the paper or the color of the printing ink. Since many printing inks bleed, spraying them to humidify them might be disastrous. Restoration denotes a treatment whose sole purpose is cosmetic improvement. The artwork only looks better, it does not last longer.

The second level of conservation denotes a treatment that may or may not make a picture look better, but above all it makes it last longer. Take a damaged print to a conservator. Only a professional should undertake such a difficult and potentially hazardous process.

The goal for lay people and conservators is preservation—the preservation of a print's inherent internal structure. Lay people are more qualified to carry out conservation in general by controlling preservation practices: the relative humidity, protecting their prints from ultraviolet light, ensuring that their prints are properly matted and framed and so forth. While conservators can certainly improve the appearance of prints, i.e. "restore" them, they do so only if the treatment will not damage the print in the long run. For instance, bleaching a print with chlorine bleach might make the print look better, but will shorten its lifetime considerably. It is important to distinguish the difference in intent. The primary intent of a conservator is preservation. The primary intent of a responsible print buyer should also be preservation.

COSMETIC RESTORATION

Secret: If you are aware of the risks, you can try cosmetic restoration of your prints.

Cleaning

The cleaning and removal of water stains can be handled by the layperson, if he takes full responsibility for possible damage. A water damaged print should be taken out of the frame and mat and placed on top of clean white paper towels. Using a mister, distilled water from the drug store is sprayed onto the print, which becomes soaked; the water lifts stains, then drains through to the paper towels beneath, carrying dirt and grime with it. After the print has dried enough to move it, it is placed between two clean white blotters and weighted flat. The blotters are replaced periodically with dry ones. You will note that the water stains have disappeared and the grime and dirt has transferred to the blotters. I usually line my first blotters with paper towels which suck up water especially quickly. Then I keep replacing blotters with dry blotters which are weighted to flatten the print. Change blotters until the print is dry.

Lifting water stains can also be accomplished by floating your humidified, water misted print in a water bath in a photographic tray placed in full sun. By a chemical process, the water on the sheet will be exchanged for the water in the tray, thus lifting out the water stains.

We used this method when a conservator recommended it to us after a horrendous flood that damaged many prints. It lifted many frightening water stains. I let the prints partially air dry and then put them between weighted blotters, replacing the blotters until the prints were flat and dry. Both cleaning procedures are risky and not foolproof and should be used with caution.

Dry Cleaning

> Secret: The basic rule of conservation is to begin with the simplest, least disturbing method first.

To remove surface dirt such as light dust, fingerprints, and flyspecks, you can "dry clean" a print. You will need white cotton gloves, a rubber air bulb, blotting paper, covered weights, erasers (see below), a needle, and a clean, soft, dry brush.
1. Wash your hands and put on the gloves.
2. Cover your working surface with a layer of blotting paper. Lay the print on the working surface, using the covered weights to hold the corners down.
3. On paper with a matte surface use one of the following erasers: a vinyl eraser, a pumice bag, or Skum-X™. Drop a small amount of Skum-X™, or squeeze some crumbs out of the pumice bag, onto the paper. Using a gloved fingertip, gently stroke over the soiled area, working toward the corners. You can also use the vinyl eraser, being very gentle with it.
4. Do *not* rest your hand on the paper. As the eraser material darkens, it is picking up soil. Use the air bulb to gently blow the soiled particles off the paper. If the air bulb is not sufficient, use the soft brush to gently brush away the soil.
5. To remove strongly adhering material—flyspecks, mud—lightly flick the spot with the needle, *without* disturbing the paper's surface.

Avoid pigmented areas during this process. Keep in mind the surface of the paper—whether it is fragile or strong, slick or matte. A crumbly artgum eraser can be used on a slick surface paper, but be very cautious. This type of eraser has been known to leave slight oily marks. Do not use a vinyl eraser on slick paper, as it may take up the paper's surface. Remember, it is easy to damage the print's paper with over-enthusiastic use of your hand as you erase.

Buckling

Buckling can be removed by pressing a humidified print with weights; by pressing a weight on top of a layer of protective felts and blotters. This remedy works best for etchings and lithographs. Buckled silkscreen prints require a conservator's care because their inks might be affected. Care also has to be taken with etchings not to press out the raised edge of the plate mark.

The cause of the buckling should be addressed. Paper is very much influenced by air humidity, so removing the artwork to a stable environment is the first step. A label stuck to the back of the print can create local buckling and an abrasion of the print paper. Take the print to a conservator for removal of the label.

Cockling

Cockling is caused by glass pressing on print paper so it cannot move and breathe as paper normally does. The paper gradually goes into waves configurations. This condition is best handled by a conservator. But the first step is to open the frame. The cause might be improper framing where not enough room was left between the paper and the glass or the edge of the frame to allow the paper to expand and contract. The remedy is to have the print re-framed and hinged with only two Japanese paper hinges at the top, giving it opportunity to move without restriction.

Tears

Tears in the edges of a print paper can be repaired on an emergency basis by gluing postage stamps on the back. A more appropriate solution is to carefully insert thin, handmade Oriental paper by means of one of the safe glues (methyl cellulose, wheat or rice paste, or library paste) to repair the tear from the back. You can also patch a torn print by using a thin strip of Oriental paper dampened with methyl cellulose or the pastes described above. Press the edges of the torn papers together and hold with the thin paper bandage behind it.

You can fill in a tiny hole yourself. This is called *in-filling*. Use two tiny pieces of Oriental paper moistened with the methyl cellulose or flour paste, and gently tap into place from the back. Press with a blotter below and above. The edges of the Oriental paper should be feathered first by tearing against a straight edge after a bead of water has been brushed along the line of the tear.

Foxing

Foxing refers to small circular patches of brownish discoloration appearing on both modern and old papers. Some think that rust specks in the paper caused foxing. Today, foxing is suspected to be a form of mold growth, resulting in a fungus. It can be caused by the sizing in the paper, and caused or aggravated by contact with acidic cardboards or animal glues in pressure-sensitive tapes.

Most foxing is caused by the print being stored in too damp an environment. Once the print is returned to stable surroundings where the humidity and temperature are low and stable, foxing will not worsen. But removal or reduction of foxing must be undertaken only by a trained conservator. Once the foxing mold has dried it can be brushed off.

Tape Stains

Pressure-sensitive and gummed tapes used to adhere prints to mats can cause severe local discoloration. The removal of these tapes from works of art should be done only by a conservator. The solvents needed to remove aged adhesive are very strong. They affect printing inks, they are toxic, and removing them causes abrasions to the paper.

Many paper tapes now on the market are mistakenly advertised as archival. They cannot be removed with water, only solvents used by conservators. Water does not dissolve this new adhesive, it merely gets it so that it rolls along and off the back of a print paper, taking with it paper fibers.

Each serious problem, such as removal of stains caused by the adhesive from tape or foxing, should be left to a professional conservator. Professional treatments involve the use of harmful chemicals and can only be used with special precautions.

Discolorations

To lift a water soluble discoloration, place a humidified print (which you dampen by gently spraying on both sides) into a photographic or plastic tray of water. The water in the sheet will be exchanged with water in the tray, thus leaching out water soluble stains and discolorations.

Weighing the Risks

A legitimate question is whether it is really worth the risk and expense to remove discoloration. The overall patina and color of the paper can be permanently changed by the chemicals used to remove stains. Also, the cost could be in excess of the value of the print.

On the other hand, you may attach a personal or sentimental value to the work of art far beyond its monetary value. So in the end you must use your own judgment in deciding whether to proceed with the restoration, after you have reviewed the problem with a professional conservator.

HIRING A CONSERVATOR

> Secret: The services of a conservator are not as expensive as you might expect.

Professional conservators have gone through a rigorous schooling at university level or by lengthy apprenticeship. They have extensive practical experience as well as theoretical and scientific knowledge. They are usually members of the national professional organization: The American Institute for Conservation of Historic and Artistic Works (AIC).

The facts are that conservators, and especially paper conservators, don't make high incomes. Salary surveys indicate that paper conservators generally make between $20,000 and $30,000 annually. Conservation treatments cost a lot because they are very time consuming and labor intensive. Relative to other services requiring less skill and involving less risk, conservation services are not expensive. Do not hesitate to ask questions of the conservator before you hire him; ask for references; ask for a preliminary consultation.

A conservator removes cellophane tape before treating with a solvent to remove adhesive stain.

The conservator repairs a tear using Japanese paper and wheat starch paste.

A layperson can become familiar with the field of conservation and restoration through the publications of the AIC which are very helpful.

The conservator's evaluation will include examination results, assessment of condition, and proposal for treatment. Often, more than one treatment is suggested, and the owner is asked to select his preference. Discussing this report with the conservator is the best way to make a decision about the treatment of a print. The technical descriptions of damage, condition, and remedies often give non-conservators trouble. The following glossary of conservation terms by Judith C. Walsh originally appeared in and is excerpted from the September/October 1983 issue of *Drawing* (Vol. V, no. 3) and is reprinted here with permission from The Drawing Society.

Abrasion of design: Rubbing, wearing, or grinding away of pigment or ink used in work of art by friction. Usually noticed along the tops of creases in the sheet and at the edges of the mat.

Abrasion of support: Rubbing, wearing, or grinding away of paper fibers by friction. Usually paper fibers in the affected areas will be "thrown up" from the sheet and can be seen as individual fibers upon close inspection.

Accretions: Small bits of foreign matter which have become attached to the surface of a sheet. Flyspecks are a common accretion.

Air dry: To take a wetted sheet and allow it to dry unencumbered in the open air.

Alkaline bath: A water bath with an alkaline solution added (1) to swell the paper fibers and flush out more dirt; (2) to render the deionized water less hungry for ions which protect the sheet; and (3) to leave some alkaline reserve in the sheet upon drying as protection from environmental acids.

Blackened white leads: The pigment white lead (and also other lead-based pigments—vermilion, red lead) can become discolored to black when exposed to hydrogen sulfide impurities in the air. This discoloration begins as a pinkish to orange tinge, then goes to a deep gray metallic color. Discoloration is reversible by applying hydrogen peroxide to the affected area.

Bleaching: The decolorization of a stain. The chemical reagents which decolor can also degrade the cellulose of the paper fibers and so must be used only when absolutely necessary. As a conservation procedure, bleaching is troublesome

Paper art is washed in filtered tap water to remove dirt and acid.

since it is always "cosmetic," that is, done to improve appearance only, and it is usually degradative to the paper.

Burnished: An area of the paper or design made shiny and lustrous by rubbing. This damage can be noted in raking light as a glossy line ("rubbed line") across an otherwise less glossy area. Usually the paper fibers are compressed by the burnishing, and usually this cannot be corrected.

Cleavage: The separation of pigment from the support.

Consumed whites: When the white highlighting in a drawing is made with chalk or whiting on an acid sheet, over time the acid in the sheet will evolve and be neutralized by the alkaline component in the white. As the carbonated white neutralizes the acid, it is itself consumed or used up, often leaving only a light area where it had been.

Crackle: The pattern of cracks in a thick paint layer caused by shrinkage of the medium in the paint, or flexing of the support.

Cupping: The condition of paint flakes which rise off the support around the edges of the flakes. These edges are easily caught and dislodged from the sheet in handling.

Deacidification: A process for neutralizing acids in a sheet of paper, leaving an alkaline residue in the sheet to protect it against further acid attacks. Most commonly, this procedure involves immersion in a water bath, although some solvent-based deacidification systems are commercially available.

Deionized water: Tap water which has passed through tanks containing resins which remove the metal ions (copper, iron, and chlorine are thought to be the most harmful) from the water molecule, replacing them with other nondamaging particles. This water is "more pure" than distilled water and is "ion hungry." It can leach out good ions (calcium and magnesium) in paper, effectively shortening the life of the paper. For that reason, some chemicals (usually calcium hydroxide) are added to wash water before bathing a work of art.

Distortions in plane: A sheet of paper has a certain "life" if it is not bound down to a stiff support. The gentle undulations and distortions in the sheet are part of its texture and three dimensionality. When the distortions become pronounced in one area or severe overall, they can be classed as: *buckles*—gentle waves over the entire sheet; *cockles*—also wavelike in shape but closer in interval; or *draws*—distortions or pulls at the corners of a sheet usually caused by tension on the sheet from mounting at the corners. When these are set and bend or break the sheet, they become *creases*. Creases differ from *folds* in that folds are deliberate and extend from edge to edge, usually bending but not breaking fibers.

Dry clean: To use various erasers on the surface of a sheet to pick up surface dirt and grime, especially prior to using a wet agent.

Dry under weights: To place a humidified paper among several blotters and under a rigid sheet, weighted down so that the paper dries flat. Sheets can also be *dried between felts,* that is, held among blotters and thick wooden etcher's felts to cushion the sheet while it dries.

Embrittlement: To become *brittle*. Suppleness in a sheet of paper depends in a large part upon the length of the cellulose chains or paper fibers that make up the paper. The fiber or chains can be shortened in manufacture or by acid attack over time. Brittleness cannot be reversed or corrected, although some treatments make handling embrittled objects safe.

Enzymes: Biological agents which are useful in rendering complex, insoluble molecules into smaller, more soluble components. Amylase (alpha amylase) converts starches into sugars which are quite readily soluble. Protease does the same thing for proteins. They are used under conditions of temperature and pH which approximate body chemistry. They must be deactivated after use.

Float wash: To place a relaxed sheet of paper on a tray of water. Surface tension will make the sheet float on the water, and by capillary action, water in the sheet will be exchanged with water in the

tray, leaching out water-soluble discoloration. (Paper will not float on most solvents.) The procedure protects friable but insoluble media, such as charcoal or graphite, from loss due to bathing.

Foxing: Small brown-to-rust-colored, colonial mold stains found on old sheets. Foxing is imperfectly understood, but recent research suggests that spots are the result of embedded metal particles, which encourage fungal activity.

Friction mount: Method of drying a badly distorted sheet which involves a mock-lining with Japanese tissue using no adhesive, only the affinity of water for water. The drawing is wetted, as is the tissue, they are brushed together to make contact, then dried between blotters, under weights. When dried, the tissue is removed.

Gouge: A groove or cavity scooped out of the sheet and often caused by broken glazing.

Humidify: To relax a sheet by minimal use of moisture, sometimes by suspending over a tray of water or over steam.

Inpaint: Color compensation done only in areas of loss of design or support. *Overpaint* is done over the original and is never acceptable in conservation.

Japanese tissue: Fine weight, long-fibered handmade papers, used in conservation to make repairs because of their strength and suppleness, and in printmaking because of their softness and beauty. They are commonly misidentified as *rice papers*.

Lacunae: Small missing part. This term usually describes wormholes in book pages but can also refer to many tiny losses in a flat sheet.

Line (or back): To affix another sheet of paper to the verso of a sheet. The secondary support can help an embrittled sheet hold together. In modern conservation, fine-weight Japanese tissues would be used, with a starch paste, and only in the most extreme cases.

Mat burn: The brown stain noted on the perimeter of sheets caused by their intimate contact with mat boards made of ground wood pulp.

Methyl cellulose: A stable, chemically modified cellulose which has many uses for conservation (for example, as an adhesive, carrier for water, or sheet size). It has the property of swelling considerably in water and remaining inert over time.

Relax: When a paper is completely humidified it is said to be "relaxed." It is made soft and slack by the swelling of the fibers. It can then be dried flat or creases removed.

Repair: A small piece of Japanese tissue applied to the reverse of a sheet to bridge a tear or cut and restores some strength to the sheet. Repairs have also been made with Western papers (called *patches*) and with tapes (called *disasters!*).

Residue of adhesive: Accretion of adhesive from former treatment or hinging, which may cause distortions in the sheet by its different reaction to moisture. Especially troublesome are overall deposits on the reverse of a sheet removed from a mount. This can sometimes cause curling of the sheet.

Spot test: A chemical test which involves placing a drop of reagent on the surface of a sheet, then reading the change in color to indicate the presence of such substances as lignin, rosin, starch, proteins.

Stain: A soiled or discolored spot in the fibers of the sheet. The stains are usually described by their origins, such as tape, light, or oil stain.

Starch paste: The most common adhesive used in paper conservation, made by cooking purified rice or wheat starch with deionized water. This adhesive remains soluble and does not discolor over many centuries.

Suction table: A porous-topped table with a vacuum suction attachment which is employed in paper conservation. The work of art is placed on felt, over the table, and sealed around the edges, and the suction turned on. Solvents, including water, can then be passed through the sheet, dissolving stains without disturbing soluble media.

Sun bleaching: The use of the sun's radiant energy in decoloring stains in paper. The sheet is placed in a tray of alkaline water and in full sunlight (or under fluorescent tubes) until the stains have reduced sufficiently (usually several hours). This procedure gives good visual results and seems not to degrade the paper.

Support: The sheet of paper, wood, linen, vinyl, or other substance that bears the artist's design. If another sheet is attached overall, it is called the "secondary support."

Tapes: Consist of two parts, the *carrier* and the *adhesive*. The carrier can be plastic, paper, or cloth; the adhesive can be gum, natural, or synthetic resin. Tapes are usually classified by the way they are affixed, and named by the carrier, for example, pressure sensitive tapes, water-sensitive tapes, Kraft paper tapes, Holland (linen) tapes, or glassine tapes. The trouble tapes cause sheets of paper is well known, and can come from either part of their structure. Recently, research into the time mechanism of pressure-sensitive tape staining has shown this to be a rapid process once it begins, completing in about one year.

Tear: Break in a sheet, severing paper fibers in an irregular pattern. Other breaks include: *cut*—hard-edge break made with a knife or scissors; and *split*—softer break made when sheet ruptures along a previously weakened area.

Thinned areas (Skinned): The localized areas in a sheet where the top layers of fibers have been removed (usually when a tape or bit of paper [mat] is removed without first softening the adhesive).

Tide lines: The brown stain at the farthest reach of an influx of water on a sheet. The water dissolves the oxidized material in the sheet, which mixes with impurities in the water. As the wetted area dries, the dissolved material concentrates at the wet-dry interface and sets as the water recedes. These stains are often difficult to move again in water.

Wash: To place a work of art on paper in a tray of pure water to remove the stains and discoloration which are water soluble. Care must be taken with the quality of water used, the way the water is introduced onto the sheet, and how the sheet is handled when wet.

CONSERVATION TIPS:

• Check conservators' references and previous clients.

• After picking a conservator ask for a preliminary written evaluation as well as a written and photographic documentation of the treatment after it is completed.

• Learn as much as you can about the field of conservation. It's fascinating, especially for print addicts.

• Talk to conservators at a nearby museum and

ask for names of qualified conservators. They can be surprisingly generous and caring.

FOR INFORMATION:
The American Institute for Conservation of Historic and Artistic Works (AIC)
Klingle Mansion
1400 16th Street, N.W., Suite 340
Washington, DC 20036
(202) 364-1036

FOR ARCHIVAL SUPPLIES:
Light Impressions
439 Monroe Avenue
Rochester, NY 14607-3717
(800) 828-6216
in New York state: (800) 828-9629

FOR REFERRALS TO CONSERVATORS:
Foundation of the American Institute for Conservation of Historic and Artistic Works (FAIC)
Klingle Mansion
1400 16th Street, N.W., Suite 340
Washington, DC 20036
(202) 232-6366 FAX (202) 232-6630

CONSERVATION OF A MUCH-LOVED PRINT

Our daughter's friend Amy brought us a badly framed silkscreen print to re-frame. It had been bought at auction and was considered a find because it dated back to the WPA era.

The print on brownish paper was made by Mervin Jules sometime during the 1930s. Its subject was a brightly naïve scene of children playing in Central Park. The pale mat was dirty and had yellowed on the outside edge of the beveled opening. However, the frame itself and the glass looked fine except for some dust. We recommended a new mat, 100% rag, and a backing of acid-free archival mat board, cleaning to remove the dust inside the molding and on the glass, and a new paper seal at the back of the frame package to prevent further dust infiltration.

When we opened the frame, we found that the print paper had turned brown because it has been glued to a wood fiber backing board. Both the glue and the backing board had discolored the print and there was nothing we could do to restore it before re-framing it.

We reviewed the issues with Amy. First, she had an emotional attachment to the subject of the print. Second, it was her first print acquisition. Third, the print had been made by a WPA printmaker: Jules was one of the early experimenters of the silkscreen technique as well as a teacher of printmaking.

Our advice was to take the print to a professional conservator, since a framer or gallery was not equipped to handle it responsibly. The conservator would remove the print from the cardboard backing and recommend any other work to be done. Our final advice was that certainly her beloved print was worth preserving, and that she should certainly find a conservator to treat it and prevent further disintegration before re-framing it.

COLLECTING
Ways to Focus Your Print Buying
11

Anthony has an addiction to English landscape wood engravings of pre-World War II rural England. His wife and children humor him as he buys every wood engraving on this subject that he can find and afford.

When asked why he makes these purchases, he replied, "I have a nostalgia for the looser, gentler landscapes of England in the 1930s. There were more hedgerows then, which provided endless inspiration to artists. There was a technical virtuosity of wood engraving from that period which is almost paradoxical, in that such an intricate, stiff medium was used to reduce huge landscapes to small, romantic, emotion-filled scenes. These scenes changed dramatically after the war when huge conglomerate developments eliminated the divisions between fields."

This chapter is addressed to the first-time print buyer who, as he becomes more experienced in buying for pleasure and decoration, becomes focused on buying certain types of prints and concentrates on buying one or more chosen specialty. A specialty can be a period, a subject, a technique, a particular artist, or a period of an artist. When a buyer of prints is focused in his purchases, the buyer becomes a print collector. A print *collector* has narrowed his special interest to a particular facet that fascinates him.

BECOME AN INTERMEDIATE PRINT COLLECTOR

Becoming an intermediate print collector is the step before becoming a focused collector, when you have certain interests and enthusiasms but you have not yet put on blinders to everything but your specialty as true collectors do. You still follow buying whims and purchase prints that strike you, but your fields of interest are narrowing and you no longer buy to cover bare walls or to match sofas.

To become an intermediate collector, buy what interests and intrigues you. The person who buys prints for the love of them, as this book advocates so often, is then an intermediate print collector. Even after all these years of handling original prints sent on consignment by printmakers all over the world, I am, and enjoy being, an intermediate print collector.

To a certain degree, everyone is a sort of collector. We collect certain types of ephemeral household goods such as postcards, stamps, and books. The type of collector this chapter highlights is different from the average taste-directed accumulator of objects. One of the identifying features of a print collector is that a true collector is so infatuated, he will travel to or telephone a shop, gallery, or auction to find and secure a type of print.

Secret: Art collectors specialize.

What makes a collector different from a buyer is that collectors set goals and limits. Gary travels across the country to shop for miniature prints twice a year. He buys what he can find using support and guidance of reference people and gallery keepers who specialize in this chosen field. If you want to become a print collector, you might begin in any of the following ways or in any mode you dream up:

1. Collect one subject: rural America, animals,

Cat prints, a subject matter often collected by print and cat lovers. From left to right: The Cat, *etching and aquatint by Gary Tricker;* Cat, *mezzotint by Joop Vegter; and* Burmese Family Portrait, *etching by Christine McGinnis.*

Etching by David Driesbach, Cat Tales.

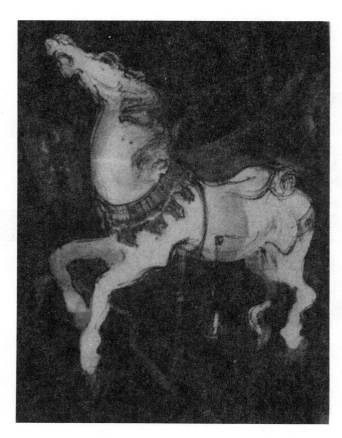

Carousel, *etching by Helen Frank.*

Mezzotint by Joop Vegter, Drop of Dew on a Leaf, a fine example of a miniature print.

cows, carousels, roses, trains, skies, woods, flower gardens.

2. Collect miniatures. This specialty is peculiar to prints. Prints in any medium that are smaller than 4″ × 4″ are called "miniatures." They can be created by unknown or known printmakers in a diversity of subjects and media or in one subject and print medium.

3. Collect one or two printmakers whose work you want to research and own and buy up their prints as thoroughly and completely as possible. One collector of Stowe Wengenroth's lithographs ran ads in all the newspapers of his state and bought many Wengenroths for $100 and $200 when they sold in print galleries for $300 to $3,500. When you collect one person's work, try to acquire early prints as well as later prints more typically shown in galleries. Ask your dealer to get these for you if they are not in his shelves or drawers.

4. Collect blue-chip printmakers or academic printmakers. Blue-chip printmakers are distinguished by the fact that they are often painters who work with master printers; they are nationally advertised; and they can be found in museum collections. Academic printmakers can and do belong in museum collections, but they usually print their own work or have students work with them to print editions.

> Secret: Buy only from recognized and reliable sources unless you are totally confident about the work you are collecting.

To become a connoisseur in a subject, do your research. Museums and libraries have areas where one can examine prints and talk about them with experts. In print rooms, special exhibits and reference books are available. Be extremely careful and only buy from reliable sources — galleries and auction houses — not from magazine ads and hotel sales. Galleries will stand behind their sales.

DO YOUR HOMEWORK

Collecting prints takes time and effort. Take time to build relationships with qualified people in the print field: print dealers, print curators, and other print authorities.

Lithograph by Stowe Wengenroth, Quarry. *One of his finest early prints, now quite rare and worth about $1500.*

You can do this by asking questions and finding out a gallery person's pet enthusiasm or latest interest. I was researching the book plate prints referred to in Chapter 2 and had just spent two days poring over many of these prints in book plate galleries, when a customer asked me to tell her about some book plate prints we had on hand in our gallery. You can imagine my pleasure in telling her about them.

Read books about prints and printmakers before you even think about collecting. There are many books about the history of printmaking and about the major periods of printmaking.

Learn about printing papers. Take time to go to your local offset printing company to learn the look and feel of the papers on which offset prints are printed. Learn to recognize cover stock, 80 pound and 100 pound coated and uncoated. Study the major 100% rag papers used by printmakers, such as Arches, Rives, and BFK. Spend half an hour at an art supply store to acquaint yourself with papers' surface characteristics, color, smooth or rough texture, and thickness. You also can see the watermarks by holding them up to the light.

Ask for a printmaker's résumé and *catalogue raisonne.* The latter is a list of his work assembled by a scholar, which pictures each and every print of a printmaker's body of work, giving the name, size, number of prints printed and by whom, and other particulars such as which permanent collection or museum collection the print is part of. There are also many checklists of printmakers' work and biographies available of major printmakers. A checklist is less formal than a book of an artist's prints, which is more superficial than a *catalogue raisonne.* The checklist is a compilation of the works available to the scholar; it is not necessarily a complete collection of the prints made by the artist. It usually includes biographical and anecdotal material about the prints and printmaker.

It does not take a lot of research to build up a feeling of a printmaker's style. Study a few books to help you pick up the major characteristics of a printmaker or school of prints.

Before I went to a major print auction where I knew *ukiyoe* prints would be sold, I read everything I could get from the library about Japanese

Watermark of German etching paper used by some printmakers.

prints. I made a list of the major artists and the characteristics I was interested in before I went and had a few cards with recent prices with me when I went to the preview before the auction. The auction went well for me because I knew what I wanted and how high I should bid to get what I wanted.

REASONS FOR COLLECTING PRINTS

To reiterate the advantages the acquiring of prints has for the average buyer:
• Print media can be treated in an infinite number of technical variations, so the collector can get involved with print media as well as the subject and/or the artist.
• Prints have a tactile quality that is very pleasurable, framed or unframed.
• Prints fascinate the viewer for many aesthetic reasons.
• Prints hold their value.
• Prints are universally available. For example, if you collect a certain subject or type of print you can look for them wherever you travel.
• Prints are inexpensive, if that is an important

factor, or expensive, if that is an option.
• Prints can be transported easily and inexpensively.
• Prints are "recyclable." They can be donated to charities such as hospitals, nursing homes, halfway houses, church fairs.

DETECTING FRAUD

> Secret: A collector carries a magnifying glass.

There is real danger that someone might try to sell you a fraud or copy when you start to collect. The easiest and most obvious way to detect a photographic reproduction is the pattern of a halftone dot screen. This looks, under a magnifying glass, something like the dot pattern seen in a color page from the Sunday comics.

Use a magnifying glass to look closely at the print under consideration for purchase. To do this properly, be sure to insist that the print be taken out of its frame and the mat lifted so you can examine the print on both the image side (recto) and the reverse side (verso). Ask yourself the following questions: What does the print paper look like under magnification: slick-surfaced or textured? thin, brownish? does it have holes?

Was it printed so that the surface of the print is dull? I will explain this with a story. My brother bought a print at an auction for $75 that looked, at first glance, like it could have been an original. Closer examination when the mat was lifted gave me two signs that is was an inexpensive copy of a lithograph. It was dull, not rich textured, and the signature was printed within the image itself, and was not made in pencil.

COLLECT ORIGINAL PRINTS, NOT REPRODUCTIONS

Since collectors want to sell their prints from time to time, it is imperative to recognize that only original prints have resale value. When selling to an art dealer, prints will only be sold at 50% of retail, but copies rarely resell at all.

Although the fundamentals of both print buying and collecting are the same, buy for aesthetic reasons; buy for pleasure; buy what appeals to you. If you collect wisely after doing reasonable research and comparisons and getting advice from print experts, you might end up with some good investments.

> Secret: Finding prints to collect takes effort.

Once again, we stress cultivating art professionals who can help you find prints and educate you on what is best to collect. The network between dealers is a small one easily accessed by telephone and overnight shippers.

However, the word gets around when a collector shops too many galleries. I recently made an inquiry for a prospective buyer and the reply was: "Oh, the man who wants Escher's such and such for a song. Not again!" You cannot play one print dealer against another as you can do with car dealers. Prints are rarer than cars and not marked up so wildly.

Besides letting dealers, gallery owners, private print and antique dealers, and auctioneers know your desires, advertise for prints on your own in the following places: small-town newspapers across your state, print journals and newsletters, and national art magazines, as well as in the Sunday *New York Times*.

Be prudent about trying to make fabulous finds of rare prints at auctions or in shops and antique stores, without getting a print dealer's advice. One of the country's best print dealer's reported to me that he faithfully shops art auctions nationally and makes less than one really great discovery a year.

> Secret: You don't need much money to collect original prints.

Being wealthy is usually equated with being a collector. This is just not at all true when it comes to prints. The most impressive print collections have been created on small budgets. Instead of buying a blouse or sweater, a print collector will at least put a deposit on a coveted print. In fact, a typical print collector would rather be in rags than

miss a print. The way some people get their jollies from a book or a special dinner, print collectors get a lift from acquiring a special print.

Let me give you some typical print prices to prove the point: a small wood engraving by WPA artist Herbert Waters—$75–$200; a silkscreen by Thomas McKnight—$1500–$2500; an etching by much-collected Philip Greenwood, who is a member of the Royal Academy and the Royal Society of Painters, Etchers and Engravers—$200–$350; cat prints by Dutch mezzotint artist, Joop Vegter—$125–$200; black and white lithographs of Cape Ann by Stowe Wengenroth—$300–$3500.

> Secret: Prints can be good investments.

My sister, an amateur antique dealer with a splendid eye, did find a Hokusai at a yard sale. She did not know who the artist was but only that the print was beautiful. She bought it for $10 and fortunately had a relationship with a sister (me) in the art business to sell it for her. I took it to the Fogg Museum for authentication and sold it a year later for $1500, which gave her a profit of $740 at 50% of retail, less 10%. If she had not such a close trust relationship to protect her, she might have been glad to sell it for $100. Cultivate your favorite art dealers if you want to traffic in prints.

COLLECT THE BEST

Especially if the prints you are buying are to be part of your collection, modest or expansive, be sure to buy the best. This is a core rule of collecting.

• Collect the most *typical* examples of a known printmaker's work (such as Jim Dine's clothing series).

• Collect prints that are technically *superb*, that are excellent examples of their medium.

• Collect the *rarest* examples of a printmaker's work, such as early or late prints that he made or "one ups," such as trial proofs and state proofs of a certain print.

• Collect the *best* examples of an unknown printmaker's work rather than inferior prints by a blue-chip printmaker. These might be inferior in print

From 1933–43, the Works Progress Administration (WPA), through the Federal Art Project, gave stipend payments to printmakers (and other artists) and in return stamped a percentage of their output, shown here in the lower left margin.

technique, in that they are not signed works, or in that the image is undistinguished.

• Collect the *best* example of the work of a period. For example, if you are collecting WPA prints, look for those bearing a WPA stamp.

• Collect the *best* prints from a place. If you are collecting white line woodcuts from Provincetown, find out who is considered the best white line woodcut artist and, if money allows, collect that printmaker and/or his colleagues and students.

• Collect the prints that appeal to you aesthetically. If there is a price difference between the prints in a body of work, be sure to buy the one you love the best, even if it is more or less expensive than the others. Remember—you will probably take your prints with you wherever you go for the next forty years, so a price difference of $100 should not dissuade you.

In your research in galleries, museums, and libraries, look for what is thought of as most typical of your chosen subject, artist, or period. Then discuss your possible choices with your favorite print dealers and print curators. Be sure always to use print professionals as scholarly springboards to sound out what they regard to be the best of the prints available to you.

> Secret: A high-priced print may not be the best work of a gallery or the best print made by the artist.

There are many reasons for a high price tag. Sometimes it is related to the number of hours an artist has spent making a print. If an artist has put seventy layers of screening onto a silkscreen rather than creating with the average ten passes, the print will cost more but this does not necessarily mean that this print will be the best print the artist has made!

Nor does a high price tag signify that this print or printmaker is the best or should even be bought. Sometimes a high price is put on a print quite arbitrarily by the artist for sentimental reasons.

A high price tag on a print or on a printmaker's

work may mean only that the work is expensively published rather than being printed by the printmaker. It can also mean that the prints and printmaker are being marketed in an expensive ad and publicity campaign in costly art magazines, by direct mail, and through brochures and telemarketing.

Secret: Try telephone shopping for prints for your collection.

Find out which galleries handle the types of print you collect. Let the gallery people know your collection needs and your budget. They will notify you when they locate prints for you and even send them to you on approval if you send a credit card number or check for them to hold while you look at the prints and take them to a print curator for approval. To locate a New York gallery carrying printmakers you collect, call the Art Information Center at (212) 227-0282. This is a non-profit service through which I have located many prints by major and minor printmakers.

SECURE YOUR PRINTS AGAINST THEFT

Security is no longer the concern of musuems and galleries alone. Nearly 500 lithographs and etchings worth several hundred thousand dollars were stolen from the New York studio of the late Raphael Soyer by thieves who broke through the medicine chest of a vacant apartment. Some time later, the prints had still not been recovered. I was aware of the gallery that had bought Soyer's estate, so when a man offered us a show of Soyer's vintage prints, I questioned their background.

My main point here is that you should keep a low profile in order to avoid becoming a victim of print theft. Privacy, which Soyer did not maintain, cannot be overrated as a security measure. If you want the spotlight as an astute collector, you cannot guarantee security.

The International Foundation for Art Research, a nonprofit service organization, helps people recover stolen art and authenticate possible purchases. They can be reached at (212) 879-1780.

The Foundation makes the following recommendations to print buyers regarding security:
• Resist the temptation to impress strangers with your print purchases.
• Document your print collection with photos or on a video as well as on a computer.
• When you lend to an exhibition, do so anonymously.
• Don't display your art near your front windows.
• When you travel, replace fine prints with reproductions.

TAKE A TAX DEDUCTION

You can keep your print collection and enjoy it for the rest of your life and still take a tax deduction by arranging to make it a gift to be given to a designated museum or library at the time of your death or at the time you have chosen. However, the tax deduction can be for only the amount you paid for the prints, not what they will eventually be worth, according to the IRS.

LETTER FROM A PRINT COLLECTOR

Just imagine the grand sweep of the legendary British landscape, from the craggy mountains of Scotland to the rolling English vales, from the rugged Welsh coastline to the gentle patchwork of the Cotswolds, the air thick with the drowsy buzz of summer, rent by storms, or stuffed with snow— all of this, remember, distilled now, concentrated, and brought to new life on a small boxwood block from which an artist has pulled an exquisite black and white print that captures the essence of that enthralling countryside.

That's why I'm fascinated by wood engravings, and why I collect them, for those unique and magical properties. Like many collectors I collect in a single area, but in depth and with a narrow focus — my collection is of wood engravings only, made in the 20th century, by British artists, of the British landscape, in black and white. While this may sound very restrictive and exclusive I don't find it so at all. The range of artistic expression is very broad, encompassing meticulous topographical depictions and muscular angular abstractions, but all created with remarkable skill and masterful con-trol of this age-old, demanding, and unforgiving medium, which requires uncommon dedication and perseverance. Wood engravings are, by their very nature, relatively inexpensive and small in scale—the largest in my collection is 8″ × 10″, the smallest is just an inch square. This preciousness of scale, however, does not diminish their power, or curtail their variety, or dilute the endless pure pleasure that they give me.

Anthony Jones

INVESTING
Selecting Prints for Investment
12

John tried to become a print investor after he read a magazine article describing the large profits people made buying original prints by name artists. The article told how prices of Chagall and Miro prints had tripled since the 1950s. When John was in Hawaii, he went into a print gallery and asked about the artists he had read about. He was shown a number of prints in elaborate frames, which were described as originals. To support that, the gallery person explained that each print was sold with a certificate of authenticity and the prints cost between $500 and $900, not as much as the article had indicated.

John bought four of these and later a few more from a limited editions print club—a mail order business that offered "investment" prints.

A few years later, when John found himself in financial difficulties, he asked an auction firm to sell his print collection. He was angry and insulted when they found his prints unsuitable for sale at a print auction because they were reproductions and re-strikes.

In truth, John was neither an investor nor even an astute buyer of art. Since many buyers consider themselves collectors, we shall start this chapter by making the distinction between a print collector and an investor.

Caught up in the hoopla of record-breaking auction prices, many would-be investors are looking at art with dollar signs dancing before their eyes. But for most would-be investors, investing in contemporary prints is a poor bet. Art experts say that the heralded art boom is taking place almost exclusively at the highest end of the market. Recognized masterpieces, not mid-range prints,

are what will appreciate in value. Investors with $100,000 to spend are often priced out of the market most likely to appreciate—old masters and the work of perhaps twenty living artists, such as Jasper Johns and Richard Diebenkorn. These investors therefore buy prints because they are told that they will appreciate in value.

A study reported in *The Wall Street Journal* quoted the findings of a Stanford University law student, who studied every contemporary art auction held at the major auction houses between 1973 and 1978. His conclusion was that less than 0.01% of contemporary art has resale value.

INVESTMENT PRINTS DEFINED

> Secret: When investing in prints, buy quality and rarity.

Investment prints are those that can be sold for a profit on what is called the *secondary market*. This cannot be done as often as many print dealers would have their buyers and collectors believe. I have heard so many dealers speculating about the skyrocketing prices of an elderly or ill printmaker's work, predicated, of course, on their rarity and scarcity, only to see the prints fade into relative obscurity within two years of the artist's death. There ought to be a documented active market for a print to be considered "investment quality." And dealers have to be interested in buying and selling the work. If you buy a print that has no resale value, it is not an investment but a purchase made because you are a collector, and you love the print and must have it.

PITFALLS OF PRINT INVESTING

> Secret: There is no resale market for most contemporary prints.

The situation has worsened over the past decade. The best galleries at least will offer to sell a print on consignment for you. Or they will offer what you paid for a print that they respect and can resell, or offer it at auction against something else they have for sale. How do you tell the difference between a good gallery and one that may try to take you to the cleaners?

> Secret: The more the gallery person talks about investment value, the more wary you should be.

Many investors have only themselves to blame. They call galleries with the question: "Who's new and hot?" Another question that is a heartbreaker for the honest print dealer: "How much do you think it will go for in five years?" I answer this question with a flat-voiced, "Not a cent more than you are paying for it, maybe even less."

PRINT FADS COME AND GO

To be a true investment, a print has to appreciate in value. You can document trends by checking auction prices of work sold in the past five years. The appreciation of artworks is a function of market activity, rarity, and fashion. There are boom-and-bust cycles. An artist's work can hit a peak of fashion one year and just a few years later be virtually forgotten.

What about "limited editions"? We often hear or read about active promotions of prints with a special, low "pre-publication" price. But the print-maker is neither recognized nationally, nor bought by museums or city and university libraries. Sooner, rather than later, the market will become satiated and the resale market for the prints will collapse. If you subscribe to one of these limited editions, do so because the print appeals to you and not to make an investment.

WHEN INVESTING IN PRINTS, SPECIALIZE

> Secret: Not all works of major printmakers appreciate in value.

I recently heard that two prints in the estate of Blanche Lazell, the leader of the Provincetown white line woodcut printmakers, were sold privately for quadruple their asking price of $600. When her heirs were paid much more than they expected, they had the rest of the Lazell woodcuts in the estate reappraised by Frank Hogan, the national expert on white line woodcuts. The price of only one other woodcut in the entire estate was changed.

Wood engraver Rockwell Kent's Self Portrait *today is not considered an investment print because there is no pencil signature and no numbered edition. However, in the future, due to an ever diminishing supply of Kent's work in the marketplace, it might hold or even increase in value.*

We bought this unsigned etching by John Marin from an antique shop for $25. Recently the print was advertised as available to the print public for $1500.

An important rule in buying for investment is to specialize as soon as possible. The art field—especially the print field—is so broad that it becomes very hard for an individual to be an expert in all aspects.

If you are particularly fond of black and white lithographs, for instance, learn all you can about artists, past and present, who have become recognized in that field. Libraries and auction catalogs are excellent sources of information. The more often an artist's name comes up, the more likely his work may be of lasting quality.

> Secret: Develop a sharp eye for investment buys.

As you specialize and increase your knowledge of the prints that interest you most, you will be able to recognize at a glance the style of your favorite printmakers, even before you read the signature.

You can discover bargains in places you least expect, such as antique shops or when traveling to foreign countries where the artist is less well known. Whenever I go to England, I haunt old print shops to see if I can uncover prints by American artists with whom I am familiar.

> Secret: Buy good prints of lesser known artists, rather than poor quality prints of known artists.

Avoid frauds, re-strikes, or copies of well-known artists' work. There are many great print-makers who are relatively unknown, whom you can research and discover and collect for a fraction of the cost of a known artist's work.

SELLING INVESTMENT PRINTS

> Secret: When investors want to sell, it can be difficult to sell at any price.

The best way to sell a valuable print is through an auction house. You do not have to have a whole collection of prints in order to sell at an auction house. If you only have one or two good prints to sell, the auction house may elect to hold them to be included with other prints from other sellers at a future date. One auction house we use has regular print sales twice a year. These are attended primarily by dealers but also by individual investors who noted a specific printmaker's name in the catalog.

Do not be afraid that your print will be sold at too low a price. The auction house will let you put a *reserve bid* on your print to protect it. A reserve bid means that you and the auction house agree upon a minimum price below which your print cannot be sold. Be aware that the auction house takes a commission, usually 10%, from both the buyer and the seller.

You can also try to sell your print independently by placing ads in art magazines, newsletters, or widely read newspapers. Generally, this works best if the work you are selling is by a well-known artist who currently enjoys an active market.

From an investment standpoint there are a few realities to recognize when you buy prints. Sometimes you *can't* get back what you paid for a print, unless you bought it from a well established gallery who will gain by standing behind a sale, and may take it as credit toward another purchase. If this happens, you can give the print to charity.

> Secrets: Prints as investments are unpredictable. When in doubt, buy for beauty.

• Prints are not difficult to resell. But if sold at auction or to art dealers, you must be ready to accept the wholesale price of the current market value of the print, since the dealers must be able to turn a reasonable profit when they sell at retail. Wholesale price is generally 50% of retail.

• You can check current auction prices of prints in several periodicals, for example, *Gordon's Prints Price Annual—Int'l.*

• There are fashions and cycles of interest in the print world. There are also periods when particular printmakers are totally forgotten.

• Market activity of a printmaker's work will send prices up. This can be carefully and artificially contrived, through ads, reviews, and gallery exhibitions, to sell the work more effectively.

• "Holding" prints is a smart move if you have something good, but you should only do this with the guidance of a reliable print authority. Years ago a prominent print dealer told me that he put his best prints in a bank vault where they would increase in value until he needed to cash in on them. Today he sells these same prints by telephone from his home. If you are merely following a trend, be careful, the price may fall. Your best guide in this is a knowledgeable gallery person or curator.

• Beware of commercial print sensations. These are often artificially created print fads and can be recognized by their *pre-publication* media coverage. Resist pressure to buy within a limited time —"get it now while the price is low...the price *will* go up..."

• Investors sell profitably internationally as well. They sell wherever money is strong. Ben Shahn's signed prints are collected today by many Japanese buyers. While it is often difficult to sell a Shahn print in the United States today, they sell for at least $1000 to $2000 in Japan.

PROFILE OF A COLLECTOR

Paul is an intermediate collector. He has always bought what he likes and rarely concentrates on one artist or type of art, but he has the eye of a true connoisseur. He seems to have known intuitively exactly what art would increase in value. He also has had a way of gleaning guidance from print and painting dealers over the years.

Recently, when he wanted funds to buy a new boat, he offered several Dubuffet paintings and prints for sale along with two George Grosz prints. He was very fond of these artworks but had enjoyed them thoroughly for almost thirty years and was glad to sell them at auction.

CORPORATIONS
How to Buy Prints for Offices
13

Dear Joan and Mary:

While you were choosing work for the hospital examining rooms, I was a coward about steering you away from just matching colors into a freer mode of choosing what you and the patients would like. I was impressed that you made the decision to select original prints, not posters for the doctors' building.

Inasmuch as your intention in this art installation was not to buy art as a corporate collection or as a corporate investment, but rather as decoration and to add warmth to those sterile rooms, I realized that you stumbled into the *House Beautiful Syndrome*, which has two dangerous parts: (a) the *blandly matching hazard*, which ends up looking more sterile and institutional than you want; (b) the *rigid color coordination hazard*, which paralyzes each decision.

My thoughts about this go beyond my task as art consultant; it is at base my own protest against the homogenization of environments that has been the dictum of the more commercial end of the art industry.

I am happy to note that the home decorating magazines of late have been praising the English country, casual, spontaneous, and personal look when buying art. That is what I would ask you to consider before you search for more art for your hospital. There are so many constraints when choosing prints for any commercial installation: budget, size, mood.

Should your colors be rigidly coordinated? Just as your gray suit was sparked by your red blouse, art can be sprinkled with color and as long as the spirit of a piece captures you and a bit of coordi-

nating color is there and the size and price are right, don't be afraid of color.

Hospital art consultants I work with suggest deliberately interjecting pieces that are not color coordinated to spice up environments. Remember, the rust chairs will be covered up by clothes and people, 99% of the time! Why then be so tied to matching them in every picture you buy for those rooms?

Instead, why not proceed as you did when you bought those rich, colorful watercolors for the halls? The warm colors of those large flowers do not match the taupes and jade greens in the reception areas. Intuitively, you chose complementary colors—the hues that are across from each other on the color wheel, and those dramatize each other just as the Christmas colors of green and red do.

Good luck arranging the prints. Let me know if I can help you find an appropriate source to direct their installation.

WHY BUY PRINTS FOR YOUR BUSINESS?

The impetus to buy prints for your business strikes in different ways. It may happen as it did to the president of Parker Brothers, who looked out of his office window at a flock of geese flying in formation against the tree-lined twilight sky and said, "We should buy sporting prints for the blue walls of the board room." Or, as you are passing an attractive window in an art gallery, you might run in to make an appointment, as the president of a small consulting firm did after his company ex-

Art on paper enhances this waiting area. Photo by John Garaventa.

panded into a new, large space which seemed sterile without pictures. Or maybe your architect will prod you to decorate the walls of your snappy new lobby and conference rooms. Buying original and limited editions prints for offices is an economical morale-building factor for a company and makes a positive statement about your company to the public.

The earliest record of corporate art buying in America is the Atchison, Topeka and Santa Fe Railway, which bought hundreds of works depicting the people and lands of the West. Art was bought by only a few American companies prior to 1940 and only arbitrarily at the whim of the

president of the firm, usually as advertising. During the 1930s, IBM and Container Corporation of America bought contemporary American prints, as well as paintings, which were used in their advertising campaigns and in their corporate headquarters. Nabisco bought Victorian prints of children eating biscuits.

I remember, as a graduate student during the late 1940s, reading *Time* magazine and noticing Container Corporation ads that were full-page reproductions of contemporary artists' work. These were impressive because they were totally different from any other ads and conveyed the innovative, dynamic, and creative style of the advertiser. Container Corporation's CEO, Walter Paepcke, bought Bauhaus art and used it to promote their image as superior designers of box containers. I was so impressed, I went so far as to apply for a job with them.

> Secret: Corporate art is a means of communicating a corporate image to clients and the public, as well as a way of giving employees a more pleasant workplace.

Studies show that 98% of corporate art purchases are not made as investments. The 2% that buys art as investments are primarily banks and brokerage houses, which admit that investment figures prominently in art selections. After World War II, the corporate building boom and competition between new firms led to art being bought for status and display in lobbies, atriums, and gardens for the first time.

During the 1950s, David Rockefeller, as CEO of Chase Manhattan Bank, bought twenty works of art to decorate offices. Chase Manhattan's collection now includes more than 12,000 paintings and prints, with many sound investments among them.

> Secret: Since 1960, 80% of corporate collections include prints.

The major explosion of corporate art buying happened during the 1960s. Prior to that, if art was bought it was to reinforce upper class male interests. In the male corporate settings of banks and law firms, conservative prints and nautical scenes predominated. High corporate profits and the office construction boom in the '60s triggered much more art buying. Today in the United States, there are more than 1200 corporate collections. Analyzing these purchases in her book *Corporate Art*, sociologist Rosanne Mortella gives us the following statistics:
• 90% of the collections were formed since World War II
• 80% of collections since 1960 include prints
• 60% of corporate collections are Fortune 500

Photo of framed prints from collection of Bank of Boston, Boston, Mass. Hung on walls of executive dining room.

A training center. Collagraph by Lucy Mueller White. Photo by Cliff Keeney.

companies now holding $2 billion worth of art
• 15% of the 1200 corporations have more than 25,000 works of art
• 40% have fewer than 300 pieces

WHERE TO BEGIN

The following decisions and actions will expedite your company's art buying.

1. Establish internally that someone has to be appointed who has the power to make the informed decision that money can be spent on art. Most companies spend $3000 to $5000 on a lobby and one conference room. A handy device is to allocate 1% of the year's gross income to art purchases.

2. Create a two or three person art committee with the power and dollars to make art selections. Give them a goal or a date when you want the art to be in place. They should have authority that is final, which cannot be overruled when the art is found. For example, the committee could be made up of the president and architect; facilities person and vice president; two or three staff members with a great interest in art; or any mixture of the above.

3. Decide on the type of artwork that best conveys your company's image. Will it be avant garde? Will it be regional? Will it be decorative? One chairman of an art committee articulated his committee's decorative goal: "We want our training center to be comfortable. The art should look like art found in someone's home—pleasant and fitting the decor."

4. Decide on a time frame for the project.

(a) To buy art in one fell swoop, in order to decorate the whole company. If you choose this method, I suggest thinking about which are your primary spaces, such as your lobby or conference rooms. Your secondary sites, such as halls, dining areas, and private offices might be reserved for less expensive works to boost employee morale. Companies usually buy at least one piece for every permanent employee's office, and allow employees to choose these pieces themselves, in many instances, from screened selections of the art committee.

(b) To buy selectively over a longer period of time. Ask your art person to develop a master plan of art purchasing for your company. If you choose the master plan, develop a direction you want your art to take. You could purchase your art over a long period of time, say, three to five years. The result of this effort might be called your "firm's collection," which might be accompanied by a folder, including your artists' biographies and personal statements.

5. Interview art gallery people and consultants. Ask your three or four best sources for a written proposal and a visual presentation, half an hour long. Give the people floor plans, rug and upholstery samples, a theme.

6. When you select your art source, work out a

contract articulating payment schedules; providing a down payment of one-fourth the budget, which should be given them upon signing the contract; providing an upset amount to them if the contract is terminated.

Valuable pieces of artwork make up only 5% of most corporate collections and are usually found in main lobby areas and board rooms. Posters and reproductions are used to decorate and enliven informal areas inexpensively. Original prints are bought for other locations for the following reasons:

• Prints are available and inexpensive. There are many name printmakers in your region whom you can support. You can also purchase prints by well-known contemporary artist printmakers, without spending as much as you would for a painting by the same artist.

• Prints can be as innovative as paintings. There is an infinite number of new combinations of prints and their media: photographs and lithography; paintings combined with printmaking; woodcuts with varnishes and metallic finishes on some layers.

• The marriage of papers and inks in printmaking gives a fresh, crisp impression suitable to up and coming corporate images.

> Secret: Prints meet a real need.

Is art important? Large and small firms throughout the United States bear witness that it is. It is evident that lawyers, doctors, and accountants, as well as insurance companies and restaurants, find that art serves unique vital functions: providing a unifying element; as a source of conversation; as a source of pride to those who chose it; as a visible statement about the self-image of the firm; as a humanizing element.

HUMANIZING THE ENVIRONMENT

Original art in hospitals and medical facilities is being used across the country as a means of offering patients and family members diversion from trauma, pain, and boredom.

Etching by Margaret Santanillo Corbeil, Poppies. *Photo by Cliff Keeney.*

Purchasing original prints by regional artists has proven an economical way for institutions to acquire interesting and meaningful artwork for hallways, waiting rooms, public spaces, and patient rooms. Many hospitals today are very conscious of their need to develop programs that demonstrate a vital interaction with the local community.

A material review of hospital art programs indicates that large medical centers such as the University of Iowa Hospital, Baystate Medical Center — University of Massachusetts in Worchester, and Duke Medical Center are implementing extensive gallery programs that offer local artists exhibition and sales opportunities. The addition of lively visual arts components in health care institutions seems to be having a very positive impact on the well-being of patients, visitors, and staff.

> Secret: Buy prints to create a suitable atmosphere for your offices.

Careful selection of prints can result in just the atmosphere you feel is appropriate for your corporate setting. What image do you want to project with your art?

Stability. Some law firms have collections of nautical prints, which they have acquired gradually since the early 1900s, implying substance and the reliability of the firm.

Glitz and glitter. Many oil firms, hotels, and restaurants choose this goal. Many law firms have eclectic avant garde prints, collected since the 1950s. This type of collection suggests a sharp, energetic business.

Established. Collecting older master prints suggests well-established firms. Buy these if you want to appear settled.

International. Avant garde print collections from European and American blue-chip printmakers/artists are bought for the corporate headquarters of many international firms.

Educated cultivation. Some companies acquire rare etchings from the 1920s and other master prints to create a refined and educated atmosphere, which adds distinction and depth to a new corporation's image.

Strength. A few strong pieces, carefully selected, subtly represent your company's stability.

Timeliness. Dynamism, humor, and sophistication are goals that companies have sought to project, by means of their buying strategies.

Quality. Quality prints project a quality company.

Creative and outrageous. Innovative, challenging prints suggest a company open to new ideas.

Soothing and tranquil. Artwork that is soothing, positive, and reassuring in subject and style has a vital role in health care institutions as well as public spaces in corporations.

Secret: Prints in offices lead to a sense of pride.

Another important reason for buying prints is the internal morale boost art gives. Clerks, secretaries, and staff will roll your artists' names out like company mascots. After I hung my three-piece handmade paper tapestries at a local law

Photo of doctor's office showing silkscreen prints by Malcolm Warr.

firm, their switchboard operator greeted me when I called with, "Oh, yes, how I enjoy your *Sun Up, Moon Down.*" Your prints will be a source of discussion around which your colleagues will unify in emotional reactions, causing people to react with pride, and to interact with each other in relation to the art. It can be a catalyst for staff pulling together.

COLORS AFFECT THE WORK ENVIRONMENT

When choosing prints as decorations, architects and interior designers can work with art professionals to find prints that produce the type of working envelope that corporate management envisions. They can pick prints in colors that have been documented to energize or soothe employees and visitors. There is psychological agreement on why people pick certain colors: purples and ultramarine blue are regal colors; yellows and greens cheer people up, and grayed colors, such as celadon green, dove gray, and mauve, soothe.

If you need to create an environment that provides shelter from the bombardment of city stimuli, pick prints that are printed in soft tints. Often, but not necessarily, paler colors are correlated with peaceful subjects and primary colors with stimulating images.

HOW TO SELECT PRINTS FOR YOUR OFFICE

Secret: Delegate print selection to a small committee rather than letting everyone vote.

An inherent problem with the print selection process is the hazards of getting too many opinions about the art and then buying nothing. I have worked these ways with firms:

The first is to work with a two or three person committee that has spent hours scouting for the perfect work of art to complement their board room; and although they consult their colleagues, the committee makes the final decision to buy or pass. I respect this method. It helps to have a team that works out the vision they set out to achieve.

Another way is to choose to be completely democratic about selecting art. This is the hardest strategy. A law firm of thirty people used this democratic method. Many pieces were brought into the conference room. Everyone in the firm voted on them by order of preference. I left after the fourth hour of voting!

Many different people can be appointed to be on committees for companies. Presidents often enjoy the role of being an art committee of one; company executives, managers, and vice presidents choose art, as well as architects, interior designers, and facilities people. Each of these different groups will bring different outlooks to the selection process.

It can be an awkward responsibility for anyone delegated to a committee because (1) company executives might vacillate about money and choices without clear direction from the CEO during the purchasing process; (2) they often are told to look into buying art and then told to cancel, due to withdrawal of funds, leaving the art dealer wondering what happened, and after offending artists they have galvanized for a project; (3) they sometimes see the art dealer and art consultant as interfering and a threat. Often times an art consultant or art dealer cannot work very creatively because of the lack of direct contact with the person who has complete authority to buy. Since the committee members who conduct the search do not determine the budget, they should be empowered to increase it, should the need arise.

A hospital in Lewiston, Maine requested some posters for their lobby, but when I spoke with them I realized that the three person selection committee was composed of the chief executive officers, all MBAs. In place of the posters, I brought them some of our most striking prints, and on the spot they elected to increase their budget and bought many beautiful original prints.

WHERE TO GET YOUR PRINTS

Secret: Galleries are not the only places to find original prints.

Let's review the sources of prints discussed earlier, and consider them from the corporate point of view.

Art studios and art schools. These are wonderful places to choose art if you make an appointment with the artist. The advantage of working directly with artists is that there is less markup in price.

Art associations. These are excellent sources of regional artists who might not be represented in galleries but might be valuable sources of local talent, which your company will be proud to sponsor and present to the public.

Art consultants. These are creative individuals whose career is to be art brokers. They will find art for your firm through a myriad of sources, sometimes nationwide. Some have a visual inventory on computer. Some space and interior designers are art consultants paid by the hour or by a markup on the art, which comes from galleries and artists. They sometimes work out very competitive monetary schemes in order to get the job. They can get art from diverse sources to you, making them worthy of the price. Many gallery owners also act as art consultants, finding artists for your firm from other galleries and artists' associations.

Art dealers. These are the artistic community's gatekeepers. They are dedicated professionals, sometimes self taught, often graduates with art administration degrees. Almost always they are idealistic and hard-working people who have done the legwork of finding printmakers whose work they showcase in their galleries. Each gallery has a stable of particular finds: some have completely regional printmakers; some carry only artist printmakers who are internationally collected; some carry master prints from the 16th century on; some carry American vintage lithographs and wood engravings from the '30s and '40s; some carry limited edition prints which are reproductions of artists' paintings, as well as original prints.

Galleries carrying noted artist printmakers are sometimes supplied by the publishers of their prints. It is usual in the art industry that when the work of well-known printmakers is sold to the gallery, rather than consigned, it means that work is more urgently pushed than prints of less recognized printmakers. Today it is also becoming usual for printmakers to select one gallery exclusively as their representative and distributor to other galleries. I recommend that you check to see if the prints are consigned to the gallery or not.

Types of Galleries

The following are some types of galleries to consider visiting when planning a corporate art purchase.

Formal galleries are often in large cities. They are paid by their commissions, not by the hour, and they do not have to be as expensive as you might think. They represent many artists. Most galleries specialize in certain artistic media: old or new, paintings, drawings, prints, photography, or sculpture. Their thrust can be contemporary or classic, decorative or innovative, figurative, abstract, minimal, or a combination.

Informal galleries can be found in seaside and resort areas as well as small towns. They often show regional printmakers and sometimes carry international, contemporary, and avant garde prints.

Cooperative galleries carry several printmakers, who pay the rent and maintain the gallery.

Mall shops frequently have posters, limited edition prints and original prints, mainly decorative, bought from many sources.

Frame shops may offer a few artists' works, reflecting the taste and the framing virtuosity of the proprietor.

WORKING WITH ART CONSULTANTS AND ART DEALERS

> Secret: Ask for written proposals from two or three galleries.

Before making print selections, talk with art professionals. If you have a working relationship with a gallery, and their prices and types of prints seem right for your firm, make an appointment to go to the gallery and do preliminary shopping. Then ask if a gallery representative can come to see your building. At this point, it is appropriate to request a written proposal from two or three art sources. Gallery owners may talk to each other and often collaborate because each gallery carries specialized art.

Here are a few suggestions about working with art professionals:

Don't call every gallery or art consultant in the city to compete against one another for one wall. One painful memory I have is of an empowered vice president who visited many galleries and picked six items to be hand delivered by each gallery, on approval, never mentioning that the items were for one small wall over a credenza. Four galleries were all called in after business hours and all resented this imposition on their time. Art professionals are small-business people, usually making great efforts to stay afloat.

Articulate your budget. Although art professionals know that budgets are subject to change, ask them what they recommend from their experience. Be frank about your constraints and flexibilities. Be aware that a gallery owner's dream is of helping a business buy good art because there can be years of good referrals and follow-up sales. But this should not be abused, such as asking the gallery to deliver artwork on an approval basis at 8 p.m. Be kind to your art professionals. Don't ask extra favors from them any more than you would other specialists from small companies.

Galleries don't deliver and supervise hanging their art, unless this is part of the contract. These services are all negotiable. It is a gallery's prerogative to deliver art or install it. Most companies hire art packers and art installers at a per hour price; art shipper charges are by the piece, according to destination.

It is fair for a gallery or consultant to ask for modest payment per hour ($25 to $50) from door to door when they are asked to make a proposal. Ideally, they appreciate a commitment to buy before coming to appraise the needs of your firm and creating a master plan for your art acquisitions. In a competitive situation, galleries and consultants will look at a space and make a proposal on speculation.

Enjoy the process of selecting prints for your spaces. The best teams I have watched picking art for conference rooms relaxed and fell in love with the works of several artists and focused on them as collectors, choosing the frames to fit the work, not the other furniture in the room. In one case, it was selecting a group of small country vignettes by an accomplished printmaker from the Cotswolds and framing them in gold frames, rather than using the mahogany of their bank's conference table and woodwork.

PROTECTING YOUR CORPORATE PRINT COLLECTION

There are problems that corporate collectors can avoid as a way of protecting their prints. After choosing a reputable dealer and selecting works of art, the corporate art buyer should make sure that the art is properly housed. Select the proper environment, and oversee curatorially correct matting, framing, and installation including the provision of security hangers.

GALLERIES SHOULD PROVIDE BACKGROUND MATERIAL ABOUT THE CORPORATE COLLECTION

Art professionals enjoy assembling biographies and artists' statements for firms. Sometimes college interns in galleries will provide this service as part of their art history studies. These statements become part of your public relations effort. Some firms produce elaborate brochures and flyers; others make videos; and many use wall labels. The *Reader's Digest* video, for instance, shows how their Impressionist painting collection was part of the founders' vision.

When you meet with an art consultant or gallery person, I recommend keeping in mind that art is communication, as well as decoration. The danger of buying art for specific spaces is that one gets color and shape specific, and the prints will be looked at as commodities, rather than the product of many hours of skilled, labor-intensive work by an artist who is trying to say something to you.

The First Bank of Minneapolis has an art collection unlike any collection amassed by any other

American bank. It is the brainchild of its former president, who collected art that would provoke discussion among his employees. I watched a video entitled "Talk Back" about how the First Bank's art collection struck their employees who were allowed to choose art they like the most and hated the most. There were many debates shown about their art collection. These conversations about art were designed to be nonthreatening forums for employees. I was impressed at the sensitivity of the interviewees' reactions to the art. The collection definitely was not seen as merely decorative or wallpaper, as other corporate collections are, by employees.

CORPORATIONS AS ART PATRONS

Professionals in the art field help artists get their work into the public view. Corporations are now the most important art patrons. Between 1974 and 1987, while museums have been retrenching, $15 million have been spent annually by businesses whose outspoken goals are humanizing and decorating new buildings, and making a show of power and riches. Fifty percent of art sold in New York City is sold to corporations; 70% of art sold in Seattle is to corporations; 20% to 30% of the yearly national art market is corporate purchases.

The unintended result of this patronage is that corporations have become art centers. Many have university-trained art administrators and curators on staff or pay for curatorial services from a local museum. Safety and care of artwork are carefully monitored; art is rotated, cleaned, and preserved by these professionals. The curator also may be responsible for selling or donating the artwork if the corporate decor changes, the firm moves, or the corporate leadership changes.

Many corporations, institutions, and hospitals have gallery spaces to show nationally known artists or artists from the community. Such a space might be a large formal gallery, such as that of Xerox® or IBM, or a hall or lobby space designated as a gallery. The curator may arrange special visual exhibits along with poetry readings, concerts, and the like, which enhance the corporate image publicly.

Massachusetts Chamber of Commerce reception area. Etchings by Margaret Santanillo Corbeil, Tulips. Photo by Cliff Keeney.

Secret: Consult museum print curators, when considering expensive prints as investments.

Museum print curators can give you safe advice about the true long-term quality of prints. It is tough to sort out all the marketing hoopla alone. Never buy impulsively for corporate investment at an art fair. Ask for the *catalogues raisonne* and museum affiliations of printmakers, dealers, and consultants who are claiming investment potential.

A CORPORATE ART-BUYING SUCCESS STORY

"The Chase Manhattan Bank art collection has benefited our corporation in many ways. Our acquisitions demonstrate our ongoing commitment to gaining knowledge of the many cultures in which we do business; the thinking processes of our employees are stimulated by the influence of art within their work environment, sometimes directly, sometimes subtly; our emphasis on contemporary art underscores our responsiveness to the present and our commitment to the future.

"We believe the collection is clear evidence that the Chase Bank is very much a part of the world in which it exists. The sense that art is something to be used, loved, understood, integrated into our everyday work lives—not revered as something beyond our grasp—is one of the real advantages in living with it as we do. By relating to art as an integral element of our work place Chase people have come to gain respect for the

creativity, the thinking, the imagination, and, indeed, the hard work that artistry requires.

"When I succeeded David Rockefeller as Chairman of the Chase Manhattan Art Committee, I asked the members of senior management to express their views as to the future direction of the art program. It is perhaps no real surprise that two themes dominated their responses: first, that we should reaffirm our commitment to the continued vitality of the program itself; and second, that quality should be the watchword underlying and driving that commitment.

Willard C. Butcher
Chairman, Art Committee
Chase Manhattan Bank

DOCUMENTING

How to Keep Track of Your Prints and Insure Them

14

Since Ken makes his living creating computer applications programs, it was only natural for him to look at the interaction of buying original prints and the computer. He contributed the following section.

Although we have never felt that a computer was the appropriate tool for many household tasks like balancing a checkbook, the wealth of data associated with our print collecting seemed to cry out for organization.

If your collecting style gravitates toward a relatively few major acquisitions, the record-keeping requirements can be satisfied by well-conceived notations on index cards, together with careful maintenance of receipts. In fact, an index card system can serve most basic needs.

But, if we were content to have only what we *need*, as opposed to what we would like to have, we would not be buying so many prints, would we?

Because I am in the computer software field, I experimented with several available commercial data base and/or flat-file manager programs including *dBase III +* from Ashton–Tate, *Reflex* from Borland International, and *Q&A* from Symantec.

dBase is probably overkill for a cataloging and reference system and is certainly the most difficult of the three for a novice to use. It is also the most expensive, by a wide margin. *Reflex* is well suited to the task, and is the least expensive. However, I found *Q&A* to be the program of choice. It is easy and intuitive to use; allows comprehensive reporting; and its "Intelligent Assistant" functions are not only useful but a lot of fun to use. I won't attempt to detail the operation of these capabilities, but I can, for example, type into the computer:

"List all the serigraphs bought in Santa Fe in 1988" No formulas, no arcane code words, the entry is made just as it appears above, and the computer quickly prints out the data.

We record all of the pertinent data about each piece, including artist, title, medium, size, edition date, place of purchase, purchase price, current valuation, framing status, etc. As with any good data base, any piece of information that might conceivably be used to extract data is kept in its own data field. For example, although we could have a "size" field that recorded height and width, like $18'' \times 14''$, by splitting the size data into *separate* height and width fields, we can extract all items more than $12''$ high, for example. Unless we were especially rigorous in always using the convention *height* $\times$ *width* in a combined data field, we couldn't extract the data as easily.

We use a simple sequential accession number, like 88–13. That indicates the thirteenth piece acquired in 1988. The program prints an acquisition label of the form:

> From the collection of Ken & Cindy Y.
> Acquisition # 88–13   Date Acq'd: 02/12/88
> Framed: 03/22/88   Frame: N72 FR SIL
> Mat: I8559   M   O8526

Obviously, not all data are applicable to each piece. The framing data tells us that it is a Nielsen N72 profile in Frosted Silver, that the inner mat is a number 8559 (Alphamat), there is no middle mat, and the outer mat is an 8526. This information is a real timesaver when you have finally achieved just the right combination in framing a piece and

TYLER GRAPHICS LTD.
250 Kisco Avenue
Mount Kisco, New York 10549
914-241-2707
914-241-7756 FAX

PRINT DOCUMENTATION:

ARTIST: *John Newman*

TITLE: *Twist in Turn*
YEAR OF PUBLICATION: *1990*
MEDIUM: *Lithograph*
DIMENSIONS: *46" x 40 3/4" (116.8 cm. x 103.5 cm.)*
EDITION: *30*
PROOFS:
PAPER: *white Rives BFK, mould-made*

PRINTERS:

Prep work for continuous-tone lithography by Kenneth Tyler; plate and stone preparation and processing by Tyler; proofing by Tyler and Lee Funderburg; edition printing by Tyler assisted by Paul Stillpass and John Hutcheson

SIGNED:

signed John A. Newman and dated in pencil lower right; numbered lower left; chop mark lower right; workshop number JN89-991 lower left verso

DESCRIPTION:

An original 2 color lithograph printed from 1 stone and 1 aluminum plate. Black was printed from the stone and transparent gray was printed from the aluminum plate.

We the Undersigned declare this information to be accurate.

Artist: Director: Date:

want to frame a companion piece. We also update the "framed" date whenever a piece is opened for cleaning or inspection.

The computer data base is obviously useful for record and insurance purposes (insurance agents and companies are really impressed by not only an organized listing, but a listing that is exactly the way they want it, a trivial matter with *Q&A*).

But once your collection grows to the point where all the walls are full, and full boxes are under the beds, and the closets are full, a good collection data base really shines. If you know your collection well, when the seasonal re-hang time comes, don't drag out all the pictures, just sit down with a size ordered or size and color ordered list of the entire collection and mentally plan the changes. I know, it's fun to have artwork covering every square foot of floor space while you plan, but it can be a lot of work.

We also use our list to plan buying trips. A list by artist and place of purchase shows us that we have purchased Stoltenberg collagraphs from five different sources over the years, but that most of the purchases have come from two galleries. That tells us that those two galleries probably had the best selection of Stoltenbergs, and that, if we are looking for more, those are the places to start.

Often we list purchases by city prior to a trip. This gives us a gallery list and shows us what was purchased in each city and gallery. Much of our travel has been focused on expanding our collection, and these lists give us a starting point when revisiting different areas. Of course, galleries change both ownership and focus, but if we were well served by a gallery in the past, the probability is that it is at least worth a visit in future.

Another useful task of a computer is to assist in the display of your collection. We have extensive track lighting in our house (more than fifty heads). It is all controlled by switching signals carried over the basic house wiring using the BSR X-10 control system. This system uses plug in and/or hard-wired modules that are individually coded to respond to action signals sent out by various control modules. Track lights may be selected individually or in groups, with each unit or group given a common "address."

KEEPING TRACK OF ACQUISITIONS

Since buying prints enables you to buy both the art of our time and old master prints, and because prints are storable and relatively modestly priced, print buyers often make multiple purchases. It is tremendously important to learn how to keep track of your acquisitions. In this chapter you will learn how to document your print collection, keeping track of what, by whom, where, for how much, and why you bought each print, both for personal reasons and for insurance purposes.

If many of your prints are stored in solander boxes or hung in other locations — schools or workshops, or lent to your relatives or to galleries for exhibition, it is imperative to keep track of them, especially if you might want to buy more by the same printmaker or at the same gallery at a later date. You might say, "Now let's see, what did we buy in Seattle in 1983 and exactly how did we frame the Peter Milton we bought in Philadelphia in 1968?"

> Secret: Document each print with complete information: personal, scholarly, and business.

No matter why you buy prints, whether you are purchasing prints for a corporate collection or buying prints as intimate reminders of experiences, it is the provenance of your print that you want to document:
• the artist
• where, when, how the print was made, and on what paper
• who owned it
• what research has said about it
• where the print or the printmaker has exhibited
• what collections, public or private, the print or printmaker is part of
• the size, description, and condition of the print
• where you bought it
• how much you paid for it
• current evaluation at auction for this or similar prints by this printmaker
• where the print is stored
• a photograph or negative number of the print
• how and by whom the print was framed includ-

ing a list of materials used with mat and frame code numbers and company sources

You can store information about your prints in many ways. The simplest system is to set up a paper file of catalog cards stored within plastic sleeves accompanied by slides or photographs and kept in a fireproof, accessible box. Or you can set up a computer file using either a data base system with text or a menu-driven system which is more specialized in its functions.

One alternative is to record your prints using a video camera. As you walk around your prints, feed information on size, price, source, current value, etc. You can even read about the artist from books or catalogs. Then store the dated and labelled videos in a safe deposit box. Such a visual print catalog could be useful in case of fire, loss, or selling a print. If a potential buyer is interested in a print you own and lives far away, you can send a copy of the video.

Plan to keep track of fourteen data fields (whether you are using a computer or simply index cards).
1. Year and number
2. Medium`
3. Artist
4. Height
5. Width
6. Color(s)
7. Provenance
8. Authentication documents
9. Location
10. Mat
11. Molding
12. Acquisition cost
13. Current valuation
14. Insurance data

TRACKING INFORMATION WITH A COMPUTER

Anyone with a personal computer can buy software packages with relational data base systems. For IBM-compatible computers, the software mentioned in Ken's discussion in the beginning of this chapter is available. Advanced Revelation software has inventory systems, and Macintosh Hy-

percard enables you to set up a card-file system that stacks layers of data. With this, you can interface many types of one-to-many information systems. The idea is to provide you, as the print scholar, with a work station providing data on your prints. Cathy Garmil, active in Boston area computer user groups, has two recommendations. Since computer technology will quickly become obsolete, do not become device dependent. She suggests that a person with mid-range computer skills document prints with a personal computer, and a museum or corporation might use a mainframe, such as a Vax computer.

If you need advice on using a computer to document your print collection, talk with an expert or hire a consultant. Jan Gartenberg, working with the Museum of Modern Art in New York, is a helpful computer-in-art person. You can also contact:

Museum Computer Network
Deirdre Stan, Executive Director
School of Information Studies
Syracuse University
Syracuse, NY 13244

LOANING PRINTS

> Secret: When a print changes location, be sure to document it.

When a print changes location, this should be carefully documented. A print-on-loan form usually includes: description of artwork—artist, title, medium, date, image size, value at purchase; appraised value; condition at time of loan; and terms of insurance coverage during loan. These terms might include the following: Borrower assumes wall-to-wall insurance coverage. Borrower is responsible for all handling and transportation. Borrower will safeguard against loss, damage, or deterioration of print from fire, extremes of temperature, and humidity. Borrower's insurance will cover loss and damage due to vermin or insects, breakage, tearing, warping, mishandling, and attempted repairs and restoration.

Document your prints in order to insure them against all risks, particularly conditions while traveling in domestic transit and overseas, and fire and theft while they are on your premises.

INSURING YOUR PRINTS

> Secret: Buy fine arts floaters to insure print purchases

Find an insurance *broker* because he will be working for you, whereas an agent works for an insurance company. Ask for a personal property floater. It can be part of your homeowner's policy or it can be a separate insurance policy taken out for your prints. If you have prints in your office, take out a commercial fine arts policy or itemize your prints under the all-risk policy covering office furniture.

These policies are called floaters because they cover items in transit, not necessarily stationary. Marine insurance covers oceanic transporting, and inland marine insurance covers the property that stays on land and over the land.

Fine arts came to be covered primarily by inland marine insurance because objects of art are subject to transit exposures and are more easily damaged than ordinary items. Marine insurers were traditionally able to provide broader coverage than fire insurers. Hence, both commercial and personal fine arts insurance coverage comes under the aegis of marine insurance policies.

> Secret: You can design your fine arts policy so it covers your collection's risk exposures.

Since an insurance policy is a written contract between the insured and the insurers, you can make sure it describes in detail proper coverage for your prints. If you lend prints to exhibitions, your coverage may include "borrowers and lenders." Be aware that risk adjustments may enhance your coverage, but may also increase your premium.

In deciding what to include in your policy, mention display cases, storage boxes, frames, even storage closets. Outline ownership of your prints as a museum does: If you are giving your print collection or a part of it, list partial gifts; if you are leaving prints to a family member, list them.

Note the location of your prints; the most limited coverage protects your prints on your premises or your prints can be insured to travel. The special term for coverage that travels with an object is *fine arts floater coverage*, meaning that the print is covered as it leaves its normal repository and is returned to it. A personal property floater on your homeowner's policy covers prints at home and in transit. If a corporate print collection is to be insured, a commercial fine arts floater policy should be taken out as part of the company insurance policy.

> Secret: In the eyes of the insurance company, the value of your prints is only the cost of replacing the paper they are printed on, unless otherwise specified.

The most important step for you as the insured print owner is to establish the intrinsic value of your prints. Have your prints appraised or use your bill of sale. An agreed-upon value for your prints should be declared at the inception of your fine arts insurance program and then gradually updated as you acquire more prints or as your prints change in value.

Values in a fine arts policy need to be monitored annually or semi-annually. You must send in to your insurer new lists of print acquisitions and updated valuations from auction records. For the very active collector, who lends and purchases frequently, monthly updates are recommended. Insurance premiums will fluctuate according to the monthly report.

> Secret: No fine arts insurance covers damage due to deterioration, wear and tear, inherent vice, vermin, or insects.

Preservation and conservation are important from an insurance point of view. I doubt if the dog urinating on Jerry's prints was covered by insurance. When rats nibbled at the handmade papers and paper prints stored in our gallery closet, the restoration was not covered. The following is a list of exclusions listed in the handbook, *Fine Arts Insurance,* by Patricia Nauert and Caroline M. Black.

• Normal wear and tear (damage caused by usual day-to-day handling)
• Gradual deterioration (the effects of time)
• Insect, moths, vermin
• Inherent vice (a quality in an object which causes it to deteriorate or destroy itself)
• Damage due to or resulting from repair, restoration or retouching
• Nuclear reaction, radiation, or radioactive contamination
• Insurrection and war
• Government confiscation

Most fine art insurance covers fire, observed thefts (not mysterious disappearances), break-ins, lightning, water damage from above (not floods), damage during transit.

No matter how many or how few prints you own, you should keep track of them either on index cards or in a computer, because one day you may need this information either to buy more, to frame others similarly, or to make a claim in case of a major loss. Take this seriously. In my experience as a gallery keeper, it is surprising how many people have told me about losing prints by theft and fire.

A LAST WORD

> Secret: Buy prints as gifts.

Dee and her friends travel with their jobs. They have a game in which they pick up small prints for each other and give them as thoughtful gifts on name days, birthdays, and Christmas. They help each other find delightful images, which end up in wall arrangements, reflecting their interest in the places they've been.

> Secret: Have a party for your printmakers.

One couple we know decided to have a party for their printmakers. They invited all the printmakers whose work they had purchased, along with the gallery people and others who had been involved with the creation of their collection along the way. It was a wonderful party, with everyone enjoying their friends' collection displayed at its best, and basking in the satisfying glow of appreciating each others' mutual talents.

And finally, this quote from a print buyer:

"Those prints have had a magical effect. If in the morning I walked through the dining room where they hung, I remembered later that day that I had done so. Owning those prints seemed to raise my level of awareness in a way that has affected my entire life."

SUGGESTED READING

The Aftermarket Art Journal.
available from: InformArt
1727 E. Second Street
Casper, WY 82601

Building a Print Collection, by Glen Warner, 1981.
available from: Key Porter Books
59 Front Street East
Toronto, Ontario M5E 1B3 Canada

The Care of Prints and Drawings, by Margaret Holben Ellis. The American Association for State and Local History, 1987.

Handbook of Print Making and Print Makers, by John Taylor Arms. New York: The Macmillan Company, 1934.

How Prints Look, by William M. Ivins, Jr. Boston: Beacon Press, 1943.

On Understanding Art Museums, by Sherman Lee. Englewood Cliffs, NJ: Prentice Hall, Inc., 1975.

Papermaking: The History and Technique of an Ancient Craft, by David Hunter. Dover Publications reprint of Alfred A. Knopf, Inc., 1943.

A Primer on Museum Security, by Caroline Keck. Cooperstown, NY: New York State Historical Association, 1966.

Print Quarterly Limited
80 Carlton Hill
London NW8 OER England

Prints: History of an Art, by Michel Melot et al. S.A. Geneva: Éditions d'Art Albert Skira. New York: Rizzoli International Publications, Inc., 1981.

INDEX